The Best 10-Minute Plays 2011

The Best 10-Minute Plays

2011

Edited by
Lawrence Harbison

CONTEMPORARY PLAYWRIGHTS SERIES

A Smith and Kraus Book
HANOVER, NEW HAMPSHIRE

A Smith and Kraus Book
Published by Smith and Kraus, Inc.
177 Lyme Road, Hanover, NH 03755
www.SmithandKraus.com

First Edition: November 2011
10 9 8 7 6 5 4 3 2 1

Manufactured in the United States of America
Cover design by Emily Kent, emilygkent@gmail.com
Book design by Rachel Reiss, rachelreiss@verizon.net
Photo on title spread and part openers @iStockphoto.com/Dragan Trifunovic

ISBN-10 1-57525-782-3
ISBN-13 978-1-57525-782-2
ISSN 2164-2435

Contents

M = male role
F = female role

▌Foreword

In this volume, you will find fifty terrific new ten-minute plays, culled from the hundreds I read last year, all successfully produced during the 2010–2011 theatrical season. They are written in a variety of styles. Some are realistic plays; some are not. Some are comic (laughs); some are dramatic (no laughs). The ten-minute play form lends itself well to experimentation in style. A playwright can have fun with a device which couldn't be sustained as well in a longer play. Many of the plays employ such devices.

In years past, playwrights who were just starting out wrote one-act plays of thirty to forty minutes in duration. One thinks of writers such as A. R. Gurney, Lanford Wilson, John Guare and several others. Now, new playwrights tend to work in the ten-minute play genre, largely because there are so many production opportunities. Fifteen or so years ago, there were none. I was Senior Editor for Samuel French at that time, and it occurred to me that there might be a market for these very short plays. Actors Theatre of Louisville had been commissioning them for several years, for use by their Apprentice Company, and they assisted me in compiling an anthology of their plays, which did so well that Samuel French has published several more anthologies of ten-minute plays from ATL. For the first time, ten-minute plays were now published and widely available, and they started getting produced. There are now many ten-minute play festivals every year, not only in the U.S. but all over the world.

What makes a good ten-minute play? Well, first and foremost I have to like it. Isn't that what we mean when we call a play, a film, a novel "good?" We mean that it effectively portrays the world as I see it. Aside from this obvious fact, a good ten-minute play has to have the same elements that any good play must have: a strong conflict, interesting, well-drawn characters and compelling subject matter. It also has to have a clear beginning, middle and end. In other words, it's a full length play which runs about ten minutes. Many of the plays which are submitted to me are scenes, not complete plays; well-written scenes in many case, but scenes nonetheless. They leave me wanting more. I chose plays which are complete in and of themselves, which I believe will excite those of you who produce ten-minute plays; because if a play isn't produced, it's the proverbial sound of a tree falling in the forest far away. In the back of this book you will find information on whom to contact when you decide which plays you want to produce, in order to acquire performance rights.

There are a few plays in this book by playwrights who are fairly well-known, such as Don Nigro and Carson Kreitzer, but most are by terrific new playwrights you probably never heard of who I have no doubt will become far better known when their full-length plays start getting produced by major theatres. And you read their work first here!

Lawrence Harbison
Brooklyn, New York

Plays for Two Actors

After

Glenn Alterman

After originally received a staged reading at Theater Schonefeld, Berlin, Germany, February 25, 2010, with Gunther Diezel and Greta Gerber, directed by Konrad Sodann. It subsequently received a developmental reading May 25th, 2010 at The Workshop Theater Company (New York City) with Gerrianne Raphael and Jonathan Pereira. The play received another developmental reading August 16, 2010 at the Workshop Theater Company with Susan Wallack and Greg Oliver Bodine.

After received its first full production in September, 2010, at the Theater at Schoenfeld, Berlin, Germany, as part of the After Folsom Short Play Festival. Cast: Terry—Anna Gedeck; Tom—Max Frobe. The Director was Max Diehl.

PLACE

A small family room, right outside the funeral parlor in a Jewish synagogue.

CHARACTERS

Terry is a middle aged woman. She is down to earth, good
   hearted, and full of life .
Tom is attractive, in his thirties or forties, polite, reserved, sensitive and soft-spoken.

TIME

The present

TERRY: My God, that was . . . !

TOM: What?

TERRY: Eloquent!

TOM: Really?

TERRY: I just had to tell you!

TOM: Thank you.

TERRY: Before you left, I needed you to know, I was . . . *so* touched.

TOM: Really?

TERRY: You had his wife in tears.

TOM: I did?

TERRY: Everyone in there was so moved.

TOM: They were?

TERRY: How did you know him?

TOM: Hank?

TERRY: Yeah.

TOM: I . . . Well actually I hardly knew him at all, just from the gym.

TERRY: The gym?

TOM: Yeah, one time when I was working out with weights, he spotted me.

TERRY: Spotted?

TOM: Yeah, stood there for support, to make sure I didn't drop the weights.

TERRY: Oh.

TOM: So I really hardly knew him at all.

TERRY: But what you said up there just now; the way you talked about him. Was like . . . was like you really knew him, like you were *brothers*.

TOM: No, hardly. . . . How did you know Hank?

TERRY: Well, to be honest I didn't really know him at all.

TOM: No?

TERRY: I do volunteer work here at the synagogue. I was just helping out this morning, saw the crowd and kind of moseyed in. Stood in the back, and heard you talking and was *mesmerized* by what you had to say. It was so insightful, so kind.

TOM: Well . . . So you really didn't know him that well either?

TERRY: No, not at all. But certainly seems like he was popular.

TOM: Yeah, lot of people here. . . . Well, was nice talking to you.

TERRY: Aren't you going to go to the shiva call at his home.

TOM: Shiva? No, I'm not Jewish, so . . .

TERRY: Oh that doesn't matter, come.

TOM: I've got to get back to work. You're going to go?

TERRY: I think so.

TOM: But you just said you hardly . . .

TERRY: Okay, alright, little confession. This isn't the first time I've gone to a funeral of a person I didn't really know. Do it all the time.

TOM: You crash people's funerals?

TERRY: Well I wouldn't exactly call it crash. But well, yeah, sometimes. It's just . . . Well, my husband died last year and we had his service here and . . . I don't know, I just keep coming back. And if there's a funeral, like today, I sometimes stop in. Generally people don't ask who I am. And I get to share some sorrow with them, to commiserate. If they do ask, I just tell 'em I knew the deceased from the synagogue. S'just a little lie. Anyway, I really like going to funerals.

TOM: You do?

TERRY: Oh God, yes! You learn so much, and not only about the deceased. People at funerals are, I don't know, so open, honest, *alive*. All their feelings are right there at their finger tips. No pretense, phoniness. Kinda ironic, huh? People being so alive at a funeral.... So you said you really didn't know Hank that well.

TOM: *(a little uncomfortable)* No, I never really said very much to him.

TERRY: But you know his wife?

TOM: No.

TERRY: *(She looks at him)* Can I ask you something?

TOM: Sure.

TERRY: *(Softly, a confidence)* Were you his...*friend*?

TOM: Friend?

TERRY: Maybe I'm way out of line here, but I think you know what I mean by friend.

TOM: If what I think you're saying...No, no, I wasn't his *friend*.

TERRY: I'm sorry, I didn't mean...

TOM: I should go.

TERRY: *(Stopping him)* But you're gay, right?

TOM: What? Yeah, so? What if I am?

TERRY: My husband, he was gay too.

TOM: Really?

TERRY: *(Smiling)* Yeah, gay, gay, gay. Gay as a goose—whatever that means. And we were married, Sidney and me, nearly thirty-two years. And let me tell you, you couldn't ask for a better husband.

TOM: Hm.

TERRY: We never really talked about it, but, well, he knew I knew. A *wink* every once in a while. Times were different back then; there was no need to talk about things like that. 'Sides why ruin a good thing, right? And let me tell ya, I loved being his wife. Every day with Sidney was a blessing. He was a good, caring man. Anyway, I feel people talk too much today. Talking's overrated. I hate Oprah and all those stupid talk shows. People always needing to reveal every...Sometimes what really matters...It's the *not saying*, y'know? The things people don't need to say to each other. The, I don't know, unspoken, that's most meaningful.

TOM: You really miss him, don't you?

TERRY: *(Sincerely, a slight sadness)* More than you can imagine. Sidney was my... He was more than just my husband, he was my *companion*. Friends and lovers, eh, they come and go. But a *companion*, that's someone so special, someone who's always there for you. We went everywhere together, traveled, did everything. We loved being in each other's company, made each other laugh. Incredible; lucky, love. *(A beat, smiling)* Y'know, for someone who just said talking's overrated, I'm going on like we're old beer buddies, blah-blah-blah. Sorry, told you, funerals.

(shaking his hand)
Anyway, I won't take up anymore of your time; was very nice talking to you...?

TOM: Tom.

TERRY: Terry. You seem like a very nice man; good listener.

TOM: There was a steam room at our gym.

TERRY: What?

TOM: Where Hank and I worked out. Wasn't very well lit, this steam room, and it was always filled with, well, steam. And one time, it was right after that time he helped me with the weights.

TERRY: *(Smiling)* When he *spotted* you?

TOM: *(Smiling)* When he spotted me, yeah. After, after I finished my set I said something like "Thank you, appreciate it". He smiled and I left, went to the locker room. Then, a little later we sort of bumped into each other...

TERRY: ...in the steam room.

TOM: Right. Accidentally, we accidentally brushed up against each other. Told you it wasn't very well lit in there. And we both stood there, just.... Didn't move, didn't say anything. Just looked at each other and... Then, almost at the same time, we touched. Just... touched each other. My hand on his shoulder, his hand on my chest. We stood there, touching, staring at each other. Didn't say anything. Was just silence, except for the sound of the steam.—Jesus, I have no idea why I'm telling you....

TERRY: Go on, please. And so, after?

TOM: After? Nothing, we just touched some more, face, hips, everything. Slowly, gently. And that was it,, that was all. We left, without saying a word. But... well, eventually it became a regular...

The steam room, we'd met there and...I know this might sound crazy, but every time we met it was more meaningful. The touches, more caring, sensitive. Then kisses, caresses, embraces. Then holding, just holding each other. He...Hank was a very loving man. Had a lot of love in him. I know that sounds...Especially since we never really said anything except "Hi" and "Bye". But I knew it, could feel it; I knew him. And sure, sometimes we did have sex but...

TERRY: *(Smiling, knowingly)* The sex wasn't important.

TOM: No, not at all.

TERRY: Didn't anybody ever walk in?

TOM: We both worked out at off hours, hardly anybody else at the gym. I guess there was always the danger. Maybe that was part of it.

TERRY: How long did this...?

TOM: I don't know, a long time, every week. And I always looked forward...But it always seemed so strange to me how little I really knew about him; I mean about his life.

TERRY: Sounds like you both knew more about each other without words, than a lot of people I know who talk all the time.

TOM: Well I didn't know he was married.

TERRY: *(A smile, softly)* You miss him, don't you?

TOM: *(Softly, sadly)* More than you can imagine. More than anyone I've ever known. I miss our meetings so much.—I quit the gym.
(A moment of awkwardness. He looks at her, then looking around.)
Well, looks like people are starting to leave. I really should get back to work.

TERRY: I should go too, yeah. Tom, what you said about him up there today touched a lot of people in that room, especially his wife, believe me. Just that you got up there in front of all those strangers and...Was very brave.

TOM: I just...I felt like I needed to come here today, that I had to. I certainly didn't plan on talking. But it's like something just lifted me out of my chair and next thing I knew...

TERRY: Well, if nothing else, you got to meet me, the loony lady that crashes funerals....I should let you go. Hey, if you're ever in the neighborhood, stop by. I'm here at the synagogue, between nine and twelve ever day. (Smiling) Who knows, maybe you and me we can catch a nice funeral together.

TOM: Yeah, sure, maybe. That would be nice. I enjoyed meeting you Terry, I mean it.
(Smiling)
You're a good listener.

TERRY: I hope to see you soon. Stop by sometime.—Be well.

(He politely shakes her hand. She smiles, leans in, gently kisses him on the cheek. He looks at her, smiles, and leaves. She stands there, watches him leave, then turns, looks back at the funeral parlor. As the lights slowly fade)

END OF PLAY

The Baby

Ron Burch

Produced in the "16th Annual New York City 15-Minute Play Festival" presented by American Globe Theatre and Turnip Theater Company on April 23, 2010. Play chosen as a finalist and performances extended to April 30 and May 1, 2010. Cast: Man—Christopher Flockton; Woman—Julie Galdieri. Directed by Melinda Buckley. Producer: Ron Burch.

CHARACTERS

Man . . . . age is flexible
Woman . . age is flexible

LOCATION

A bedroom

TIME

Now

A man and a woman prepare for bed.

WOMAN: . . . I just couldn't believe it.
MAN: I know.
WOMAN: Who does she think she is?
MAN: I don't—
WOMAN: I mean really.
MAN: Yeah, I know.
WOMAN: And the way their kids—
MAN: Yes.
WOMAN: I mean can you believe . . .
MAN: I don't know.
WOMAN: What?
MAN: I guess, I don't.
WOMAN: What?
MAN: Didn't bother me.
WOMAN: Really?
MAN: Yeah.
WOMAN: Well.
MAN: No, not really.
WOMAN: I guess it wasn't that bad.

MAN: I played with one of them.

WOMAN: You did?

MAN: Uh huh.

WOMAN: Seriously?

MAN: What's wrong with that?

WOMAN: You just don't seem to know your way around kids.

MAN: Well, I was an only child....

WOMAN: You run from them.

MAN: I don't run....

WOMAN: I've never even seen you talk to one before.

MAN: I just never got used to them.

WOMAN: You actually played?

MAN: Yeah. In the back when you all were having wine.

WOMAN: I thought you were in the bathroom.

MAN: I was.

WOMAN: I thought you were having a serious problem in there.

MAN: When I came out, there he was, looking kind of sad.

WOMAN: So what'd you do?

MAN: We threw a ball for awhile.

WOMAN: Oh.

MAN: It was fun.

WOMAN: That wine they had was terrible.

MAN: Was it?

WOMAN: Yes.

MAN: I'm not much for wine.

WOMAN: I know that.

MAN: I thought they were nice.

WOMAN: Yes, they're a nice couple. I'd never met her husband before. Their baby was cute.

MAN: It was nice of them to invite us over.

WOMAN: They seemed disappointed.

MAN: They did?

WOMAN: Yeah.

MAN: In us?

WOMAN: I think they thought we had kids and were going to bring them over.

MAN: Where'd they get that?

WOMAN: I have no idea. You think she'd know better.

MAN: Hmm.

WOMAN: What?

MAN: Nothing.

WOMAN: I mean she's worked with me for, how many years?

MAN: Five, isn't it?

WOMAN: No, six. Six years. I just thought she would know me better.

MAN: I guess she doesn't.

WOMAN: Doesn't what?

MAN: Know you better.

She looks at him.

WOMAN: Something wrong?

MAN: No.

WOMAN: So she said, "Do you have kids?" And I said, "No," and it was just weird.

MAN: Maybe they were uncomfortable.

WOMAN: With what?

MAN: That we don't have kids.

WOMAN: Why would they be uncomfortable?

MAN: Maybe they thought it wasn't by choice.

WOMAN: What do you mean?

MAN: Some people want to have kids and they can't. They don't have a choice. It causes them pain.

WOMAN: I know that.

MAN: So maybe, all I'm saying, is that it was awkward for her.

WOMAN: Yes, but she knows.

MAN: She knows what?

WOMAN: How I feel. So she shouldn't have been uncomfortable.

MAN: Mmm.

WOMAN: What are you saying?

MAN: You know what I'm saying.

WOMAN: What?

MAN: I don't want to talk about it.

WOMAN: You brought it up.

MAN: I didn't bring anything up.

WOMAN: Don't get this way.

MAN: I'm not.

WOMAN: You're starting.

MAN: I'm not starting, you're starting.

WOMAN: Okay.

MAN: Why are you asking me?

> *Beat.*

WOMAN: What does that mean?

MAN: It doesn't mean anything. Okay? Not a thing.

WOMAN: You could have been nicer tonight.

MAN: Mmm.

WOMAN: Seriously. I'm in there, drinking wine with them, treading water conversationally.

MAN: You wanted to go.

WOMAN: Yeah and then you disappear.

MAN: I told you where I was.

WOMAN: That's not the point.

MAN: You always have to be right, that's what it is.

WOMAN: What do you mean?

MAN: Changing the subject.

WOMAN: I'm not.

MAN: Okay, whatever. I thought they were nice.

WOMAN: I know.

MAN: The way they . . . interacted.

WOMAN: What're you talking about?

MAN: It was nice. When their son came in and he had that problem with his homework.

WOMAN: Yeah.

MAN: And the pictures they had on the fridge.

WOMAN: What pictures?

MAN: On the refrigerator.

WOMAN: I didn't see them.

MAN: You know family photos and stuff. Drawings.

WOMAN: Their kitchen could use some updating. That white dishwasher was totally out of place.

MAN: Uh huh.

WOMAN: Did you see it?

MAN: No.

WOMAN: What?

MAN: Nothing.

WOMAN: What?!

MAN: Just about dinner.

Beat.

WOMAN: I saw you looking at her.

MAN: Who?

WOMAN: Mandy.

MAN: I wasn't.

WOMAN: No, I saw you. You were staring.

MAN: No.

WOMAN: You sure?

MAN: Yes, I'm sure. I wasn't looking at her like that.

WOMAN: Like what?

MAN: Like what you're insinuating.

WOMAN: Then what were you looking at?

MAN: I don't know. All of them.

WOMAN: Why?

MAN: I was just thinking about the pictures on the fridge.

WOMAN: Stop.

MAN: Okay.

WOMAN: Why do you do this?

MAN: You know.

WOMAN: I know.

MAN: You know why.

WOMAN: I wish you would stop. Really.

MAN: Okay.

WOMAN: I'm.

Beat.

MAN: We were throwing the ball. Their son's name, the one I was with, is Bobby. We were throwing the ball and he said to me, "You're not very good at this." And I said, "At what?" And he said, "At throwing the ball. You need to practice." That's what he said. You need to practice.

Long pause.

WOMAN: You know the reasons why.

MAN: I know.

WOMAN: We've talked about this.

MAN: Yes. I know.
> *She gets into bed.*

WOMAN: Baby?

MAN: Yeah.
> *He sits in a chair.*

WOMAN: Remind me to write her a thank-you note for dinner.

MAN: Okay.
> *He remains where he is.*

WOMAN: Are you coming to bed?

MAN: I'm not sure.

WOMAN: I thought maybe we could fool around.
> *She laughs. He looks at her.*

MAN: Mmm.
> *Lights fade.*

END OF PLAY

Blood

Aliza Einhorn

Blood was first produced by the Fusion Theatre Company as a winning entry in their annual short works festival, "The Seven," June 10 to June 13, 2010 at The Cell Theatre in Albuquerque, New Mexico. Festival producer: Dennis Gromelski. The play was directed by Robb Sisneros. Veronica was played by Jen Grigg and Rosa was played by Tahirih Koller.

Blood had its second production at Manhattan Theatre Source's EstroGenius, A Celebration of Female Voices, in New York City, October 20 to October 23, 2010. Festival producer: Jen Thatcher. The play was directed by Heather Cohn. Veronica was played by Melissa Macleod Herion and Rosa was played by Anna Lamadrid.

TIME

Present day

SETTING

All sets and staging are at the discretion of the director.
It can be bare bones or approximate the various "places." Most of all, the setting is the mind and the heart and the conversation between the two women.

CHARACTERS

Veronica . 20s to 30s, a dancer. Any ethnicity.
Rosa . . . . 20s to 30s, a matador. Latina.

Lights up on Rosa and Veronica.

VERONICA: "Lead with the heel, lead with the heel!" My teacher barks at me.

ROSA: In Spanish, it means killer: *matador.*

VERONICA: But today I can't focus.

ROSA: I'm not afraid of what I am.

VERONICA: I tried the waltz, I tried the foxtrot—

ROSA: And when I enter the arena, I feel brave, elegant. Humble.

VERONICA: —the *samba, flamenco, tango.* I had the best gancho in all of Brooklyn!

ROSA: My father was my teacher. And his father before him.

VERONICA: My legs? My legs are like knives.

ROSA: Strange to think about it now—

VERONICA: Feet and legs to DIE for.

ROSA: They thought I was too sensitive.

VERONICA: Knives, swords—I'm violent!

ROSA: Too sensitive for the ring.

VERONICA: I'm an angry woman. Give me blood!

ROSA: I didn't mind the blood.

VERONICA: I said to my teacher: "Show me the most violent of all the dances!" So she taught me the *pasodouble*.

(Pause.)

Tuesday night, it's after my class, I'm in a bar, having a beer, chatting with the guys, and a bullfight comes on the T.V. The stupid pussy *bartendress* wants to change the channel but I tell her NO. She flips her long hair in my direction. Fuck her. But it's like I'm hypnotized, *stuck*. I can't stop watching the harsh afternoon sun and the small woman in the center of it all, like a tiny god.

(Squinting eyes as though watching TV.)

What on earth is she wearing? I had to write her a letter.

ROSA: I am not a violent person, but I need violence to make me happy. Understand?

VERONICA: I do. You're like me. Tell me everything.

ROSA: My mother would give me a candy to suck on at the start of every match: purple, red, blue, striped and sweet, because I would cry. Because I fell in love with every bull my father killed. Agility, harmony. Grace. That was my Papa.

Sweetness and light: my mother.

VERONICA: Dear Rosa: I knew we were the same when I saw you on T.V., and I wanted you to know how rare that is—a true understanding of souls. I'm an American, born and raised in New York City. Have you been here? The protesters call you a killer, but I know the truth! You're an artist, a woman against nature, against beast, against the world, herself! But what do you want? To live? Or to die? And if that bitch tries to change the channel one more time I swear I will cut her throat.

ROSA: It was a long letter. At the end, she wrote: "The bullfight is a metaphor—for love. I understood this today as I watched you. Please write me back. Love, Veronica. P.S. I am a dancer and today my teacher taught me the pasodouble."

VERONICA: Dear Veronica: Let me tell you a thing or two about love. Love is angry, love is brutal, love is soiled, love is ugly. I want an ugly love. Are you ugly enough for me? Love, Rosa.

ROSA: And since you enjoyed the fight so much, and you claim to understand me, answer me this: What does the bull want?

VERONICA: The bull is an animal!

ROSA: Does he want kindness?

VERONICA: He wants to survive, to live another moment—

ROSA: Does he want peace?

VERONICA: He's a beast of the field!

ROSA: Maybe he wants to fall in love.

VERONICA: Dear Rosa: I fell in love with the *pasodouble*. And what I love most about it is the death. I die at the end of every dance. My teacher is the *matador* and I'm the bull. Everytime. Understand?

ROSA: I do. You're like me. See this scar? And this one? And this? *Cornadas*. I want to show them all to you.

VERONICA: I want to see them all.

ROSA: When I was a girl, my father said to me: be the woman that you are! Dark, brooding, empty of light, shattered vessel, be proud. Here, drink. Is this blood, Papa? He laughed at me. Tomato juice. And when I was a girl, he broke my arm. I have a picture, I'm wearing a cast, he's smiling a huge smile, standing beside me. He broke it so I would know pain. He said I wouldn't know it otherwise. I never told anyone that story.

    (Pause.)

Let me see you.

VERONICA: I'm too ugly for you to see.

ROSA: But you're a dancer.

VERONICA: Believe me!

ROSA: I thought all dancers were beautiful.

VERONICA: No.

ROSA: Perhaps that is what the bull wants—to dance.

VERONICA: He wants nothing! What does the dancer want? What does the wood of the floor want? What does the *clackity clack* of the shoes want? And the legs and the elbows and the teeth and the ass! And the balls! What does the body want?

    (Pause.)

It was another night at the bar after my class. I was exhausted, hungry. The usual *bartendress* on duty, wearing next-to-nothing, as always. I'm not saying she's a slut or anything but there's something . . . too open about her. I'm not jealous, that's not it. She has this confidence. Pride. The way she sidles up to the bar and does whatever it is she does with the bottles, money, change, tips, tits. Whatever. She's . . . really beautiful.

ROSA: I didn't mean to upset you.

VERONICA: You didn't.

ROSA: You didn't write me for two weeks.

VERONICA: I'm sorry. I was busy.

ROSA: Are you still my friend?

(Pause.)

Everything. Everything was as usual when I entered the ring. The hot afternoon, I was sweating in my *traje de luces* as I looked to the seats in the shade, and I looked to the seats in the sun, and I thought I saw my father, and I thought I saw you, Veronica. I thought I saw your face. Was it? Was it you?

VERONICA: No. And no, I don't have a boyfriend. The bartender, she always asks me, every time I come in: "Where's your boyfriend?" Supposed to make me feel bad, I guess. Feel sorry for myself. Don't you think I would if I could? Don't you think, I say to her, I would be rich, famous, beautiful, with a dozen boyfriends? If I could? Now shut the fuck up and let me watch my show. "What's the matter with you," she says. "Why are you always so angry?" she says. "And how can you watch that barbaric shit? Don't you feel bad? For the bull?"

ROSA: I feel bad all the time. I'm not a happy person.

VERONICA: Why not?

ROSA: I have nothing.

VERONICA: But you have—

ROSA: Blood. All over me.

VERONICA: A *matador* with a guilt complex? Oh please. You have the adoration of the crowd—they love you! I long for such applause!

ROSA: They don't know me.

VERONICA: They remember your father!

ROSA: And they hate me because I'm not him!

VERONICA: So why do you do it?

ROSA: When you wrote to me I thought finally! Someone understands! Okay, you're an American, but true understanding runs deeper than the blood of a nation. And your New York City runs with blood doesn't it? *Doesn't it?* I thought we were the same. I see that we're not. You don't understand me at all!

VERONICA: But I do! Wait!!
> *(Long pause.)*
> I don't know what she wants from me. I'm not Ginger fucking Rogers. *Don't move your hips like that. It's not a samba.* I do my best, but she's always pushing pushing pushing. Women think they know everything. I told her about Rosa.
> *(Pause.)*
> Another Tuesday night, nothing special, my body aches. Miss Bartendress brings me my drink and makes sure to bend forward so I can see it all and she tells me her name. I don't know why she does it, I've been coming here all year without a name. She turns on the T.V. "Fine," she says. "Place is empty. You seem like you had a hard day. Watch whatever you want." *Anything?* "Anything." It felt like she had been waiting for me. And the bullfight began. It was Rosa.

ROSA: I felt elegant, courageous, humble.

VERONICA: And something made me turn away. I couldn't watch, I made her change the channel.

ROSA: The trumpet sounded for the first *tercio* and when I saw this bull, I knew.

VERONICA: Then I asked her to change it back—we went through this a couple times.

ROSA: I understood him.

VERONICA: It was so hot in there.

ROSA: I felt him.

VERONICA: Felt like the room was on fire.

ROSA: I loved him more than all the others. I knew.
> *(Pause.)*
> And then. And then. The *tercio de muerte.* The trumpet sounded again, the faena would begin, I entered the ring alone.

VERONICA: You know . . . how it is . . . when someone dies? You get that feeling like you knew it was gonna happen?

ROSA: The sun was dripping down—down my neck into my collar, eyes burning, I needed shade.

VERONICA: Somehow the body knows.

ROSA: So I put the *muleta* over my head, and I heard the crowd gasp—

VERONICA: Oh my God—

ROSA: —gasp for air.

VERONICA: Jesus Asshole! *Asshole asshole asshole!*

ROSA: As I charged the bull.

    (Pause.)

    It was fast, it was bright, it was blood blood blood GIVE ME BLOOD! And the crowd roaring in my ears: Rosa. Rosa. Rosa. *Mas cornadas da el hambre.*

    (A beat as lights dim a little.)

VERONICA: I got one last letter after she did it. I was hoping there would be another—that maybe one of them got lost in the mail.

ROSA: *(Very tired/quiet tone)* See this scar here? And this one? And this?

VERONICA: She said she was gonna give me a gift, special for me and no one else. No one else. No one. NO.

ROSA: Send me a picture. Please? I don't want to be alone.

VERONICA: And she told me to go to the bar on Tuesday night.

ROSA: It won't be long now . . .

VERONICA: And watch the fight.

ROSA: Any moment . . .

VERONICA: I thought maybe I'd get an ear in the mail, or a tail.

ROSA: There's so much blood. Do you hear them? They're singing my name.

VERONICA: They do that, you know, with the ears. And the tail.

ROSA: *Jesu Christo* . . .

VERONICA: Like souvenirs.

ROSA: Hold me.

VERONICA: Souvenirs . . .

ROSA: Hold me while I die. Love . . .

VERONICA: Rosa.

    (End of play.)

Curveball

Brendan Burke

Original Production: June 16th, 17th, and 18th, 2010, Manhattan Rep, New York, NY, Ken Wolf, Producer. Cast: Kevin—Joel Turner; Megwyn—Ashley Diane Currie. Crew: Director—Brendan Burke; Sound and Lighting—Abi Gale; Music—Harry Whitaker; Assistant Director—Steve Koster. Special Thanks to Brad Fraser.

CHARACTERS:

KEVIN: .... 28. Taller. Athletic. Former college baseball star. Now works as a loan officer for a major, soon to be defunct bank. From Grosse Pointe, Michigan.

MEGWYN: .. 29. Attractive. Former actress, now pilates instructor. From Ventura, California.

SETTING

Their apartment. 48th street and 8th avenue. Manhattan. 2008. A spacious one bedroom in a doorman building.

Kevin is seated on a couch, center stage. He looks out towards the audience. He passes a baseball between his hands, anxiously. Megwyn enters. . . . she carries a yoga mat, and a duffle bag.

KEVIN: I'm done.
    They're done.
    With me.
    They're done.
MEGWYN: What?
KEVIN: The bank. It'll probably be another day, and then it'll be official.
MEGWYN: Are you sure?
KEVIN: A bunch of them are going under. It's not over.
    (pause)
KEVIN: I just got the email. Pretty much all the guys on my floor. Gonna be done.
MEGWYN: I . . . ok.
KEVIN: People saw it coming. It's not all that surprising.
MEGWYN: I know. I know, I saw on the news at the gym.
    (pause)

MEGWYN: My dad called me from Long Beach about an hour ago. He's supposed to land at two.

KEVIN: Oh, he's coming today?

MEGWYN: Yes. *(she walks into the next room)*

KEVIN: Didn't I tell you I was going out to Davis' this weekend?

MEGWYN: What? *(she re-enters)* I thought I told you about this a couple of weeks ago.

KEVIN: Sorry.

MEGWYN: You're going out there, to Long Island? Why?

KEVIN: Davis has a couple of transfers from Southern schools, he wants me to pitch to them in the gym there. They gave him a whole gymnasium on the campus

MEGWYN: Can you not do this another weekend?

KEVIN: They're only here this weekend.

MEGWYN: *(takes a breath)* My dad's going to be disappointed.

KEVIN: Look... please?

MEGWYN: Well, what am... what should I tell him?

> *(pause)*
> Kevin, do you have to be like this right now?
> *(pause)*
> What is it that happens to you out there when you're in a gymnasium in the middle of nowhere pitching baseballs to college kids?
> Seriously?
> *(pause)*
> Seriously.
> *(he starts to collect some things in a bag)*
> What?

KEVIN: Meg. I wanted to wait it out... a bit... but I'm going to tell you... just gonna tell you now, this spring I'm going to be leaving, for awhile.

MEGWYN: What?

KEVIN: I'm gonna go home. I'm gonna take Davis up on an offer.

MEGWYN: What?

KEVIN: What?

MEGWYN: What did he offer you?

KEVIN: He just got a job managing an A ball team back home.

MEGWYN: And?

KEVIN: And, he offered me a spot in his starting rotation.

MEGWYN: How long have you known about this?

KEVIN: A couple of weeks.

> *(pause)*

> I mean, about when he got the job or . . . .

MEGWYN: *(interrupting him)* . . . about when you decided to do this?

KEVIN: I was almost . . . I wanted to, and then . . . there . . . and I got word about this thing this morning. Was it.

> *(pause)*

MEGWYN: A lot of people are going through this stuff right now, Kevin . . . a lot of people are losing . . .

KEVIN: . . . I've got nothing left here . . .

MEGWYN: . . . oh, thanks . . .

KEVIN: . . . not one SPECK of me is happy working in finan . . . .

MEGWYN: *(shocked)* You're gonna just leave? You're not even officially laid off yet, and now you're going to leave your life, move back to Michigan and play minor league baseball.

KEVIN: Ya. *(collects himself)* Yes.

MEGWYN: Where?

KEVIN: Lansing. The Lansing Lugnuts.

> *(pause)*

> *(she laughs, hysterically)*

MEGWYN: Are you kidding?

> *(pause)*

> Kevin?

> *(pause)*

> What does . . . I mean, what does that mean?

> *(pause)*

> Seriously, Kevin, what does that mean?

KEVIN: It means . . . that . . . I'm going to move back there. In the spring.

> *(pause)*

MEGWYN: So, what?

> *(pause)*

> So?

> *(long silence . . . their shared discomfort is manifesting itself physically in both of them)*

MEGWYN: So that's it.

> *(pause)*
>
> You're done with me.

KEVIN: I'm sorry.

MEGWYN: Kevin, you just got word that you might be let go from your job, It's not even a done deal yet. Please take thirty seconds, and get a grip....

KEVIN: I've made up my mind.

MEGWYN: I REALLY think that you should think about this more.

KEVIN: He talked to me about it about a month ago.

MEGWYN: And you didn't even think to consult me in any way about you just packing up and leaving for Michigan? Is this baseball some kind of fucked up excuse to . . .

KEVIN: . . . I wasn't sure how things were gonna fall with the bank . . .

MEGWYN: . . . and did you HAVE to tell me about this while my dad is on his way here? Really? You ARE aware of how ridiculous this is going to sound?

KEVIN: I'm sorry.

MEGWYN: So what? What are you going to do? You're just gonna start a minor . . . league . . . career? You're twenty eight years old . . .

KEVIN: . . . yeah?

MEGWYN: Then what?

> *(pause)*
>
> Yeah.
>
> *(Kevin is visibly shaken)*

MEGWYN: You're just gonna leave?

KEVIN: Leave what?

> *(phone rings)*

MEGWYN: Fuck!

> *(she hits the 'silent' button on her cell phone)*

KEVIN: I didn't wanna do this to you.

MEGWYN: Right. You didn't WANT to fuckin' pull this a few hours before my dad gets here . . . right?

KEVIN: Stop.

> *(silence)*

MEGWYN: Are you . . . . like, do you need some kind of help?

KEVIN: No.

MEGWYN: Do you have a disassociative disorder?

KEVIN: No.

MEGWYN: What is your intention with this?

KEVIN: I wanna play....

MEGWYN: ... you wanna play....

KEVIN: Ball.

MEGWYN: .... you wann...

> *(Kevin stands)*

KEVIN: ... yes.... yes... yes, I wanna play fuckin' ball. What the fuck else is here for me now!?

MEGWYN: Where do you think you're going to go with this?

KEVIN: I don't know. I just know that I don't want this anymore.

MEGWYN: This like, what? This like, your life?

KEVIN: Your life.

> *(her cell rings again)*

MEGWYN: FUCK! *(she hits the silent button again)*
> Your life.
> I just... I can't anymore.
> That's my dad. His flight was probably delayed. *(almost in tears)* Do I call him back and tell him to just not come?

KEVIN: Do what you need to do.

MEGWYN: *(pleading)* I think you need to just cut this out.

KEVIN: Cut what out?

MEGWYN: THIS.

KEVIN: "This" what?

MEGWYN: THIS! Do you not see how you might be a bit old to pursue this?

KEVIN: Look at this. Look at your life. Look at this world you've built around yourself. Just look.

MEGWYN: What about it?

> *(pause)*

KEVIN: I don't know. This apartment. I don't knowwwww. This apartment. Visits with friends I don't... I... like I just don't have any... like, that I just don't give a fuck about, ok? The brunches, dinner parties, and all this stuff you do? It's great, and I love you, but I'm just.... I can't. I feel like a caged animal here. It keeps me up. I can't focus on what could be one of the worst careers in finance, ever.

MEGWYN: It's your apartment, and your friends, and YOU picked
your career Kevin. Nobody picked it for you.
   You're bi-polar or something, I swear to god. Just not that
long ago it seemed like this was a good situation for you. I
thought we were on the same page here, hello? I think you need
to just take the weekend, and chill . . .

KEVIN: *(cutting her off)* . . . no no no . . .

MEGWYN: Well what am I gonna do, Kevin? It's been two years with
us here. What am I supposed to do, just go on as if you never
existed?

MEGWYN: *(to herself)* I'm down to two days a week teaching now . . . .

KEVIN: What?

MEGWYN: I'm going to have to start bartending again.

KEVIN: So that IS what this is about . . .

MEGWYN: OH no, don't you even TRY to play that shit with me. I
took care of myself, and my brother AND my dad for years before you. That type of bullshit might work for your boys, and
their little fuckin' trashbag girlfriends, but don't you pull that
shit with me!

KEVIN: Okay-ay.
   (pause)

MEGWYN: You hear me?
   (Kevin looks at her, guilty, shameful)
   (she embraces him) Why?

KEVIN: Shit happens, Meg. I'm not going to have many, if any more
opportunities like this. I can't let all *(seeking)* . . . THIS *(referring to their shared apartment, belongings, friends)* be 'it' for me. I
just won't . . . I CAN'T do it.

MEGWYN: You're being a real fuckin' asshole. It's not two thousand
two anymore, Kevin, and you're not a college baseball star now.
You're just another loan officer who's about to get the axe, just
like the rest of the guys on your floor. Can we both please get a
grip? Just find out how to file for unemployment online, and
start looking for something else, like ALL your boys are doing
right now, as we speak.
   (silence)

KEVIN: I've been MORE than supportive of you, when you were
working more, and . . . .

MEGWYN: . . . I stopped auditioning because I wanted to . . .

KEVIN: . . . because you wanted to, what?

(pause)

(he gestures in sarcastic reference to the apartment) Exactly.

(pause)

MEGWYN: It's a sex thing, isn't it?

KEVIN: NO, it's not just that . . .

MEGWYN: . . . oh it's not JUST that. You don't fuckin' think I smelled this?

KEVIN: What do you mean?

MEGWYN: You leave for work and kiss me like I'm your grandma.

KEVIN: Please.

MEGWYN: *(mocking)* Guess the ole' tread came off the tires, huh? I guess you . . . .

KEVIN: *(stopping her)* . . . Jesus, Meg . . .

MEGWYN: No seriously. How often now? Huh? Hardly ever?

KEVIN: WhatEver . . .

MEGWYN: Right. Can ya just admit it?

KEVIN: Admit . . .

MEGWYN: . . . that you WANNA go ride on a bus in the Midwest in a bus and fuck 19 year olds?

KEVIN: . . . what?

MEGWYN: What do you want from me? You want me to act like a 19 year old for you? I can . . . you want me to act like the co-eds back at Central fuckin' Michigan? Because I can . . . .

KEVIN: Oh, for fuck sakes.

MEGWYN: No, no. I want to. I'll be a freshman. I just signed up for a rush, and now I'm checking out all the sorority houses allllll over campus. *(mocking)* 'wow, aren't you Kevin Keller . . . the senior who pitched a two hitter last season against Ball State *(she grabs his belt)*. Do you want me to come over? Maybe hang out for awhile before I go to my afternoon class?

KEVIN: Meg. Cut it out. *(he pulls away from her)*

MEGWYN: I mean, that is what you really want, right?

KEVIN: I'm not built for this shit, Meg. *(she persists)*

Cut it out. *(she stops)*

I've been pretty good to you.

(she stares at him)

KEVIN: I let you move in with me after only a few weeks. I never made you....

MEGWYN: ... but it was THAT bad?...

KEVIN: ... I let your little brother stay here while your dad was, you know, before???..., getting dried out???...

MEGWYN: ... has it really been that bad? Has it been the hell that you're making it out to be?

KEVIN: No. It wasn't. It wasn't at first, but things change.

MEGWYN: That's MY fault?

KEVIN: I didn't say it was your fault.

MEGWYN: *(stoic, fighting tears)* ... Yeah, well, you know what Kevin, not everybody has all the options open to them Kevin....

KEVIN: I know all of this Meg, and I'm sorry, I...

MEGWYN: Thanks Kevin. I appreciate it.

KEVIN: Ohhhhh.... *(he goes to embrace her)*

MEGWYN: *(she rejects him)* I think you're fuckin' crazy Kevin.

KEVIN: I'm not crazy.

> *(pause)*

I'm scared.

MEGWYN: Something is wrong with you. Seriously wrong. I don't know what I'm gonna do. My dad's alone, and now I'm alone now, and I'm fuckin' scared.

> *(he embraces her more forcefully this time, and holds on)*

KEVIN: You'll be fine.

MEGWYN: Why is that your answer for everything? It's gonna be 'fine'. How fuckin' easy is this for you?

KEVIN: ... I just renewed my lease. Just take this front room, make it into a bedroom, and rent it out to one of your friends. It's not all that difficult to....

MEGWYN: *(she pushes him away)* I'M NOT TALKING ABOUT THE FUCKING APARTMENT!

> *(pause)*

KEVIN: I'm gonna go. I'm just gonna go out there now.

> *(pause)*

MEGWYN: This is not happening.

> *(Kevin walks into the bedroom.)*

MEGWYN: This is not fuckin' happening.

> *Meg sits on the couch, and cries.*
>
> *He re enters carrying a sports bag, filled with clothing, and a glove attached to the bag. He stands and looks at her briefly.*
>
> *He exits.*

Dogma Afternoon

Kate McCamy

Produced in May 2010 by The Drilling Company at the 78th Street Playhouse for their Faith-themed evening of one-act plays. Directed by Kate McCamy. With: Amanda Dillard—Evan; Mickey Carpenter—Adam.

CHARACTERS

Evan is a young hip girl, 20s, with little tolerance for stupid.
Adam, 20s, not stupid but incapable of reining in his anger at the world.

PLACE

A spare room with a table, at least two chairs and a red corded telephone.

TIME

Present.

Evan, an attractive, trendy young woman, sits at a table doing the crossword puzzle. A telephone is on the table.

EVAN: Hmm, Heavenly father...
> *(Counts to four)*
> *Adam, a young man enters, he holds a piece of paper. He sees Evan and takes a second to collect himself.*

ADAM: Oh hi Evan.

EVAN: Hey.

ADAM: Ah, Adam, we worked together a coupla weeks ago...

EVAN: Yep.

ADAM: You get this from Harrison?

EVAN: Oh yeah, so not paying attention to that shit.
> *(back to crossword)*

ADAM: I can't believe that micromanaging pissant wants us to use a script. What a waste of tax payers money... This is almost as bad as the Census...

EVAN: Oh yeah how's that goin?

ADAM: I quit. My boss was fired by his boss who is an inept asshole, just like this place, a microcosm of the bigger picture. The higher up the bureaucrat the more incompetent a tyrant.

EVAN: Host.

ADAM: No Tyrant.

EVAN: Host, four letter word for . . . never mind.

ADAM: Huh? I rest my case, we just sit here doing crosswords!

EVAN: Ah, yeah and from a lot of points of view this is a good thing.

ADAM: Yeah, sure, you're right. Evan, how do you deal with the politics and hypocrisy of this place?

EVAN: I smoke a joint.

ADAM: Oh. Sure, I mean . . . why didn't I think of that? . . . Next time. How can you deal with that idiot high? You stoned now?

EVAN: No Adam . . . .

ADAM: I thought you said . . .

EVAN: Dude you believe everything you hear?

ADAM: Oh no course not. But I wouldn't say anything anyway, I mean I'm not . . . a snitch or nothin'. I mean Harrison is a waste of air space anyway, runs this tiny little operation like, like he is God and we're his minions.

EVAN: I dunno do ten people make a minion? Relax, we know he's a schmuck, even he knows he's a schmuck. I wouldn't want his job.

ADAM: But he's ineffectual, does nothing but get in the way, what does it cost the tax payers to employ that jerk?

EVAN: 16.32 an hour.

ADAM: What? That's all he makes?

(pause)

Did you know they spent 9 billion dollars on another moon expedition? Speaking of wasting money. I mean what the fuck? Didn't we already go there? And this is after firing Pluto!

EVAN: Yeah, 9 billion is a lot of bread.

ADAM: Think about it, Evan, one billion dinner rolls on top of each other would go from here to the moon. Think that times 9. Now that is a lot of bread.

EVAN: Now that is a waste.

ADAM: Exactly.

EVAN: I mean the bread, well both actually. You always measure things in dinner rolls?

ADAM: It helps give perspective. OK Evan, I'm going to let you in on something, alright, look, this whole system that they're running...

EVAN: What system, here?

ADAM: No, much bigger. The, Corporate Greed Machine, well let's just call them the.... Illuminati for now.

EVAN: You mean like the church? Or the Masons?

ADAM: Bigger, but now instead of using the wrath of God, they're using fear of foreclosure. These guys are powered by greed. Not faith. Just growing, amassing more and more power and money.

EVAN: So what, they meet once a month on Monster island and plot the next bailout?

ADAM: Exactly. Hey. You don't believe me? Ever notice how newly elected Presidents get really old fast?

EVAN: Yeah, It's a stressful job...

ADAM: They're sat down and told the real deal and they go gray, like, Bing! overnight. Happens all the time.

EVAN: What're they told?

ADAM: I imagine it's kind of like the Sith Lord telling them,"Keep us at war so we make money, keep the population distracted so they don't notice."... diabolical evil laughter...

EVAN: That's crazy...

ADAM: Sure is, this whole recession, manufactured. The middle class was getting too powerful so boom, economic downturn, make everyone worried about survival, like in the old days, so we're too busy to notice that laws are being changed left and right. Facebook and twitter was invented to lull the masses into a state of catatonic complacency in the guise of communication! Now they can do whatever the fuck they want. They're harvesting.

EVAN: Harvesting?

ADAM: Yes, like praying mantis'.

EVAN: Praying mantis harvest?

ADAM: Preying on the innocent, as usual. The banks Evan, follow the money, the banks own the houses. People got to live some where. Get us all scared about terrorists and then when that begins to wear off they pull the plug on our middle class illusions.

EVAN: That's a pretty bleak outlook you got there Adam.

ADAM: Well, it all adds up. Hey think about it, anytime something bad happens a celebrity dies. You notice that?

EVAN: Ah, no . . .

ADAM: They do. And they go in threes? Or so they say. Michael Jackson, Ed McMahon, and Farrah . . .

EVAN: Oh yeah I remember that, poor Farrah, she got the shaft even in death . . .

ADAM: Yeah and the media is complicit! What those headlines covered up were all the fucking bailouts. Oh and they made that crap up about the threes. Just to make us sit around waiting for celebrity number two and three die. Instead of paying attention, HELLO!. People are either evil mongers or sheep being lead to the slaughter house. you know what? Basically people are stupid or suck. . . . Especially Celeste . . . Shit.

EVAN: Celeste?

ADAM: Never mind . . . forget I said that . . .

EVAN: Oh, your girlfriend?

ADAM: No! Ex!

EVAN: Ah, the break up thing. So, how long?

ADAM: 6 years.

EVAN: OK well that is a long time. Almost common law right? I understand, I dated a guy for like 2 years. The whole time his relationship status was single, then went to it's complicated then to in a relationship, but it wasn't with me apparently. That was a bite.

ADAM: Bite is right, it still feels raw.

EVAN: How long ago did you split? They say it's a month recovery for every year involved.

ADAM: That is totally inaccurate. We, ah, dated for about in or around 5 months, 2.4 weeks. Close to the pivotal 6 months mark . . .

EVAN: I thought you said 6 years?

ADAM: See, that is why I know for a fact that month to year recovery ratio is bullshit.

EVAN: Ah, Adam?

ADAM: Yeah?

EVAN: How come you're working here?

ADAM: Well, because it's a good thing to do, you know help out people . . .

EVAN: Yeah, but what about helping yourself? You seem like . . .

ADAM: Like what? What?

EVAN: It's just that you seem a little intense.

ADAM: Intense? I care, is there something wrong with that now?

EVAN: No . . .

ADAM: So why are you here?

EVAN: Oh ah the experience, and the credit, for college, the money of course though it sucks ass . . .

ADAM: How can you do that?

EVAN: What?

ADAM: Just be so accepting? You know what that makes you? A sheep.

EVAN: Hey if I was a sheep I wouldn't be here OK? You know what? Fuck you. I am not accepting anything, I'm here to do something proactive. Yeah the world is fucked up but there's good stuff too. I see the beauty, the trees that grow through the cement. How did you get passed the psychological test anyway? As I recall one of the requirements was a cheerful positive disposition?

ADAM: Hey I'm a positive person, I believe that deep down there is light in everyone's soul, that we're programed to want to do good from the first moment we look into our mother's eyes.

EVAN: Hah! You're a moaner.

ADAM: A what?

EVAN: You bitch and moan about everything that's wrong with the world and all your conspiracy theories but what good is that doing us? Right now?

ADAM: Hey well, I feel better knowing the truth. Life is hard. At least the bubbles aren't there to pop.

EVAN: Hard? What do you know from hard? My mother's life was . . . Her dad was murdered by an evil motherfucker and then they beat her dog, Silky so badly that his back leg had to be removed, and the people would say to her how sorry they were about the dog, not her because they couldn't see her pain. But Silky was fine. Ran around, chasing balls, sniffing and doing all the things dogs do but with three legs. He didn't know any different. Anyway, the point is, we get some bumps along the way, you know? We're all damaged goods in the delivery of life but, well, we get there. If we try . . .

ADAM: I ah, my.... My mom was, well she, I guess she wasn't as lucky or, well as strong as your mom. She didn't have a three legged dog to...

EVAN: Was? She dead?

ADAM: Yeah, she had just finished redecorating her new apartment, my folks had split, and, well I use to joke that she hated the wall paper, but she picked it out. I don't know... look, you're right, it's not all bad, I mean there are good things, like...

EVAN: Like what?

ADAM: Ah, beer?

EVAN: That was you joking right?

ADAM: *(impulsively)* I meant to say... you, you're good. That's why I come here... to be with you...

> *Phone rings. They both jump and Evan answers it.*

EVAN: Hi Harrison. Uh huh, really? Ok, sure.

> *(To Adam)*

They want to talk to a man...

ADAM: A jumper?

EVAN: No, a popper. Was your mother... did she?

ADAM: Yes. A jumper.

EVAN: So sorry..

> *She hands him the phone. Adam looks at the script.*

ADAM: *(reading from script)* Hello, this is Adam and I'm here to help you through this difficult time... no I don't need to know your real name. Just tell me what's got you so down... down is trite... OK in a morass of misery... Yes... Well you should think about the people who care about you... I'm sure there is some one out there who cares... Really? Well, we care here, that's why we're here. Life is a gift, really. I know... but it is... I know, no... I really do know... Hey I haven't had sex in 6 years, it ain't the end of the world.

> *(clearly straying from script)*

Yeah. No, I meant no it's not worth killing yourself over, really. No woman ah, person is worth it....

> *Evan is taking notes on a form.*

ADAM: No you have a right to be angry. We all have things to be angry about. You just have to find a way to deal, you know? Something outside of yourself that you can just trust, like a three legged dog.

Yeah God works... exactly, yes he does. That's basically what the Bible is right? A how to behave book for dummies, right?

Evan gestures for him to keep him on the phone. She makes some more notes, keeping track of the time.

ADAM: Me? Well sure, I mean I know all the cliche parts... I'm well there is a lot to read and read into... hey whatever works for you is good. No Jesus was cool no doubt.... yes answer the door it's a sign, a miracle maybe? Or it's one of my colleagues, just happened to be in your area, just checking... to make sure you're OK.... Hello, hello?

EVAN: They get 'em?

ADAM: Yeah.

EVAN: Wow. Nice work. Hey you OK?

ADAM: I strayed from the script, just a bit.

EVAN: So fucking what!

ADAM: I just hate being phony.

EVAN: But you weren't.

ADAM: All that bible shit..

EVAN: Hey, that's what he needs to believe in, let him. Like you said, we all have to believe in something, out side ourselves. Otherwise we drown in our own Narcism or conspiracy theories... You were good, really.

ADAM: Yeah?

EVAN: Yeah. You wanna go out... for a beer or something?

ADAM: Now?

EVAN: After our shift dumb ass.

ADAM: Oh, right, of course, sure. Yeah, I mean yes I do, would love to.

Blackout

Eighth Wonder

Jon Spano

Original Production Information: May 10, 2010, Times Square Arts Center. Director—Stephen Field. Cast: Jon Spano (Barry); Val Davison (Melissa). Producers—Jon Spano and Stephen Field.

CHARACTERS

Melissa. . . a woman in her thirties; loquacious
Barry . . . . a man in his late forties; reserved, wry

TIME AND PLACE

The present. Around Noon. The Lyceum Theatre in New York City.

SETTING

Two seats in the mezzanine section of the Lyceum Theatre.

The rumblings of a crowd gathering inside the Lyceum Theatre in New York City. . . .
Lights come up on Barry, sweating, already seated in a row of the theatre's packed mezzanine section, his jacket on the one remaining seat beside him. He stares out, downstage, towards what is presumed to be the stage of the Lyceum. He wipes sweat from his brow then fiddles with his program, a glamorous black-and-white headshot of a woman on its cover.
Melissa enters hastily and out of breath, squeezing past those already seated. She carries a large purse and her own program.

MELISSA: *(To those she steps past.)* Excuse me. So sorry. Thank you. Excuse me, please. . . .
(To Barry.)
Is this seat taken? Is this your jacket?
(Barry begrudgingly takes his jacket from the empty seat. Melissa "plops" into the seat. She addresses Barry, almost a verbal assault, but she's very friendly. Too friendly. The kind of person you hope you don't sit next to on a plane.)
MELISSA: Uff . . . ! I think this is the last seat in the house. I thought I almost wouldn't get in! I overheard an usher say that people started lining up outside the theatre at seven a.m.!
UNSEEN ANNOUNCER: Ladies and Gentlemen: Welcome to the Lyceum Theatre. As you take your seats, please remember to turn off

your cell phones. The memorial tribute to Lydia North will begin in approximately fifteen minutes with an introduction to her life and career by Hal Holbrook.

MELISSA: Wow! Did you hear that? Hal Holbrook! Just look at this crowd. Lydia always sells out the house.

BARRY: Even from the beyond.

> *(Barry smiles at Melissa. She's made him uncomfortable with her forwardness. Melissa noisily takes a roll of candy from her purse. She pops one in her mouth and offers one to Barry, already annoyed by her constant chatter.)*

MELISSA: I wouldn't have missed this for the world. Lydia was my all-time favorite.—Would you like a mint?

BARRY: Actually I'd like a drink.

MELISSA: Sorry all I have are mints. Oh and Cherry Hall's cough drops from when I had a cold.

BARRY: *(Taking the mint.)* I'll take the mint.—Unwrap your candy before the show starts, right?

> *(Barry discreetly puts the mint in his pocket. Melissa takes out a compact and checks her makeup. More noise. She applies a bit of lipstick. Suddenly:)*

MELISSA: I just saw Bernadette Peters and Kristen Chenowith downstairs.

BARRY: You should go say hi! Ask them for their autograph!

MELISSA: I tried to get here early to sit in the orchestra section, but my manager wouldn't let me leave. So I told him I had an appointment with my OB/GYN? To which the dumb Greek said,

> *(thick accent)*

"Can't you wait until your day off to take care of these female things?" To which I replied, "Female things aren't always a matter of convenience." That shut him up for the rest of the morning, which was just fine with me. Silence is golden I always say.

BARRY: If only it were contagious.

> *(Melissa looks around, bites her tongue. She pulls a bottle of water from a crinkling plastic bag in her purse and gulps. Then, tentatively as she leafs through her program:)*

MELISSA: So um, did you take the day off work too?

BARRY: No I'm here from L.A.

MELISSA: I was born in L.A.! But I don't remember a thing about it. My father moved us—my mother, my sister, and me—moved

us to New Jersey when I was two . . . Bet you just got off the
plane, right? You do look a bit peaked, if I do say so myself . . .
Are you an actor?

BARRY: Depends on who you ask.

MELISSA: You are, aren't you? I knew it!

BARRY: What was your first clue?

MELISSA: Oh I can always tell . . . We have a different energy than normal people . . . . Maybe I've seen you in something?

BARRY: I was in a couple of slasher flicks. In one, I play this psychopath from L.A. who goes to see *Wicked* . . . and sitting next
to him is this woman who won't stop talking. So he whips out a
meat cleaver and –

MELISSA: Oh will you stop! I'm just asking because you have a familiar face. A nice face. Nice eyes. You'd be good in commercials, if
I do say so myself . . . That's so stupid: "If I do say so myself."
Because I'm talking, right? I said it. So why say, "If I do say so
myself"?

(Pause.)

So did you ever do one?

BARRY: Do one what?

MELISSA: A commercial?

BARRY: Yes, for K-Mart: "Santa's making his list! Let Mr. Blue Light
make yours!"

MELISSA: That was you? WOW! I'd love to do a commercial. But until
my big break, I'm just a waitress.

BARRY: Then I'll take one quiet seat in the mezzanine, please, with a
little elbow room on the side. Hold the talk!

*(Melissa looks off, hurt by Barry's abruptness. Barry tries a
bit of damage control.)*

BARRY: Um . . . I admire people who can do that. Wait tables. It's
tough work.

MELISSA: It's mostly humiliating. Most actresses I know are wait-
resses. Or go-go dancers. I'd do that. Strip. Pole dance, whatever. If I were really skinny . . . But as far as my acting is
concerned? I'm no Lydia North . . . . I act for the fun of it. And
I love going to auditions. You meet so many interesting people.
And that's fine. That's enough. Because I love theatre. Even if I
can't be a part of it in the way I dreamed of . . . . I'm Melissa.

BARRY: Barry.

(They shake hands. As he withdraws his hand, Barry winces slightly. There's a sharp pain in his gut that he tries to hide. Melissa doesn't notice; she's looking at her program. Barry's pain subsides.)

MELISSA: So what do you do now? Since you don't act anymore?

BARRY: I own a dog-walking service. "Whisker Walkers" I call it. Twelve employees. Fifty-three dogs. Hey what do you get when you mix a Poodle with a Great Dane?

(Brief pause. Melissa can't guess.)

A Great Pain!

(Barry laughs. Melissa finally gets it; laughs.)

MELISSA: *(Laughing too much, too long.)* Oh that's funny!

BARRY: No it isn't.

MELISSA: *(Moving on; leafing through event program.)* Um, nice program don't you think? That it's a nice photo?

BARRY: *(Studying program cover; a headshot.)* Yes. It's something in her eyes.

MELISSA: In my scrapbook I have an old review of *Ransom For A Dead Man?* Where Walter Kerr wrote that Lydia North is the eighth wonder of the world! —What's your favorite performance? Of Lydia's I mean.

BARRY: It's so hard to say.

MELISSA: I know, right? Because there're so many. It's like asking what do you like better, filet mignon or lobster tail? If you don't eat meat, it's easy to pick... but I like surf and turf.

BARRY: Irish Moonsong.

MELISSA: Oh you saw that?! I am so jealous! You must have been very young. Rumor has it that *Irish Moonsong* is when Lydia started drinking a lot. But I don't believe all that. People gossip about anyone who's famous... Just rip our idols to shreds! And if you're a guy and you're a famous actor, then all the rags say you're gay—even about George Clooney. But I know he's not.

BARRY: Oh, did you sleep with him?

MELISSA: What? No! Don't be silly! I mean not that I haven't thought about it. I just know because he's so manly you know? He could be your husband or your friend or your daddy or –

(Catching herself.)

Oh dear I, I didn't mean anything by that. I mean who cares who Tom Cruise secretly bonks or artificially inseminates? I don't. Not anymore since he started talking to aliens and jumping up and down on Oprah. On her couch I mean. It's just that when you're famous people say the—

> *(Barry gasps, an uncomfortable exhale. He takes a handkerchief from his pocket and wipes the sweat from his face.)*

MELISSA: Hey are you okay?

BARRY: Yes. Just... I'm a little warm. It comes and goes.

MELISSA: Oh I am just so rude! I'm not even considering how you must—You're in mourning, right? I mean, we all are. We'll never see another Lydia North play again.

> *(Melissa's sad for a few moments then, remembering something, giggles.)*

BARRY: What's so funny?

MELISSA: When I was like nine, my mother took me to see Lydia in *Anne of Green Gables*. Oh for years after that I wished that I was Anne.

BARRY: Children wish for silly things.

MELISSA: And I thought that one day we'd do plays together.

BARRY: Well there it is: life as dreamed versus... life as lived.

MELISSA: Oh don't get me wrong. I was a happy kid. Devoted father and a great mother... a saint really.

BARRY: Yours too?

> *(Melissa suddenly sniffs the air: there's an awful smell. She sniffs again, looks around.)*

MELISSA: What's that odor? Oh my god do you smell that?

BARRY: *(He does, but plays dumb.)* Smell what?

MELISSA: That...! I think it's coming from the man sitting behind us. You know, a person reaches a certain age and wearing "Depends" should just be mandatory!

> *(Barry squirms, looks around for another place to sit.)*

BARRY: Are there really no other seats left?

MELISSA: Oh Barry please don't move. The smell will go away.... Or, or is it me? I'm bothering you aren't I? One time a guy sat next to me and my mom on a plane and he changed his seat because I wouldn't stop talking.

> *(Sniffing the air again: it's bad.)*

Ew! The Polaski Skyway!

BARRY: The what?

(Melissa searches her purse for a bottle of spray perfume. She finds it; discreetly sprays the air.)

MELISSA: That smell. What it reminds me of. The Polaski Skyway. It's this bridge in New Jersey just outside Manhattan? There's all these smokestacks and factories and these green-black ponds and canals full of sludge. So if anyone from Newark ever says to you "must be something in the water" they're not kidding...! But no, it's something else, something...

(Recognition.)

Oh!

BARRY: What now?

MELISSA: Well when my mom and I were on that plane? She was really sick. And between the chemo and all the meds she had very distinct reactions... Odors. Hey maybe that guy on the plane didn't change his seat because of me. Maybe he moved because of my mother's *(unsaid: smell)* ... Well it doesn't matter now anyway. The smell's gone.

(Putting away perfume; moment to reflect.)

Doctors say certain cancers can run in the family. I'm always getting checked. It's scary how this tiny thing inside you scarfs away at your guts and grows to be so much bigger than you.

BARRY: Disease is humbling. It tells us that it's, it's what you can't see that kills you.

MELISSA: *(contemplating)* Maybe... You know I never asked.

BARRY: About what?

MELISSA: About you.

BARRY: Oh I grew up in Oakland. Only child. Father was a nerdy math professor at Berkeley. Kind of a cliché, actually. And my mother? A-number one. Stellar by all accounts. I couldn't have done better.

MELISSA: Go on...

BARRY: No I, I think they're about to start the program...

MELISSA: Maybe we can go to Starbucks after the memorial and... and talk.... I'd like that. I'd like that very much.

BARRY: I would too but. I have a flight back to L.A.

MELISSA: Oh.

(Barry winces; he stifles a sound, trying to repress his pain, which is worse now. He takes a flask and a bottle of pills from his jacket pocket. He swallows a pill, quickly chasing it with a large gulp of liquor. Melissa is alarmed.)

Hey you can't drink in here! What's wrong with you? People are gonna—

(Barry puts the pills and flask back in his jacket. He's short of breath. Melissa sniffs the air: the smell is back. She leans in towards Barry and sniffs him: it dawns on her!))

Oh... Oh my! Oh dear! It's, it's you. It is you, isn't it? You, you're. It's your medications! Oh God I... I'm so... I'm so—I wish I could just keep my mouth shut!

BARRY: It's all right. You're rather refreshing in this air.

MELISSA: You know, despite everything that went on with my mom, she kept a really positive outlook. I think that helped.

BARRY: I'm sure it did.

MELISSA: And your mother must be so worried about you.

BARRY: Oh. No... In fact she'll never know... And she wouldn't have wanted to... She died. Of...

(Referring to his sick body.)

... of this.... Coming to this event is, quite literally, my last wish. —When I was thirteen I saw a full-page ad in the L.A. Times for this play called *Irish Moonsong* at the Mark Taper Forum. And the ad had a picture of Lydia's face. And I pretended for a moment, just like you did when you saw *Anne of Green Gables*, that Lydia might adopt me—

MELISSA: Acting. And our mothers. Lydia. We really have so much in common if I do say so my—

BARRY: —because my foster mother told me that my real mother died giving birth to me. But I knew, even as a boy, that that was a lie. I knew my mother was alive and well.

MELISSA: But if you know that it means you found her.

BARRY: Yes.

MELISSA: Where was she?

BARRY: She was... on stage.

(Barry salutes the stage with his flask: a long, hard look.)

MELISSA: What...? Oh God. Oh no. No, no, no, no, no.... You're lying! Don't you dare make up something like that about –

(Melissa is dumbfounded. Barry winces in pain: this one is the worst yet.)

BARRY: *(Forcing a deep breath.)* I took one look at that ad and I felt this string between me and Lydia connecting us . . . through the eyes. And so I bought a ticket. To *Irish Moonsong*. And I was . . . awed watching her up there beneath the lights. She was so . . . spectacular.—And when the play's over I go to the stage door and I write the stage manager a little note to see if I can meet Lydia. And the stage manager says, "Barry? Lydia would love to say hello, and he brings me inside to the greenroom. And there's a handful of her friends already there, just waiting. Her manager. An assistant. A guy she was engaged to. And then coming down the hall, I hear "the voice!" And when Lydia enters, the whole energy of the room shifts and you know you're in the presence of a star. She's sipping a glass of white wine, saying hello to everyone. And then suddenly Lydia twirls around to face me: It's the moment I've been waiting for! She smiles at me and offers her hand . . .

(Acting this out a bit; extending his arm.)

But then she blinks a couple of times. And there's a, a pause. The awkward kind. And then she jerks her hand back and the smile disappears from her face . . . The others see Lydia, standing frozen . . . and a hush comes over the room. It's just me and Lydia, staring into each other's eyes.

MELISSA: *(Looks from program cover to Barry.)* Because . . . oh my god . . . Of course! They're the same!

BARRY: I remember a smudge of lipstick on her front tooth. And then came seven seething words:

(Ferocious whisper.)

"WHO LET THAT FUCKING KID IN HERE!?"

(Hard sigh.)

And, and she whirls around and her wine spills over the top of her glass and she disappears down the hallway . . . Gone. And everyone's staring at me, like I've done something wrong! And I ran out of the theatre . . . ran back to the bus stop. Back to Oakland. And I never saw another Lydia North play again.

(Wincing in pain.)

MELISSA: Are you—?

BARRY: *(Grabbing his jacket.)* Gotta go.

MELISSA: No. Stay. Please.

BARRY: *(Rising hastily to exit.)* It was nice to meet you. Melissa. Thank you for the mint.... Enjoy the show.

> *(Barry stumbles and almost falls. He steadies himself.)*

MELISSA: Barry...! Wait. Don't go.

BARRY: *(To those he must step over; out of breath.)* Pardon me please. Excuse me. Pardon me.... Ma'am I said excuse me!

MELISSA: BARRY!

> *(Barry is gone. Melissa is about to go after him. Then she is suddenly distracted, as the lights start to dim and the offstage announcer speaks:)*

UNSEEN ANNOUNCER: Ladies and gentlemen: Please welcome Mr. Hal Holbrook!

> *(The crowd begins to applaud. Melissa looks back-and-forth between Barry and the stage, torn between the two. Melissa falls back into her seat, looking straight ahead, a heartbreaking look. A spot on Melissa as the applause grows louder and the lights fade to black.)*

THE END

A Fellow of Infinite Jest

Don Nigro

A Fellow of Infinite Jest was first presented at the Edinburgh Fringe Festival as part of the White Room Theatre's Big Bite-Size Breakfast in the Assembly Rooms at George Street, Edinburgh, Scotland on August 7th, 2010 with the following cast: Kemp—Nick Brice; Shakespeare—Russell Shaw. Tech Manager—Andy Cresswell. Director—Clive Wedderburn, with help from consultants Shirley Jaffe and Julian McDowell.

CHARACTERS

Kempe (50)
Shakespeare (35)

SETTING

A nearly deserted tavern in London late one night in the year
1599. A wooden table and some chairs, surrounded by darkness.

Will Kempe, most famous comic actor of his time, known for his
spirited jigs, bawdy jokes and merriments, a slapstick comedian, song
and dance man. An original shareholder, with Shakespeare, Burbage
and others, in the Lord Chamberlain's Men, Kempe most likely orig-
inated the roles of Dogberry in *Much Ado About Nothing*, Peter in
Romeo and Juliet, Bottom in *Midsummer Night's Dream*, Costard in
Loves Labours Lost, and Lancelot Gobbo in *Merchant of Venice*. Some
believe he was also the original Falstaff, although others think this
unlikely. What is known is that in 1599 Shakespeare seems to have
changed his mind and killed off the immensely popular fat knight off-
stage in *Henry V*, about the same time as Will Kempe left the Lord
Chamberlain's Men for good, morris dancing his way from London
to Norwich. Kempe probably died in 1603.

> *Let those that play your clowns speak no more than is*
> *set down for them; for there be of them that will them-*
> *selves laugh to set some quantity of barren spectators to*
> *laugh, too, though in the meantime some necessary*
> *question of the play then to be considered. That's vil-*
> *lainous, and shows a most pitiful ambition in the fool*
> *that uses it.*
>
> —HAMLET (III.2.38–45)

(A tavern. Night. Shakespeare sits writing at a wooden table. Kempe moves into the light, holding a sheet of manuscript. He's been drinking, but he's not drunk.)

KEMPE: What is all this shit?

SHAKESPEARE: *(Continuing to write, not looking up.)* To which particular shit are you referring?

KEMPE: This speech you've stuck into this Hamlet thing you've been working on. All this shit about sticking to the script. What is all this shit?

SHAKESPEARE: It's just a rough draft.

KEMPE: What are you trying to say?

SHAKESPEARE: It's fairly clear, I think. Hamlet instructs the players to speak the words as they're written, instead of making them up as they go along.

KEMPE: Hamlet's an arse wipe.

SHAKESPEARE: I'll give that note to Burbage.

KEMPE: This is not meant as a personal criticism, Will, but, really, this Hamlet thing is a reeking piece of cow flop. The gravedigger is all right, I suppose, but what have I got to do otherwise? Where are the jokes? Where's Yorick?

SHAKESPEARE: Yorick is dead.

KEMPE: That's the problem. That's my part. Yorick is my part. Why does Yorick have to be dead? I could liven things up a bit as Yorick. I might even be able to save this turkey for you, although I doubt it. But I can't do much if Yorick is just a skull. I can't play a skull. Unless I do a bit of ventriloquism. What the hell is the matter with you? I'm telling you frankly, Will, and I hate to say this, but I really think your powers are in decline.

SHAKESPEARE: You think so?

KEMPE: You've been going down hill ever since Titus Andronicus. And where's the Henry Fifth play you promised us?

SHAKESPEARE: It's nearly done.

KEMPE: I want to do more Falstaff. Falstaff, a man can sink his teeth into. Not all this morbid, melancholy Dane shit. What the hell are you wasting your time with this old rubbish for, anyway? Falstaff's the man for me.

SHAKESPEARE: Falstaff's not in the new one.

KEMPE: What?

SHAKESPEARE: Falstaff's not in Henry the Fifth.

KEMPE: You're joking. Don't try and joke with me, Willy. You're no good at that. That's my area.

SHAKESPEARE: I'm not joking. Falstaff's not in Henry the Fifth.

KEMPE: Falstaff's not in Henry the Fifth?

SHAKESPEARE: No.

KEMPE: Falstaff is not in Henry the Fifth?

SHAKESPEARE: No.

KEMPE: Well, where the hell is he, then? Hiding behind a tree?

SHAKESPEARE: He's dead.

KEMPE: Falstaff is dead?

SHAKESPEARE: Yes.

KEMPE: Falstaff is dead? He's dead?

SHAKESPEARE: Yes.

KEMPE: Falstaff is dead. And Yorick is dead.

SHAKESPEARE: Yorick is very dead.

KEMPE: Have you lost your fucking mind?

SHAKESPEARE: Possibly.

KEMPE: If Falstaff is dead, and Yorick is dead, then where does that leave me? What the hell am I supposed to do? Just dance the jig at the end? Is that all you're leaving me? I just do my jig at the end, and that's it?

SHAKESPEARE: No more jigs.

KEMPE: What?

SHAKESPEARE: No more jigs at the end.

KEMPE: You're putting the jig in the middle? Well, that's an interesting thought, but—

SHAKESPEARE: No more jigs. No more making personal comments to the audience. No more improvisations. From now on, we're sticking to the script.

KEMPE: The script?

SHAKESPEARE: Yes.

KEMPE: We're sticking to the script, are we?

SHAKESPEARE: Yes.

KEMPE: Do you know what I do with the script?

SHAKESPEARE: Not much.

KEMPE: I wipe my stinking arse-hole with it. That's what I do with the script.

SHAKESPEARE: Yes. I've noticed.

KEMPE: What are you saying?

SHAKESPEARE: I'm saying from now on, there are no more jigs, no more making up your own lines at the spur of the moment and blurting them out in the middle of the performance, no more stopping the show to make jokes about the audience. No more of that. From now on, we just do the lines I write. That's it.

KEMPE: That's it, is it?

SHAKESPEARE: That's it.

KEMPE: You decided this all by yourself, did you?

SHAKESPEARE: We decided. All the shareholders.

KEMPE: I'm a shareholder.

SHAKESPEARE: We had a meeting.

KEMPE: Now you're having secret meetings?

SHAKESPEARE: You were invited. You didn't show up.

KEMPE: I had a very important engagement with a clockmaker's wife.

SHAKESPEARE: I'm sure you did.

KEMPE: So you all got together behind my back, and decided to shove me out? Is that it?

SHAKESPEARE: We didn't decide to shove you anywhere. We decided no more jigs, no more improvisations during the performance, no more talking to the audience unless it's in the script. That's what we decided.

KEMPE: Burbage too?

SHAKESPEARE: It was unanimous.

KEMPE: You're a liar.

SHAKESPEARE: You can ask them.

KEMPE: No more jigs. No more jokes. No more talking to the audience. What the hell is left for me? What's left for me, then?

SHAKESPEARE: What's left for you is to be an actor. An actor who learns his lines and says them the way they were written.

KEMPE: Oh, the lines, the lines, the precious lines. You're so damned precious about your stupid damned words. Precious, precious, precious. Honey tongued Shakespeare. This ain't your damned stupid Venus and Adonis masturbational fancy ass poetry, Willy.

This is the theatre. I'm an entertainer. We're entertainers. We're comedians. Comedians. We live by the seat of our pants. We make it up as we go along. The script is just a little road map. Something to blow our noses on and light our pipe with. The script is a jumping off point. That's all it is.

SHAKESPEARE: Well, there's not going to be any more jumping off. You can like it or you can not like it, but that's the way it's going to be, from now on.

KEMPE: You did this to me.

SHAKESPEARE: We all decided.

KEMPE: You did this to me. It was you that put them up to it.

SHAKESPEARE: They all agreed.

KEMPE: I didn't agree.

SHAKESPEARE: You've been outvoted.

KEMPE: You can take your damned votes and stick them up your wife's fat ass, you ungrateful, back-stabbing little sewer rat. I made you. I picked you up when you were nobody, a little shit-faced hayseed nobody, fornicating with sheep in Stratford. I gave you a job holding the horses, cleaning up horse shit, doing all the muck work. You were nobody. Without me you'd still be back there in fucking Stratford-Upon-Goat-Piss shoveling muck with your whore of a wife and your loony old bankrupt dad.

SHAKESPEARE: That's enough.

KEMPE: It is enough. It's more than enough. I've had enough of you, with your precious script. Your precious words. You're so fucking precious about your words. This is not how we did it in the old days. In the old days we were making it up as we went along. And people loved it. It was exciting. It was reckless. It was alive. Anything could happen. The script is a damned straight jacket for a bunch of cowards too stupid to trust their own wits in the moment. Fuck the script. I don't need any goddamned fucking script and I don't need you. I don't need any of you.

SHAKESPEARE: You make my work look stupid. You throw in dumb jokes older than Methuselah. You make obscene gestures at the audience. You throw fruit at them. You make animal noises. You interrupt the flow of the play for ten minutes of standing on your head and making farting noises. And I've put up with it all these years because you took me out of Stratford and gave me a chance. Don't tell me I'm not grateful. I've always been grateful. I will always be grateful. But I can't stand by and watch any more while my life's work is turned into a damned monkey festival. The same stupid jokes. The mockery of what I've written. The interruption of the story to insert completely irrelevant vulgar slapstick routines that were old when Alfred the Great was sucking on his wet nurse. We just can't have this any more. That sort of thing is over. You're just going to have to adjust.

KEMPE: *(Building to a fine rage.)* Or what? Adjust or what? Do you think I'm going to knuckle under to this sort of political bullshit? I don't need you. I don't need this damned company. I don't need any of you. I'll go out on my own. I'll dance my way to fucking Scotland, farting Greensleeves as I go, and the people will follow me. Nobody will pay any attention to you. The theatre is not a building. The theatre is not a piece of paper with a bunch of chicken scratching on it. I am the theatre. Flesh, blood and gonads. You are just a bunch of fucking words. Precious, precious, precious bullshit. Four hundred years from now, they'll remember me, not you. Nobody will have heard of you. This will be the Age of Will Kempe. I am the theatre. You are nothing. You have always been nothing. You will always be nothing. Nothing. Nothing.

(Kempe storms out rather magnificently. Shakespeare sits there. Puts pen down.)

SHAKESPEARE: He hath borne me on his back a thousand times.

(Shakespeare drinks. A moment. Kempe returns, a bit calmer.)

KEMPE: Treachery. You know it's treachery.

SHAKESPEARE: Worse. It's art. That was good, though. You built that speech beautifully. Can I use that?

(Pause.)

Look. I'll make you a bargain. If you'll stay, I'll bring Falstaff back. He won't die. We'll put him in Henry the Fifth. But you must say the lines as written. Do you understand? Word for word, as written. No jigs. No capers. No improvised asides. No commenting upon the buck teeth of the village idiot in the front row. Just trust the damned lines. Trust the play. You're a wonderful actor, a very great actor, when you just trust the play. But you must swear to me. You must swear it right now.

KEMPE: Do you hate me so much, you would murder the best damned character in the history of the world?

SHAKESPEARE: I don't hate you. I am immensely fond of you. But you must say the lines as written.

KEMPE: NOBODY TELLS ME WHAT TO SAY. NOBODY.

(Pause.)

SHAKESPEARE: Then Falstaff is dead.

KEMPE: What about the Henry Fourth plays? What about Merry Wives? How are you going to do them, without me?

SHAKESPEARE: Pope can play Falstaff.

KEMPE: Pope? Pope?

SHAKESPEARE: He's done it before, when you were ill.

KEMPE: Pope can barely pee in a pot.

SHAKESPEARE: He'll say the lines I wrote.

KEMPE: You're an arrogant, arrogant, vicious little turd.

SHAKESPEARE: I thought I was nothing.

KEMPE: You're worse than nothing. You're a damned writer.

(Pause.)

All right. So be it. Falstaff is dead. And this company is dead. And I'll dance on your grave. I'll dance a jig on the smoking ruins of this theatre. You'll see. I'm what the people want. Not you. Dancing. Jokes. Jigs. Clever patter. The old routines. That's what people want.

SHAKESPEARE: Nevertheless.

(Pause.)

KEMPE: You were my friend.

SHAKESPEARE: I am your friend.

KEMPE: You were a son to me.

SHAKESPEARE: I am your son.

KEMPE: You're a fool.

(Kempe turns and goes out. Pause.)

SHAKESPEARE: Yes.

(Shakespeare looks sadly at nothing for a bit. Then he picks up his pen and begins to write again, as lights fade. Darkness.)

The FQ

Andrew R. Heinze

The FQ premiered at the 16th Annual New York City 15-Minute Play Festival, at the American Globe Theatre, May 1, 2010, with Sally Burtenshaw (Sami) and Nick DeSimone (Burt). Producer—American Globe Theatre (& Turnip Theatre Company), Liz Keefe, Executive Director.

CHARACTERS

Sami (female; 40)
Burt (male; 40)

TIME

The present.

PLACE

An office.

At Rise: Burt sits behind his desk holding a script. Sami sits across from him holding a script.

BURT: Withdraw your script? Withdraw your script? You can't withdraw your script! My future is in this script. So's yours.
> *(Phone on Burt's desk rings. Burt eyes the caller ID, grimaces and picks up.)*
Hi Ronnie ... Sami's still here ... I know we're at deadline, it's just that ... Yeah, a problem, a little problem ... I'm not sure exactly. But whatever it is I can handle ... No, I ... But Ronnie ... But Ronnie ... But Ronnie ... Hello?
> *(Burt hangs up phone.)*
This is bad. This is very bad. Look, Sami, do you want to spend the rest of your life where you are right now, so far off Broadway you're in New Jersey? This is television. This is *cable*, and cable is where America lives. Where do you think Shakespeare would be working today? Off Broadway? Hah! He'd be on cable. Why? Because he was a success. A money-maker. He knew great art is great entertainment.
> *(pause)*
Do you have any idea how much money we're going to make when this show takes off—your show?

SAMI: My show? My show?
> *(waving script)*
> This is not my show, Burt. It's all fucked up.

BURT: You mean you're stuck? Frustrated? Lost touch with your muse?

SAMI: I mean literally fucked up.

BURT: Literally fucked up? What does that even mean, *literally* fucked up?

SAMI: You've inserted the word "fuck," and every conceivable variation of the word "fuck," into every line of my script.

BURT: Now wait a—
> *(Sami leafs through the script, scanning the pages.)*

SAMI: —We've got "fuck you," "fuck me," "fucking A," "mother-fucker," "starfucker," "buttfucker," "brainfucker," "fuckbuddy," "fuckable," "for fuck's sake"—

BURT: —I know there's—

SAMI: —"How are you?" becomes "how the fuck are you?" "Beautiful day" becomes "beautiful fucking day." And I love this: after a tremendous personal ordeal, Samantha says "I love you" to James, and James says "I want to fuck you like a drill bit in a chunk of knotty pine"?

BURT: I liked the metaphor but—

SAMI: —You know, Burt, I'm sitting here imagining you improving the Bible: In the fucking beginning the Lord created the fucking heavens and the fucking earth and the Lord looked on his creation and said, "What the fuck?"

BURT: Sami, it's not me, it's the culture of cable. I didn't create it. I just feed it. Cable needs the F word or cable dies. If cable dies, I die And you die. Why do you think the networks are fucked? Because you can't say fuck there.

SAMI: You realize, don't you, that most people don't say it one tenth as much as people on TV? You do realize that?

BURT: Around here they do. You should hear—

SAMI: —Take that nurse show. Every other word out of her mouth. I used to work in a hospital and I can tell you that's not how nurses talk. Think about it. If nurses went around the halls talking like that. You think people would put up with that? Pa-

tients? Families? Supervisors? But you say this is real. Real life, you say.
> *(mimicking)*
> "We've got to show real life." I've got news for you, Burt. In real life nurses don't talk like dockworkers.

BURT: They would, if they watched more TV. Which is why we're here, isn't it? Look, it's not just about sprucing up the language. You've got a story about a couple of writers and nothing *happens* between them!

SAMI: Nothing happens?

BURT: You know, no erotic interplay.

SAMI: You don't really mean erotic interplay, because there is erotic interplay. You mean—

BURT: —Sex.

SAMI: Which explains what you did to Scene 7. Samantha and James are frantically brainstorming but they're stuck, can't figure out how to end their script, and they're past deadline. So what do you have them do?
> *(reading from the script)*
> "James jams Samantha against the wall, reaches under her skirt and rips off her undies in a violent yet graceful motion of his powerful right arm"—

BURT: —See? Now they're up against the wall figuratively AND literally! Adds texture to the scene.

SAMI: *(reading)* "Each thrust of his hips stimulates her to conceive a new line of dialogue"
> *(Sami looks up at Burt, then continues reading.)*

SAMI: "Within seconds the script is complete and Samantha climaxes, screaming, "fade to black!"

BURT: I know, I know. Originally I had her scream "I'm dying," but I couldn't work that into the story arc.

SAMI: You're flushing my story down the toilet!

BURT: Is it perfect? No. Do we have a few stylistic differences? Of course. But Sami, you've got to understand, I've got big money behind this script. I've got serious commitments behind this script. This script is my make-or-break moment. This is my life we're talking about. I lose this baby, after all the hype I dished out about it?—I'll be road kill on the media highway.

SAMI: I'm not going to—

BURT: —I pushed for this project. Pushed! For you!

SAMI: For me?

BURT: Am I enunciating badly? Yes. For—

SAMI: —The project you were supposed to be pushing is not
        (lifts the script)
    this. And if *this* isn't put back to what it was when it was my
    project, you can find yourself another pilot to push.

BURT: Another pi . . . There's no other pilot. I have no other pilot.

SAMI: Well, you better find one because *this* pilot
        (lifts the script)
    is not preparing for lift off.
        (Very long pause.)

SAMI: Burt, look. I want this to happen. But you're putting me in an
    impossible position.

BURT: How about we modify?

SAMI: Modify. OK, maybe we can modify. How?

BURT: We could change some of the fucks to frigs.

SAMI: Fucks to frigs?

BURT: Some of them, sure.

SAMI: Fucks to frigs. Instead of "beautiful fucking day," "beautiful
    frigging day?" Like that?

BURT: Exactly! What do you think?

SAMI: Are you insane?

BURT: What? You don't like?

SAMI: Don't like? That sounds ridiculous. It's worse than fuck. It's
    like soft porn. If you're going to fuck up my script, fuck it up.
    Don't frig it up.

BURT: Now we're talking. So, are we on the same page?

SAMI: No, we're not on the same page. You're on *these* pages
        (lifts up the script)
    and I'm on the ones that were there before you *frigged* them
    up.

BURT: Are you telling me you won't allow any changes?

SAMI: I'm telling you I put my soul into this project. I thought we
    were going to pioneer a whole new concept of TV drama, some-
    thing serious but not dull, bold but not sensational—

BURT: —Sami, you can't—

SAMI: —You think I haven't dreamed every night for a year of seeing this on the air? You think I didn't put everything else on hold? My mother's dying of cancer—cancer!—and she said she'd hold on to see the pilot.

BURT: She said she'd hold on for the pilot? So how can you let her down over a few edits?

SAMI: A few edits! Your "edits" would not only kill her, they'd kill me. You think I could go back to the theater after this? Believe it or not, Burt, I've got a reputation. As an artist, not a cable whore.

BURT: Now *there's* a title for a mini-series: Cable Whore. See, you've got an instinct for the mass audience. If you'd just be a little flexible about the scripting process—

SAMI: —If you'd just be a little passionate about your art, or is it all about the money now? Christ, you used to read Wallace Stevens on summer vacation! Now you spend your days inserting obscenities into other people's prose. What happened?

BURT: Hey, this isn't college, so hold the lectures. I have a family to support.

(pause)

Had a family to support.

SAMI: Had? What happened—

BURT: —I shouldn't have said.

SAMI: No. Tell me.

BURT: Oh, what the hell. My wife left me and took the kids. She said I wasn't going anywhere. Said I wasn't a driver, wasn't a winner. She called me a loser.

SAMI: Gosh, I'm so—

(Burt's phone rings; he picks up.)

BURT: No. It's bigger than I thought . . . Yeah . . . No, she's adamant . . . Adamant . . . It's like determined, but more so . . . A-d-a-m-a-n-t . . . Right. Listen, Ronnie, can I bend on the fucks? . . . She hates them . . . I explained about cable . . . Yes, I told her it's real li . . . How many? . . . OK.

(Burt hangs up.)

It's the FQ.

SAMI: The FQ?

BURT: The Fuck Quota. A main character has to say it at least once every two minutes. Reality TV has put us under A LOT of pressure. We meet the FQ or we lose market share.

SAMI: Don't you see how ludicrous this is?

BURT: Sure. So, will you do it?

SAMI: No, I won't do it.

(pause)

Burt, we're better than this. I can work with you if you'll work with me. You've got to man up to Ronnie or Donnie or whatever his name is and tell him this

(holding up the script)

is about more than his fucking bottom line.

BURT: You don't man up to Ronnie. Ronnie's a man-eater. I man up to Ronnie and my cable connection is cut. Permanently.

(Sami stares at Burt until Burt picks up the phone, pushes a button and addresses RONNIE.)

She won't budge . . . She won't fudge either . . . Right, won't budge or fudge. Listen, Ronnie, this show could be something special, it could blow the top off . . .

(Burt hangs up.)

He said if I can't train you there are other bitches in the pound.

SAMI: He said that?

(Burt nods. Sami reaches to pick up the phone.)

Where's redial?

(Sami pushes a button.)

SAMI: Ronnie? Samantha. Listen. I think Burt and I have worked this out . . . Yes, that is fabulous. Tell me what you think—ready? "Ronnie enters." . . . Yes, there's a new character named Ronnie. He's a crude, power-tripping media executive. So, Ronnie says to Samantha, "Hi," and Samantha replies, "Don't 'Hi' me, you cunt-faced motherfucking fuckbucket."

(Sami hands the phone to Burt.)

BURT: OK . . . OK . . . OK.

(Burt hangs up. Pause, as he stares at Sami.)

BURT: He says he loves that you added the Ronnie character, and the dialogue rings true, and he never heard the word "fuckbucket" but it should be in the dictionary. Says you can keep the script how you want, so long as you keep the Ronnie character.

SAMI: Keep a stupid, self-centered boss who everyone curses at?

BURT: What do you say?

(Long pause.)

SAMI: I like it.

BURT: And it's real.

(Lights out.)

End of play

grunge is dead

Katharine Sherman

Grunge Is Dead was presented as part of the 16th Annual
New York City 15 Minute Play Festival presented by
American Globe Theatre and Turnip Theater Company
on April 22, 2010. It was directed by Phil Gates. Kate
Gleason produced the night of plays and the cast was as
follows: Tessa—Caitlin Johnston, LEO—Dylan Kam-
merer. It was also produced in Los Angeles as part of the
Eclectic Company Theatre's 7th Annual Hurricane Season New Play Festival & Playwriting competition in August 2010, directed by Kerr Seth Lordygan. The cast was
as follows: Tessa—Erin Treanor; Leo—Dave Buzzotta. It
was developed and produced at Bowdoin College in
2009 under the direction of Cait Hylan with the following cast: Tessa—Natalie Jimenez; Leo—Sam Waterbury.

THE TIME

The present or a few years ago

THE PLACE

Tessa's bedroom

CHARACTERS

Tessa. . 17–25, maybe her hair is dyed an unnatural color; alternative-ish clothing—she does a lot of drugs, she has
massive circles under her eyes, she hasn't left the house
in days

Leo . . . the same age as Tessa; maybe he has dreadlocks; a little
bit of a hippie; same kind of alternative-ish clothing

*The set is an incredibly grungy no pun intended well maybe a little
apartment:*

*A bed, or a mattress on the floor. beer cans and empty bottles of
cheap wine and handles of cheaper hard alcohol. clothes strewn
around: denim and flannel, ripped tights, boots, makeup. a stereo, tapes
and CDs spilling around it—even if music comes from a laptop or ipod
speakers, it's important that there are tapes and CDs everywhere.
magazines, a few empty junk food containers, empty and half-empty
packs of cigarettes, photographs with smudgy black fingerprints.*

*Part of the mess—present but not immediately noticeable—are bot-
tles of thick black acrylic paint, some empty, some half empty, some
full; paint on the bottles themselves, crusty, messy. smears of black paint
all over the room as if from handprints—on the sheets, on the magazines . . .*

Balled up blackened tissues or cotton balls or towels

*A bowl of water, and clean tissues or cotton balls or towels, and
soap.*

Sitting on the bed or near it or one on, one off: Tessa and Leo.

Tessa's hands are painted black.

As the lights come up, Leo has taken one or both of Tessa's hands and submerged it/them in the bowl of water. Throughout the play, he is cleaning the paint off of her hands.

Silence

TESSA: there was a moment of silence

LEO: what?

TESSA: nothing
silence

LEO: how long was it

TESSA: i don't know
silence

LEO: like that?

TESSA: probably
i don't know
silence

TESSA: remember the magic flute?

LEO: yeah

TESSA: there's like an ordeal of silence in that.
like, silence is something you have to get through.
silence

TESSA: remember that time when your parents were away in eighth grade and we got wasted and i really wanted to take a bath and i started filling it up and then we passed out naked under your bed and it flooded?
beat

LEO: yeah

TESSA: they were so mad about the water damage
beat

TESSA: that's fucked up
beat

TESSA: you know that's fucked up right
beat

TESSA: leo. you know that's—

LEO: yes i know it's fucked up whatever i paid them back
pause

TESSA: leo?
beat

TESSA: leo?
> *beat*

TESSA: leo—

LEO: what

TESSA: where are we
> *Leo sighing*
>
> i —

TESSA: please?

LEO: we're in a hot air balloon that crash landed in the middle of the ocean

TESSA: so it splash-landed.

LEO: ha
yeah
it splash-landed in the middle of the ocean, and now we're just floating around, but we've got a picnic basket with us, so we're fine.

TESSA: what's in the picnic basket

LEO: four bottles of andré and a pint of ice cream

TESSA: what kind

LEO: vanilla
vanilla bean

TESSA: we better eat the ice cream fast. before it melts.

LEO: we can make andré ice cream floats

TESSA: awesome
> *pause*

LEO: okay. tess—

TESSA: your turn
you have to it's your turn i have a good one you'll really like it i promise

LEO: . . . . where are we

TESSA: we're in a treehouse in the rainforest. it's totally camouflaged and—and green and shit so you can't even tell we're there. but we are. and the snakes are all totally poisonous but they're our buddies and we hang out. and we don't have to wear clothes, and it's so hot and humid that it's like—that second right after you turn the shower off, but before you start to feel cold. but it's like that all the time, and we eat—plants—and talk to monkeys and it's awesome.

LEO: awesome
> *beat*

TESSA: where are –

LEO: you know you should get out of here. go for a walk. get some fresh air.

TESSA: i don't wanna go for a walk i wanna stay with you
i mean
will you come? on the walk?
> *beat*

TESSA: walking's overrated.

LEO: how's school

TESSA: fine

LEO: tessa.

TESSA: what it's fine
i assume
i
imagine
i'll go back next week
> *beat*

TESSA: did you ever listen to the pussycat dolls?

LEO: *(amused)* no

TESSA: have you—heard of them

LEO: nope.

TESSA: oh. well i don't listen to them either. i really don't. but at my job they used to always have like mtv or whatever on, so you'd have to watch it because you were bored, and the shit's so damn catchy. it's the catchiest shit ever, and i'm like well fuck it grunge is dead i guess i'll just listen to the pussycat dolls, and they have this one video where they're in the desert? and the one chick's playing the piano? and if you think about it there are so many music videos where people are playing pianos in the desert and it's like why? why would you take a piano to the desert, that's just impractical, it would go out of tune ... but anyway, they're in the desert, and it's really funny because there's only one girl they let sing, like, ever, and there are like twelve other girls in the band who don't do anything but dress provocatively and wriggle
i kinda wanna be a pussycat doll

       i wouldn't have to do anything
       i guess i'm not hot enough though
LEO: babe
       you're hot enough
TESSA: you don't even know what they look like.
LEO: you're hot enough
TESSA: you wouldn't say that if you knew what they looked like
LEO: listen. i—
TESSA: remember when you set the bed on fire?
LEO: that was you
TESSA: nuh-uh it was you your side was flamier
LEO: your side went up too
TESSA: do you think we both fell asleep with cigarettes? is that what
       happened?
LEO: seems likely
TESSA: maybe they both went up at the exact same time. like, whoosh!
       symmetry.
       and i was like, what do we do! and you were like stop drop and
       roll and i did but i wasn't on fire the bed was.
LEO: yeah
       silence
TESSA: you know we never filled a watermelon with vodka. we were
       going to do that.
LEO: right
TESSA: i mean i could do it
LEO: if you want
       watermelon's good on it's own though
       especially in the summer
       you can spit seeds at people. be a cute little machine gun. they'll
       never know what hit them.
       beat
TESSA: i like you
       beat
LEO: did you eat today?
TESSA: probably
       whatever we've got ice cream in the picnic basket
LEO: tess—

TESSA: here's what i've been thinking about. hot air balloons and ice
    cream and requiems and trials.

LEO: trials

TESSA: yeah like ordeals. like shit you have to go through. to prove
    yourself or whatever. remember the day layne staley died? and
    we skipped school and painted our hands black and listened to
    jar of flies on repeat all day

LEO: don't follow

TESSA: —

    —

    i feel like no one even knows who he was anymore
    does that always happen? after you die? i don't think it does

LEO: does if you start listening to the pussycat dolls

TESSA: shut up
    it's too damn catchy
    i can't help it

LEO: tell me something

TESSA: about what

LEO: about you

TESSA: remember when we were smoking on the roof and we dropped
    your dad's video camera off it

LEO: yeah

TESSA: because he would always bring it to all your wrestling matches
    and you hated it

LEO: i know

TESSA: so i wanted to film us running around naked or something and
    switch all the tapes but you just wanted to drop it off the roof
    is that the difference? is that how we're different?

LEO: tessa
    tell me how you're doing

TESSA: well i was thinking about the magic flute—you've seen it,
    right? that—that movie where it's a recording of a stage per-
    formance but it always zooms in on this little girl in the audi-
    ence, on her face, and she smiles when something good is
    happening and when something bad's about to happen you can
    tell—from her face—because i was remembering the part where
    they have to go through the trials—like prince tamino has to go
    through all this shit to prove himself worthy of princess

pamina—or maybe it's prince pamino and princess tamina, i can never remember—and then there's papageno and papagena, and i always thought it would be funny if our names were almost the same. like if your name was tesso. or if my name was lea. i guess that makes a little more sense. anyway first it's—it's silence, which is hard because you think the other person doesn't love you anymore, and it like breaks your heart not to be able to –

LEO: tessa

TESSA: –talk to them, i'm almost done i swear, so tamino—pamino— whatever—he makes it, even though it makes pamina think he doesn't love her anymore, and she's about to kill herself but then these three boy sopranos come down in a hot air balloon and tell her not to, so, she doesn't, but then –

LEO: tessa

TESSA: then it's—oh first we have to see papageno go through the same thing, and he kinda fucks it up, but it works out, and –

LEO: tessa listen

TESSA: and the—so tamino—plays the flute, the magic one, and it gets them through water and fire and –

LEO: babe

TESSA: where are we
leo where are we
> *beat*
we're in a, we're in a park, and it's spring, and there's a carousel, and we
we
where are we

LEO: listen to me
i died

TESSA: *(shaking her head: the opposite of mm-hmm)* mm-mm mm-mm mm-mm mm-mm mm-mm

LEO: i died, babe

TESSA: so what are you a ghost

LEO: no

TESSA: then did i die too

LEO: no

TESSA: i thought maybe i'd died too

LEO: you didn't
    listen tess i can't come see you anymore
TESSA: why not
LEO: you know exactly why not
TESSA: not yet
LEO: i really
    gotta go
TESSA: wait leo
    leo
    i was thinking about it i was thinking about—trials—ordeals—
    and like the magic flute and they go through fire and water and
    that's what we did, right? we flooded the house and we set the
    bed on fire but we made it
    we made it
    and then i was doing more—more research on it and i guess i
    always thought it was to prove yourself worthy of something—
    the trials were—but on wikipedia it said that it was for proving
    your—guilt, or your innocence, if you were accused of some-
    thing, and there were three kinds, there was—there was water
    and for that you'd like get submerged in a stream or whatever
    sometimes with a millstone around your neck and you were in-
    nocent if you survived—and for fire it was walk across coals or
    something and if you didn't have any injury or if it healed you
    were innocent—and if not you were just—executed—and the
    third kind—the third kind was—
LEO: tess . . .
TESSA: no listen the third kind was trial by ingestion, and if you were
    accused you had to eat a piece of barley bread and then see
    what it would do to you, like if you vomited or if your legs
    swelled or something so so listen listen was that the third trial?
    the third ordeal? when you—took too much was it—failing the
    trial of ingestion—because it's like, we were proving ourselves,
    but trial by—by ingestion is like—what were we guilty of
    what were we guilty of leo
    what were we guilty of
        beat
LEO: i don't know
    babe

you're gonna be fine
i really gotta go
TESSA: wait
leo wait
was it on purpose did you do it on purpose
leo did you do it on purpose
don't leave
LEO: i have to
get up, okay
TESSA: can i go with you

he shakes his head
and then
he isn't there anymore
and maybe she puts music on
and she reaches for a bottle of black paint
and squeezes some into her palm
and rubs her hands together
and paints them black.

lights down.

Halfway to Paradise

Carson Kreitzer

Halfway to Paradise was originally produced at Bedlam Theatre (Artistic Directors Maren Ward and John Bueche), as part of their Twenty Ten Fest, April 16, 2010. It was directed by Jennifer Elwood; the lighting design was by Ariel Pinkerton; the set and costume coordinators were Jason Overby and Telsche Thiessen; the dramaturg was Sarah Slight; and the stage manager was Kristin Campbell. The cast was as follows: Sarah—Shana Holmes; Nurse—Kari Kjelkseth.

CAST

Sarah (teens)
Nurse (30s-40s.)

SETTING

A simple, spare, beautiful space: a hospital, a field, the night sky.
The hospital should not be visible at first, or at the end.

TIME

October 3, 2006.

(At first we just see Sarah. She is dressed modestly, her head covered in white.)

SARAH: You can't see the stars like I can.
  Here, a mile outside of Paradise.
  Electricity drowns them out. In town. In the cities.
  But here. Black is black. And the stars shine by the thousand-thousand million.
  Like ants. each one individual. can pick it up, feel the six legs tickle your hand. Each one individual, but if you let your eyes go a little bit un-focus, they're a snaking pattern of glittery black on emerald green, glittery black on red-dirt brown.
  Stars're just like that. Go out on a cold night, heart beat slowing down,
  breathing slow, you and your brother huddled close for the cold.
  and more and more stars pop out at you
      (Slowly, behind her, we become aware of a hospital bed. A nurse is present, checking machines, making her rounds. It's the middle of the night.)
  voices low in the dark
  Is that Cassiopeia?

I see the three—that's Orion's Belt. Big and little dipper, and the North Star.

And all the thousand thousand with no names. Just up in the sky, singing God's praises.

(I don't think I've ever seen such an awful thing. As my brother's face. When he had to leave. And I had to stay. You're crawling on god's green grass and then someone's picked you up. Thousand times bigger than you.)

Next day at school we drew them out. The ones we could remember.

And were sent back, to lie on the cold damp grass more evenings. Till we could see more and more.

(looks straight at the audience.)

I know people think the Amish don't have fun, but we have fun. We work hard. Everyone works hard. But there's time to be a child. And to learn things you don't really need. Like Cassiopeia.

We make a choice. When the time comes.

We decide to stay. No-one is here who doesn't want to be. And we know that—we'll have time to do the thinking. Time to decide if we want to go out into the world.

Where things are different.

I don't think I'd want the other life.

(smiles, with a bit of mischief)

but I was looking forward to making up my mind.

The other lives—like stars out there.

I could grow up to be different. Zippers and electricity. Have a radio at home. A husband who is not Amish. Children who are not Amish.

And I would not be Amish.

(shakes her head)

I can imagine—but I can't really imagine.

Not to know the first light of the sun over the green mountains. Getting up so early you can see your breath. Leaning your face against the warm, hairy hide of the cow you're milking, sleepy like you are.

Bringing in the milk to Mama. Brother finds a few eggs. Sitting together at the big wood table. Scarred in places you remember. Your place at table. Your place in the world.

Then walking to school together. My brother and me. Day and
day and day and day. The walk there. The walk home.
A mile out of Paradise.
School's halfway in between. We had kids from Nickel Mines.
Kids from Paradise.
*(We become more aware of the Nurse. The machines. Perhaps
the sound of an EKG machine. The ghostly breathing of a
ventilator.)*
Now the story spreads. Mouth to mouth to mouth. And then
it's done. We all know. The rest of the world comes by to take
pictures
and wonder why our faces don't look different
they always think we look sad
can't tell the difference.
but we
we know the difference.
now the story has spread.
The rest of the world hears on radios, televisions. For one day,
for two.
I hope someone is looking after my brother Daniel now.
My father and mother sit in a strange English place.
They don't believe in electricity.
But then, they don't believe in violence, either.
And I am in the English world, attached to both.
(The English world made this problem. The English world can
try to fix it. They are very sad, the doctors, the nurses. The sur-
geon whose job it is to cut through flesh, re-make the human
body a different way. Not during the operation, but after. His
hands shake. His head bowed, in the corridor. Like he's praying.
Maybe he doesn't have a church, either. We don't have a church.
We have the school building. All that isn't homes, or barns, or
field. Why build a house for God when he is everywhere?)
This is my moment of decision.
I leave the world I know
and in this English world I sleep
cut open and sewn carefully back together, I am become a quilt
now, telling stories like any other.
He said he was angry at God. He said you better pray I don't
shoot you.

I said shoot me. And leave the others alone.

Man doesn't know how to strike a bargain.

NURSE: angry at god. so what. so fucking what. angry at god.

boys and women sent out of the room. girls tied up with plastic ties. The Amish. For fuck's sake.

ten girls shot. five are dead. so far.

worked a full shift then went home. sat at my kitchen table and cried. came back today.

I don't now what to do with this anger. want brass knuckles, want knives. want knives growing out of my knuckles. want machine-gun fire to spit from my eyes.

Ten Amish girls. Lined up in front of the blackboard. Tied up with plastic. Shot at close range.

Their parents out in the hallway. Like they're from another time. Fucking... Buggies. In the hospital parking lot. Mothers and fathers stoic and stunned, in their homespun. In the hallway. Sitting on the naugahyde benches.

And then he shot himself. Big fucking deal. How about you just kill yourself to begin with. Just kill yourself. Just fucking kill yourself.

Makes me want to believe in heaven. Makes me want to believe in hell. I don't. I can't.

But my god, can you imagine the weight of ten little Amish girls' souls? Pressing down on you, can't breathe for all of eternity?

But nothing will fix it. No punishment will fix it.

And the Amish have a barn-raising. Build a wall around Lancaster County, Pennsylvania. Keep the outsiders out. Let no one in.

Who could blame them?

SARAH: From here I can see...

my brother Daniel.

My brother Daniel leaves.

I am a hole in his side.

Daniel. Don't leave for me.

You couldn't have stopped him.

twelve years old.

Couldn't stop the man with guns, the man who is the earthquake in our world.

don't leave for me.

Leave because you fall in love with a girl
and she sings in a band. Loud, with electricity.
But she likes good food, raised right, so she comes to buy jams
and preserves, when you're manning the table
your eyes meet and she smiles like electricity.
Leave for her, to join the English world for her
don't leave for me
I'm all right.
I float, between the worlds
in this cold bright place
in this dreamless
electric sleep
I make my decision
I could be like this nurse
wear blue jeans with zippers
and hospital shoes.
working, with strong firm hands that do not shake
this is good.
a way to be, in the world.
Her mouth is a hard line, now
she does what she can for us
fierce, like an animal.
I like her.

NURSE: Come on, you're a strong little girl.
You're the one
you're the one said
Shoot me. Leave the others alone.
Thirteen years old. Never known anything but this stretch of
land
Leave the others alone.
I can hear your voice as you say it. Calm. Sure.
I'm sure, too.
You're gonna pull through this.

SARAH: Maybe I'll leave—be a nurse
strong hands and glass tubes and hospital shoes
maybe I'll stay—be a teacher
show where Cassiopeia is.
If you lie back in the dark and get very quiet
if you let your eyes adjust

NURSE: pull through

SARAH: Maybe I'll leave and sing in a band. Loud with electricity.
Maybe I'll stay
lean my head against the hide
of the sleepy cow
bring the milk, warm from her body
in to my mother
in to my own house
churn till the butter comes. Sweet and white.

NURSE: pull through.

*(over next, hospital EKG beeps slowly fade into crickets.
wind. quiet.)*

SARAH: I go back

NURSE: Please. Little girl.

SARAH: not my gun not my world
I go back to the animals in the barn, settling in for the night
gets dark when the sun goes down and we don't try to change
that, not much. I wouldn't give up candles, not for anything.
Not for this.

NURSE: come back to us.

SARAH: Blackberries. end of summer. the way they burst on your
tongue.
Last days of summer, and the nights getting cold.

NURSE: come back.

SARAH: It wasn't fair of him to send you out, Daniel. A burden you
shouldn't have to keep. I know you would have taken my place
if you could. As I tried to take the place for the others. But we
can't have things how we want. All we can do is live the way
we're meant to live.
You know what that is, Daniel. You know.

(smiling, strong.
A glow on Sarah, gaining intensity.)
Let your gentleness be known to all men.
The Lord is at hand.

(blackout.)

—*end of play*—

It Was Fun While It Lasted
or
I Wouldn't Drink That If I Were You
or
You Have 4 Hours to Vacate the Premises

Laura Eason

Originally produced as part of City Theatre's Summer Shorts Festival 2010. Adrienne Arsht Center, Studio Theatre, June 3–27, 2010. Epstein Center for the Arts, Silverman Auditorium, July 1–3, 2010. Directed by Barry Steinman. Cast: Loyalist—Chaz Mena; Messenger—Erin Joy Schmidt.

CHARACTERS

The Loyalist: . . . . . older than the Messenger, a person of large
mind, deep soul and earnest, passionate
convictions. Listed as 'L' in the script.

The Messenger: . . . younger than the loyalist, young in general,
very amiable, and just the messenger, you
know, so don't get mad at him or whatever.
Listed as 'M' in the script.

(Casting note: The actors are referred to as 'he' in the script but
could be either gender.)

LOCATION

The Loyalist's office.

SET/PROPS

A table or desk with some papers on it and a chair.

COSTUMES

For both, something that could read non-specific 'uniform' of
some kind—a melange of government/business/ military/radical/anti-
establishment outfits/uniforms—that comes off as its own thing. The
idea should clearly evoke that there is an organization that these two
guys are a part of but nothing too rooted in reality. Whatever the idea,
both characters should be dressed in different versions of it, clearly
different ranks/stations/status.

TIME

In an imagined funny but off-kilter very near future.

The Loyalist ('L') sits working at his desk. He is very focused.
If there is a door, there is a knock. If there isn't a door, the Messenger ('M') just enters into the space.

M: Hey. They, uh—
    (Pointing offstage)
    They said it'd be OK if I came in.

L: Oh. Sure. Come on in. I wasn't expecting anything today...?

M: Oh, no, I don't have a delivery.
    (A beat.)
    Didn't they, uh... didn't they tell you I was coming?

L: Uh, no. You're from—?

M: From 'upstairs'. Yeah. They said they'd call you.

L: *(Concerned, nervous, standing)* No...?

M: OK. Well. OK. Well, you should sit down.

L: *(Very nervous)* I should sit down?

M: Not like—
    (With a deep voice)
    'You should sit down'
    (Regular voice)
    Just, you should sit down.

L: *(Sitting)* OK.

M: So, first of all they said to tell you—and I see why now—'cause you're, like, a little freaked, right? Right?!
    M laughs and L can't help but laugh a little nervous laugh, too.
    Well, don't worry, 'cause they said to tell you—first—that you've been great. Super loyal and all of that. And a seriously good worker, and, like, so dedicated and focused all these years, always giving it 100% and all that—!

L: OK...?

M: So, because you are so their guy, they wanted you to be one of the first to know. So, that, you can make plans and stuff.

L: Plans?

M: Yeah.

L: For...?

M: The disband-tion. Wait—is that the right word? Disbanding? Dis-em-band-ment, maybe?

L: Disbanding what?

M: The country.

L: *(Thinking he misheard)* The *country?*

M: Yup.

L: *(Unable to process)* Our country?

M: Yup. I know, it's kinda sad, right?

L: *(Still in disbelief)* Our *country?*

M: Yeah, you know, I wasn't sure at first when they told me, either, because, you know . . .
> *(He thrusts his arms out)*
. . . THIS was, like, such a good idea. But, we have to admit, everything's kinda gone in the shitter recently.

L: I don't know that I . . . ?

M: So, they're disbanding it.

L: And, and what? Starting something new?

M: Fleeing.

L: *Fleeing?!*

M: Yup.

L: Like running away?

M: Running away exactly!

L: Where?

M: Different places. Some north. Some south. Some undecided, I think.

L: But we've worked so hard! Things have been rough recently, sure, but overall, things have generally been going well for a long time—

M: Yeah, that's where you're kinda wrong. It's all, uh . . . how do I say this—they realized that we've basically been going down the wrong path.

L: The wrong path?

M: Yeah, you know, they say it all seemed good at first. I don't know personally, cause obviously I haven't been around all that long, but it seems like it was all really inspiring generations or whatever ago, and, like, everyone was doing everything for the right reasons and were selflessly dedicated to this big, beautiful dream for the future—

L: Yes, I know. It's been my life. My whole life.

M: Wow. So, this must *suck* for you.

L starts to walk around, still stunned.

But for a long time now, and you probably feel this, right, that it's been going kinda south. Like, nothing is working the way it should or really turning out well at all. So, pretty much everyone is just going to go their own way—do the next thing.

L: The next thing? I'm *(actor's age)* years old! I've been working at this for *(between ten and twenty)* years! Working to prove that what we believe is possible, putting it into action—this has been the work of my entire life!

M: It's a tough break, man, it really is.

L: Why are they giving up so easily? We've had tough times before—?

M: Have we?

L: Yes, of course!

M: I don't know, to try and get out of this would just be so . . . hard.

L: But—? Maybe the solution, the next great idea is right around the corner—

M: Sorry, man, but that's a little . . . blah, blah, blah.

(In a slightly mocking tone)
'The next great idea is right around the corner—'

L: But it's true, I mean the next great idea could really be—

M: *(Charmed)* They were not kidding when they said you were totally charming, so positive and hopeful—

L: Seriously, seriously, there has to be another way of looking at this—

M: Look, everyone gave it a good shot, right? Clearly, not everyone was as 'above board', or whatever, as you, but they tried. But with the way things are going, they'd rather be spending time with the family, or whatever, so they're all heading to their island places—

L: But what about *everyone* else?

M: Who? Like, *the people*?

L: Yes.

M: *(Realizing)* It's a tough break.

L: I think I need a glass a water.

M: Oh, I wouldn't.

L: What?

M: Have a glass of water.

L: Why?

M: They've discovered some things. Some things about the water. So, you shouldn't drink it.

L: I shouldn't drink the water?

M: Naw. I mean you *can* but, you probably shouldn't.

L: But the studies said conclusively that the rumors about the water / were—

M: *(Quickly)* You know, I don't mean to hurry you along or anything, but news of what's up is starting to leak out already 'cause some dumb-ass booked like six private planes heading out of town in a super obvious way that was, like, so clearly...
  (Waving his arms above his head)
  'Crisis!!'—but, uh, if you want to go, you need to decide really soon. Like this afternoon.

L: This afternoon?

M: By around four-ish. Does that work for you?

L: But my family.. our things... what...?

M: No sweat. You have a good couple of hours to get it together, and there isn't much more time than that anyway with the fires coming.

L: The *fires*?

M: Yeah, there's been some small explosion—mines or refineries or chemical plants or something—and it's putting some stuff out into the air that's not so great—not that the air's been so great lately anyway!

L: OK. Well, I guess, I guess we'll go. We'll go.

M: OK. Well, a car'll be here at four—

L: Wait! Wait! What about the new guy? The new guy everyone was so excited about? Is he staying?

M: *(Charmed)* They said you'd ask me about him! They were like, 'He's so committed, he's going to ask about the new guy and see if he's staying or not'—

L: Is he?

M: I think he might be. But nobody thinks it's a good idea. I mean, seriously, the guy'd have to be crazy to want to stay and try and figure all this out—

L: But he has some good ideas—

M: Maybe a couple of years ago it could have done some good, but . . . Look, everybody tried, well, most people tried, and, if you look at things in a certain way, you have some things to be proud of, on at least a couple of fronts, but now it's time to move on and—

L: But we gave hope to people all over the world.

M: Did we, really? I think we mostly made them fat and sold them a lot of crap.

L: That's not even close to the whole story—

M: Right. We also made them think that being rich and being happy were the same thing.

L: That's not what we were trying to say! That's not what we were trying to do!

L sits down and starts looking at his papers.

M: Well, you did try, right? When you look back, you'll always know you tried.

  (A beat.)

So, you have my cell if you need anything. I need to get going—

L: Don't bother sending the car.

M: You really shouldn't.

L: If the new guy thinks we can get through this, then . . .

M: Really?

L: Really.

M: It's probably not going to turn out well.

L: Probably not.

M: And, so, what? Down with the ship and all that?

L: I guess.

M: Alright, man, you sure?

L: Yeah.

M: OK. Well, best of luck to you. I admire it. I do.

L: Do you?

M: No! I think you're a dumb-ass! Save yourself while you can!

L: But we all were supposed to be in it for each other—

M: That's what everybody said . . . but . . . come on!

L: Right.

M: Well, good luck.

L: Thanks.

M starts to go.

Make sure you tell them I'm not leaving.

M: OK, but I don't think they're really going to care.

L: Tell them anyway.

M: OK, man. Good luck.

L: You, too.

L gets up and give M business card out of his pocket.

Will you tell the new guy I stayed. That I'm here?

M: I will.

M goes to exit and turns back.

You didn't know things were going down a bad road?

L: I knew certain things weren't exactly what they should be, I guess we didn't look at all the studies the way we should have, I think we talked too much about the money and not enough about the consequences, and all the frigging plastic, we should have seen where that was headed... but I thought it would all work out. I think our *intentions* were good...

M: Right. Well, you know, man....

M pauses trying to think of a great exit line. He struggles for a second, then a second more, and then, unable to find it, gives up and exits.

L looks to his papers on his desk. The sound of fire and explosions. He looks up, then, back to the paper. He picks up his pencil, ready to write.

L: Step one.

END OF PLAY

The Lady and "The Tyger" or William Blake's "How I Met Your Mother"

Trace Crawford

"The Lady and 'The Tyger' or William Blake's 'How I Met Your Mother'" premiered at Lakeshore Players Theatre, 6th Annual 10-Minute Play Festival, June 3–6, 2010, White Bear Lake, MN. Cast: Woman—Allie Munson; Man—D.W. Surine. Directed by Brian Sherman.

"The Lady and 'The Tyger' or William Blake's 'How I Met Your Mother'" received its first New York production by Rapscallion Theatre Collective, 4th Annual Salute UR Shorts New Play Festival, July 8–11, 2010. Cast: Woman—Blair Lewin; Man—Geoff Borman. Directed by Rachel Park.

CHARACTERS

Man: .... Late 20's, gives off a "permanent grad student" vibe.
WOMAN: .. Also late 20's, full of eccentric, neurotic energy.

SETTING

Somewhere in the city.

TIME

The Present.

(Scene: Somewhere in the city—the present—maybe it's a bus stop, maybe the edge of a fountain, maybe a grassy hill, or even, God deliver us from triteness, a park bench. What matters is that it houses an individual keeping to himself, exemplifying stillness, in an environment that otherwise could be crowded and hectic.)

(At Rise: A man, late 20's, gives off a "permanent grad student" vibe, sits reading a paperback copy of William Blake's Songs of Innocence and Experience. A woman, also late 20's, full of eccentric neurotic energy, enters and makes a bee-line straight for the man.)

WOMAN: DON'T TOUCH ME!

MAN: *(Quite startled.)* What?

WOMAN: *(Quietly.)* I said . . .
      (Not so quietly.)
      DON'T TOUCH ME!

MAN: I'm not going to touch you.

WOMAN: Don't touch me. I'm telling you I don't want to be touched.

MAN: I'm not going to touch you, lady. What the hell's wrong with you?

WOMAN: Just don't touch me.

MAN: Lady, I'm not going to touch you! Jesus!

      (man goes back to his reading, attempting to be dismissive, but eying her unusual behavior with a mix of both suspicion

and intrigue. woman slowly crosses behind and around him,
encircling him, almost like she's stalking him, then quickly
sits next to him, a bit too closely.)

WOMAN: Why not?

MAN: What?

WOMAN: Why not?

MAN: *(Is he annoyed or fascinated?)* Why not what?

WOMAN: When I said not to touch me, you acted like the idea of it,
the very thought of it was utterly grotesque. Surely, I'm not all
that repulsive to you, am I? I simply want to know why when I
asked you not to touch me, you reacted like I had told you to
give an erotic massage to your uncle.

MAN: *(Is he repulsed or amused?)* What?

WOMAN: Why did you act like the idea of making physical contact
with me would be the worst thing on earth?

MAN: *(Rising, a bit flustered.)* Lady, I don't want... would you just...
I mean... What the hell is wrong with you?

WOMAN: What the hell is wrong with me?

MAN: Yes, what the hell is wrong with you?

WOMAN: Nothing the hell is wrong with me.

MAN: Something has to be wrong with you. I was just sitting here by
myself, minding my own business, not bothering anyone, then
you came running over, screaming at the top of your lungs, and
practically pounced on top me.

WOMAN: *(Rising, as well. Perhaps on her hands and knees.)* Pounced!
Ooooh, I like that. Pounced! Pounced like a tiger!

MAN: What?

WOMAN: Pounced like a ...
(Beat.)
"tyger, tyger, burning bright!"

MAN: What?

WOMAN: *(Lunging towards him.)* Pounced like a "tyger, tyger, burning
bright!"

MAN: *(Incredulous and anxious.)* What are you *talking* about?

WOMAN: "Tyger, tyger burning bright. In the forests of the night."
William Blake. Your book.

MAN: *(Relaxing some. Maybe a quick laugh)* Oh. Yeah.
(Beat. Uncomfortable.)

Look, I don't know you...and you're kinda freaking me out
here. I just want a place to sit by myself and read. So...
(Sitting back down.)
Just—just leave me alone, OK?

WOMAN: *(Beat.)* You want to be left alone.

MAN: Yes.

WOMAN: By me.

MAN: Yes.

WOMAN: You want to be left alone by me.

MAN: Yes.

WOMAN: You want me to go away and leave you alone and never have
to see me again.

MAN: Lady, that's not what—

WOMAN: You want me to go away, disappear off the face of the earth,
walk off of a cliff or off the top of a building or something and
never, ever, show my face here again.

MAN: Now, I didn't say that I wanted—

WOMAN: You wish that while I was walking away from you, dejected
and despondent, I was hit by a bus and knocked unconscious.
Then, as they were attempting to breathe life back into my
bruised and broken body, a stampeding herd of water buffalo,
or something, came along and trampled me into the ground,
mixing my, by now disfigured, carcass in with all of the garbage
and sewage and everything else in the street that no one wants
to claim as their own, until my remains were eventually torn
asunder and rendered into absolute nothingness by the chemical additives at a water treatment plant.

MAN: What the—

WOMAN: Ha! Well the joke's on you. I'd still be in that water and then
one day you'd go to the kitchen and turn on the sink to take a
drink and WHAMMO! I'd be inside you—actually physically
within you—part of you forever, mixed in with your DNA or
metabolism and whatever—and you could never get rid of me.

MAN: *(Beat.)* What is *wrong* with you?

WOMAN: *(Sitting next to him again.)* I bet *then* you'd wish that you'd
have touched me.

MAN: *(Beat.)* I thought you didn't want to be touched.

WOMAN: What?

MAN: Like, two minutes ago you were just screaming about not wanting to be touched.

WOMAN: I was?

MAN: Yes!

WOMAN: Are you sure?

MAN: What?! Of course I'm—What?—
    (Rising to leave.)
    Alright, that's it. I'm done.

WOMAN: *(Rising as well.)* Calm down, calm down.

MAN: What do you mean, calm—

WOMAN: OK, look, I'll level with you.
    (Is she serious?)
    That's just my conversation starter.

MAN: Your conversation—

WOMAN: *(Interrupting.)* —starter.
    (Absurdly slow.)
    Sstaaaaaaaaarrrrrrrrteeeeeeerrrrrrrr.
    (Normal again.)
    My conversation starter. I use it sometimes to help break the ice
    when I see a person that I think looks like they could be inter-
    esting.

MAN: Really?

WOMAN: Really.

MAN: *(Beat.)* That could quite possibly be the strangest thing I've
    ever heard.

WOMAN: Seriously? How so?

MAN: You mean you actually go up to people and scream at them to
    leave you alone in order to get them to pay attention to you?

WOMAN: Works every time.

MAN: That makes no sense.

WOMAN: Sure it does.

MAN: How?

WOMAN: How doesn't it? Reverse psychology. Look, *we're* talking
    aren't we? Would we still be having this conversation if I had
    simply come up to you politely and said something trite like
    "What's your name?" or something? I don't think so. You'd have
    ignored me or gotten up to leave, or whatever.
    (Incredibly charming.)

But, as it so happens, you instead paid attention to me and now here we are engrossed knee-deep in an engaging and enlightening conversation.

MAN: *(Beat. Then, his defenses melting, sitting back down and laughing...)* There is *definitely* something wrong with you.

WOMAN: Why? Just because I didn't follow the prescribed initial conversation script? Just because I choose to live outside of the plot lines of a typical "how we met" story? How sad is it that being original must mean that there's something wrong with me?

MAN: It's not just that you were original. Your whole attitude, demeanor—it just screams... "off."

WOMAN: *(Beat. Then quickly ...)* Well, I don't think so.

MAN: *(Beat. Genuinely intrigued by her.)* So why touching?

WOMAN: *(Feigning ignorance, perhaps trying to charm.)* Hm? Are you talking to me?

MAN: *(Laughing, despite himself.)* Yes, of course I'm talking to you.

WOMAN: Just wanted to be sure.

MAN: So why touching? Why did you scream about not wanting me to touch you? You could have come at me yelling about anything that you wanted. Why did you choose to scream about being touched?

WOMAN: To put it simply, because touching someone instantly goes right to the center of who they are.

MAN: I don't see.

WOMAN: There is no possible way to make a stronger connection between two people than with the simple act of touch. Laying hands. Making physical contact with another. It goes right to the core of our being. Makes a bond stronger than words ever can. We could talk for an hour and even have amazingly stimulating conversation... but in that incredibly brief moment that we hold hands, or hug as we part or... kiss...

(He looks at her quickly.)

an electrical connection is made between our souls that is stronger than any words we could have said.

MAN: Are you serious?

WOMAN: Of course I am. Think about when you kiss someone for the very first time. I mean every other kiss is great too, or can be... but that first one—that first time you make contact—that one is magic. That one can move mountains. Why? Why is that one simple act so monumental that it can actually stir your soul?

MAN: *(Beat.)* Touch?

WOMAN: *(A victory!)* The power of touch!

(Beat.)

You like Blake?

MAN: Sure.

WOMAN: Tell me what you like about him.

MAN: Well...

("Since you already mentioned this poem earlier.")

"The Tyger"... I love how he explores the... contradictory reactions that a—well, in this case a tiger—but really for that matter, any situation where you take a personal risk can generate. You're terrified, repelled. But also at the same time... transfixed by its beauty and power. It's like staring directly into a perfect storm.

(Beat, as he looks directly at the woman. Why does she make him so uncomfortable?)

And he proves his point by using language that can have multiple meanings, so the more you read it, the more you realize that all of your reactions—the repulsion and the attraction—are both genuine and true. It's beautiful.

(Is he talking about the poem or her?)

Oh, and he does it with style. Take the line, "What the hand, dare seize the fire?" In just seven words, he shows us the danger, but also the excitement, involved in taking risks, especially risks that involve connecting with someone who's new... or different... and therefore intensely frightening.

WOMAN: "What the hand, dare seize the fire."

MAN: It's beautiful, isn't it?

WOMAN: Personally, my favorite has always been Gibran. You know, The Prophet? He lived in Greenwich Village and wrote these stories and poems about the nature of love and stuff. Well, one of the things he writes about is love at first sight. He says that love is a connection between the souls of two people. An intertwining, a touching of the spirits in an electric way, and unless that connection is made instantly, it never, even after years, can be forced to exist.

MAN: A touching of the spirits?

> *(Beat. He looks at her.)*

I like that.

WOMAN: I thought you'd see it my way.

> *(A long, possibly uncomfortable pause.)*

Well, I'd better go—life's not all strange conversations in the park

> *(or bus stop, or whatever)*

you know.

> *(Starts to leave.)*

MAN: *(Standing.)* Wait—

WOMAN: *(Turns around. Coy? Excited?)* Yeeeeeesss?

MAN: *(Crossing to her.)* I . . . well, I was wondering . . . Would—would you like to go get coffee or something, I mean, if you don't have somewhere urgent you need to—

WOMAN: Yes.

> *(First, witty banter.)*

I mean, there was this fire that I was going to go try to seize across town . . .

> *(Quite serious now.)*

but there's one heating up right here that I'd like to keep my eye on . . . so, yes. Yes, I would love to go get coffee or something with you.

MAN: You know, this has got to be the oddest way I've met somebody in my entire life.

WOMAN: I don't know.

> *(She takes his hand. Slowly, HE looks at their now clasped hands—at last touching—then to her, feeling the electricity between them. They both smile.)*

What's normal?

> *(They walk off, still holding hands as they "burn through the forests of the night.")*

Look at Me

Susan Westfall

Look At Me was originally produced by City Theatre for its annual Summer Shorts Festival, June 3–27, 2010, at the Adrienne Arsht Center for the Performing Arts of Miami-Dade County, Miami, Florida. Cast: Eddie— Scott Genn; Celia—Breeza Zeller. Directed by Avi Hoffman. Stephanie Norman, Producing Artistic Director.

CHARACTERS

Eddie . . finally home but not really there. Twenties–early thirties.
Celia . . who has been waiting for him. Twenties–early thirties.

SETTING

A bedroom, dimly lit by a lamp or two, some candles. It is dark and shadowy but for the bed. The bed is large and made. There is a nightstand and an arm chair is nearby.

TIME

The present

Eddie sits at the foot of the bed. He's in jeans and a shirt which he doesn't look quite comfortable wearing. His hands are on his knees, his eyes are closed. He opens them but doesn't look around when Celia enters. She turns off the music, the Elvis Presley version of "Fever". A lamp is dimly lit and there are candles. Celia has been waiting a long time for Eddie to come home. She is wearing a filmy negligee. She lies down on the bed behind him. She is nearly touching him, but doesn't. Both look a little nervous.

CELIA: I love you Eddie . . . *(Beat)* Do you love me?

EDDIE: I dream about you.

CELIA: I dream about you too.

EDDIE: On lookout when there was nothing out there to see, I could see you.

CELIA: How did you see me?

EDDIE: You were lying down. I could see your curves, your breasts, your hips, your sweet, sweet ass . . . in the shape of a certain mountain on the horizon. Shit, Celia. I was supposed to be looking for something else out there. Someone else. But I was always looking for you. And then right at dawn, didn't matter what season it was, I would see you, like you were smiling at me over your shoulder. Then the sun would come up and you'd just melt away. Fucking broke my heart.

CELIA: I'm here now.

EDDIE: Yeah.

CELIA: Come to me, Eddie.

He doesn't, but he's smiling a little. She reaches for a picture on the nightstand.

CELIA: I see you in a frame by my bed. The picture I took of you just waking up? It's the last thing I look at before I go to sleep. That's why I dream of you, that picture. And there you are waking up when I wake up. And sometimes I wake up and imagine I feel your hands on me, all over me, and I don't get out of bed so fast. You know what I mean?

EDDIE: Over there the women, they walk by when we're on patrol. They're covered head to toe in their robes. Burkas. Just their eyes showing, and shoes. It's supposed to make them modest. But if there's two of them walking together, you hear them whispering to each other, and you can feel their eyes on you.

Celia has slid around and beside Eddie. She takes his hand and holds it. He lets her.

CELIA: You're a good looking man, Eddie. All of you men in uniform? I bet those women wanted to look at you. Maybe it made them hot under those, what did you call them?

EDDIE: Burkas.

CELIA: Burr... kahs...

EDDIE: Yeah, well. Their men catch them looking at us, they might get buried up to their necks and stoned to death.

CELIA: No shit? That's awful... *(Beat)* Do we have to talk about this?

EDDIE: Those women, they were either stupid or brave. Sometimes they'd slow down so you could take a good look. Maybe one of them would turn and look back over her shoulder, with these eyes that made you want to see what the rest of her looked like. It was a turn on... but I'd pretend it was you under those robes. Oh yeah, I'd wonder, what would Celia be wearing under there. Or not? Once the Captain caught me smiling, thinking about you darling even if I was looking at this woman, and he pulled me up and got all in my face and says... *(Eddie hears it all over again, whispers)* ... "Eyes forward, Soldier, before you fucking get us all killed." Just for looking.

Eddie shivers suddenly. He pulls his hand away.

CELIA: Shit, Eddie ... I mean, my God. You must have been so horny! Well, here I am, baby. All yours.

Celia is laughing, and finally Eddie is laughing a little too. She puts her arms around him but he shifts, suddenly at a loss what to do with his hands, his body, uncomfortable with what he's telling her.

CELIA: Come on ... You know you want to know what's under my robe.

Eddie's still. His eyes are closed. Now he's breaking her heart.

CELIA: I want you so bad Eddie. Don't you want me?

Celia lifts her nightie a bit, flirting, trying harder.

Or is it you just got so used to looking, you aren't used to touching? (She laughs low) I bet this is the kind of thing would get me in trouble with those freaks back there.

Celia puts a foot on the bed beside Eddie, and puts his hand on her leg as she lifts the nightie higher. She waits for him to take the hint. He doesn't. He lifts his hand off and it's like he's slapped her. She walks away, her back to him. They are silent.

CELIA: I don't know who I thought I was waiting for.

EDDIE: I'm sorry.

She watches him from across the room. Eddie shivers.

CELIA: I'm so happy you're home, but if I did something or said something wrong—

EDDIE: It's not you, okay? I'm just really tired, is all.

CELIA: Yeah ... Me too. It's been a long day. Let's go to bed. Is that alright, if we go to bed? I mean if you don't want to fool around, you could just be on your side, and I'll be on my side, we don't even have to watch the Tonight Show ... (beat) It sucks anyway. But you should get undressed. Okay? Here, let me help you.

Celia is back on the bed behind Eddie, trying to unbutton his shirt, but he gently pushes her away.

EDDIE: Don't.

CELIA: Don't what? Honey, I'm just trying to help you off with your shirt—

EDDIE: No, I'm cold—

CELIA: So you'll be more comfortable in bed—

EDDIE: I'm okay like this.

He pushes her away.

CELIA: Well, I bought you pajamas. You never used to wear anything, but another wife, she said her husband came home and right off ditched his camos for some pj's, and . . . . you want me to get them for you? Maybe, just for tonight? Until you get used to things, again . . . Like me? (beat) Eddie, you can't sleep in your clothes—

EDDIE: I've been sleeping in my clothes and my boots and my helmet and my pack for awhile now, Celia, with a fucking cocked and loaded gun in my hand. Where is my gun?

CELIA: You don't have a gun. I wouldn't let you in this house if you had a gun. Besides, you don't need a gun anymore. You're home. And you're not going anywhere.

EDDIE: I can't believe I used to sleep naked.

CELIA: We both did.

EDDIE: Well, now I can't.

CELIA: Fine . . . I don't care. You've been living a fucking nightmare, okay? I thought I was but I've just been here and alone. Now we're together again, husband and wife. And I want you to know I've waited for you, and kept myself up! In fact I go to the gym so much I look better than you remember, okay? I'm not buff, but I'm trim. There's guys, hot young men, I fend off that make passes at me. They can't believe I'm married and waiting around for you.

She drops her robe. The nightgown is very sheer. She spins for him. Drapes it on him.

Imagine I'm your bride again, in my pretty, pretty nightgown, and you can't wait to tear it off and make love to me.

EDDIE: Make love to you?

CELIA: Yes, Eddie. I want you to make love to me. Or fuck me.

EDDIE: Fuck you? I can't look at you.

She moves fast and slaps him hard and he falls back, stunned.

EDDIE: You bitch.

CELIA: Now look at me.

EDDIE: Jesus, Celia, that hurt.

He puts his hands up, but she pulls them down, gets in his face, and takes his face firmly in her hands.

CELIA: Now. You're looking at me.

EDDIE: Yeah? Well, I don't see you.

CELIA: I know that.

EDDIE: I'll never see you again . . .

CELIA: I know that.

EDDIE: I'm never going to see anything ever again.

Eddie pushes her away and stands, stumbles, is searching for something.

EDDIE: Shit, I suck at this. Do you see it?

Celia gets a white cane for him. He takes it, begins to tap his way around the room.

CELIA: Watch out. The chair's in front of you. Remember the chair you liked to read in? Everything's exactly as it was before you left, okay? They said it would make it easier . . .

He finds the chair, sits. This was home. She comes around and perches on the edge of the bed in front of him. Slowly she reaches out and touches him very gently on his knee.

CELIA: Okay? Now what?

EDDIE: *(He reaches out with the cane and taps her.)* I need to tell you what happened—

CELIA: You were on foot patrol, and there was an i.e.d . . . that's what I was told.

EDDIE: Yeah? Well. It had been quiet, like maybe things in this village were getting back to normal. People were out which they aren't if the Taliban are creeping around. So I guess I, I let myself relax? It's fucking exhausting, Celia, waiting to be killed. Anyway, this woman starts to come towards me, and she's looking right at me, no lie. We are looking straight at each other, and she murmurs something as she gets closer. It was so strange fucking bells should have gone off. My buddy, he tried to move me aside? Away from her? But I started to follow her, which was dangerous and against orders—

CELIA: Oh, Eddie. This happened because you followed some woman . . . ?

EDDIE: It was a trick, Celia. I walked into a trap. Those fucking lunatic fanatics see we're lonely, and because we are, sometimes we let our guard down, to look. You know, try to catch a woman's eyes under her veils. Just to see if she's noticed you, can see the man under all the camouflage and hardware, see I'm not there to hurt her, or anyone. I need her to look at me so I know I'm ... still alive. So when this woman walked past me and my buddy, it's like I just forgot the war for a minute. Maybe I believed I was following after you... Then she drops her robe and it's a boy! Little bastard is laughing his butt off at me, and takes off running. And I go tearing after the little shit, so I can catch him and kill him. And my buddy is running after us telling me to stop and let him go—and that's when he steps on the fucking IED. The last thing I saw, still see, was him and the shrapnel. Then, nothing... Until you came to me in a dream. Or maybe it was the coma.

Celia pulls him up, holds him, then takes the cane from him.

EDDIE: Hey! I need that—

CELIA: Trust me.

She guides him to the bed, takes his face in her hands.

CELIA: When you dream about me, what do you see?

EDDIE: I see you perfectly. I think.

CELIA: Let's find out.

She places his hands on her face.

EDDIE: This is stupid.

CELIA: It's not. This is how you're going to see me from now on. *(She puts his hand on her hair)* My hair is long again. Which is a pain in the ass to take care of. And I color it now.

EDDIE: It's not brown?

CELIA: It's lighter. *(Moving his hands)* What color are my eyes?

EDDIE: Blue. Ish. Blue-ish. *(He trails down to her mouth)* You have a beautiful mouth Celia.

She takes his hand and kisses it, and puts it on her breast.

EDDIE: I can't.

CELIA: But I love how you touch me.

EDDIE: You know why they took my gun away? I told my shrink I should be dead for what I did. For what I did to you. I'm blind. My career is over. I don't know what the hell else I'm going to do. But I don't expect you to stick around while I figure it out, or because you feel sorry for me. You don't deserve any of this fucked up shit. And I don't deserve you. Could I sound any more sorry for myself?

He leans against the head board. She curls up beside him, her arms around him.

CELIA: I imagined if this day ever arrived, when you came home, it would be like it was our first time. Remember? That day we couldn't tear our eyes off each other, and we just knew the minute the bell rang what we were going to do. Remember how impatient we were getting into the back seat of my car? And then getting out of our clothes? You had on a shirt almost like this and I couldn't wait for you to unbutton it so I reached up and pulled it over your head, like this . . . *(He lets her pull his shirt off. She strokes his chest)* Then we were all over each other, our hands exploring, our mouths tasting, me checking to see if you were scared, and you asking if I was scared. And we could have stopped like before, but I wanted you so bad I didn't even take off my dress. I just pushed you back a little, like this *(she lays him down)* and then I climbed on top of you, like this . . . *(she lifts herself onto him)* And we eased into each other . . . like this . . . *(He is reaching up to her, finally touching her, feeling her respond, and pulling her down into him, and they kiss.)* And when we came up for air, I looked to see if you felt as happy as me. And you had as big a shit eating grin as I'd ever seen. Remember what you said? *(His arms are around her as she looks down at him.)*

EDDIE: I love you Celia.

CELIA: After that. You said, let's do it again and again and again and no matter what happens let's never stop. I'm willing to try if you are.

EDDIE: Are you sure? We'll be alright? I don't know. I can't see what's in your eyes. You're going to have to help me. Just don't pity me.

Eddie runs his hands over Celia, first gently and then more urgently when she responds.

CELIA: Sure, Eddie. Whatever. So. What do think? Shall I turn off the light?

EDDIE: What light? *(He raises her arms and she lifts her nightgown over her head.)*

End of play.

Magnolia Day

S. D. Graubert

Production History: Yellow Springs Corner Cone 10 Minute Play Festival, Short list, 2010; Wagner College, June 2010; Festapalooza, Mind-the-Gap Productions, May 2010; Writes of Spring, May 2010, HB Studio; Winner, Nantucket Short Play Festival, Summer 2009; Source Festival, DC, 2008, where it was reviewed as 'the best of the relationship plays' by the Washington Post.

TIME

Present

PLACE

Marie's living room, New York City

CHARACTERS

Marie . . (early 20s) About to get married.
Lisa. . . . (mid 20s) Marie's older sister.

Marie twirls in front of Lisa.

LISA: So, what are you, like, an eight?

MARIE: Six!

LISA: *(Jealous but covering)* Wow. You're gonna be one skinny bride.

MARIE: Three dress sizes!

LISA: How'd you do it?

MARIE: Work out.

LISA: *(Disappointed)* Oh. *(Hopeful)* But then you can eat what you want, right?

MARIE: Pretty much. I mean, no sugar, no red meat, no fried foods, no starch, no simple carbs, no, um, did I say fried foods? No fried food, no wheat, no dairy, no alcohol, no gluten, no genet-ically-modified soy, no caffeine, so, yeah, apart from that, I can pretty much eat what I want.

LISA: Wait. Caffeine's fattening?

MARIE: Addictive.

LISA: Totes. But fattening?

MARIE: Sugar, in your kidneys, no, spleen, somewhere in there—

LISA: So, wow, it's like drinking sugar—

MARIE: And white bread? That's like eating sugar.

LISA: No!

MARIE: Totes McGoats. *(As if this most important fact in the world)* Turns to, like, sugar, in your stomach. *(Triumphant)* It is so good to see you, Lisa!

LISA: Well. Couldn't miss Magnolia Day—

MARIE: But we're not doing Magnolia—

LISA: —You didn't want to meet at the Bakery, so—
> *She pulls out a lidded bakery box.*
—I brought the bakery to you!

MARIE: Lisa, no, no, I told you, no Magnolia Day, not this year, not with the wedding and everything—

LISA: I see you once, maybe twice a year—

MARIE: And I promise to change that—

LISA: And this is Magnolia Day—

MARIE: But I'm getting married in two months! Three weeks and four and a half days.

LISA: Jeez, it's one day, Marie. Live a little.

MARIE: Do you know how hard it is to be on the wagon? I went through it all with my food therapist.

LISA: You have a food therapist?

MARIE: All brides have food therapists. She said sugar is my crack.

LISA: She di'nt!

MARIE: And she's right! Once I start, I just can't stop.

LISA: 'Till you're hanging out on the corner, offering sex for cupcakes.

MARIE: It's hard, Lisa. Not like coal mining hard, but hard.

LISA: You were a coal miner? Was that, like, when I was fighting injustices in South Africa?

MARIE: You were fighting injustices in South Africa?

LISA: No-wuh.

MARIE: Lisa, God! You know what I'm talking about!

LISA: It's a few little, teeny tiny cupcakes—

MARIE: From the Magnolia Bakery!

LISA: That's the point.

MARIE: NO-wuh! I am absolutely not gonna do Magnolia Day this year, I can't, I won't, it's absolutely not gonna—
> *Lisa opens the box, resplendently filled with cupcakes.*

They look so pretty!

LISA: All the colors—

MARIE: —And the sprinkles—

LISA: —Gotta have the sprinkles—

MARIE: How do they make them look so good?

LISA: —And taste so good—

MARIE: I guess one won't hurt.

LISA: You're the best.

MARIE: The frosting!

LISA: I know—wuh!

MARIE: How do they make it stay up?

LISA: I got your favorite.

MARIE: Chocolate with the lilac frosting?

LISA: And mult-coloured sprinkles. And I got your other favorite.

MARIE: Strawberry with the oreo chocolate frosting?

LISA: And the chocolate button on the top—

MARIE: —And my other favorite?

LISA: Vanilla with the purple frosting, and the yellow sprinkles.

MARIE: *(Squealing/screaming-panicked)* OH, MY GOD!

LISA: I KNOW, I KNOW, I KNOW, I KNOW!

MARIE: I DON'T KNOW WHICH ONE TO CHOOSE! THEY LOOK SOOOOO GOOOD!

LISA: And taste SOOOOOO good.

MARIE: All bunched together like that—

LISA: All cosy in their box.

MARIE: Like best friends—

LISA: Yeah—

MARIE: Like an army of best friends.

LISA: Or sisters.

MARIE: A family—

LISA: The Cupcake Family—

MARIE: The Cupcake Family in their little box house.

LISA: All together in their little house.

MARIE: All scrunched together in their little box house.

> *Marie claws at her chest, distressed.*

MARIE: Rubbing against each other. Getting crushed.

LISA: Marie—

MARIE: Fighting for room—

LISA: It's the lid, the frosting, sometimes it sticks—

MARIE: I can't—

LISA: You can scrape it off—

MARIE: Can't breath—

LISA: The frosting, like you said, it's just that it's—

MARIE: How many are there in there? One, two three—

LISA: Fifteen.

MARIE: Fifteen.

LISA: ... Yeh—

MARIE: Fifteen? Fifteen cupcakes from Magnolia Bakery?

LISA: It's Magnolia Day—

MARIE: I know it's Magnolia Day—

LISA: Your last Magnolia Day as a singleton.

MARIE: God! / God!

> *Lisa, playfully holds a cupcake, as if it's speaking to Marie.*

LISA: Marie ... Marie..

MARIE: I love my thin self; I believe I can do it. I love my thin self; I
believe I can do it.

> *Lisa holds up a second cupcake.*

LISA: Marie. Hullo, Marie—

MARIE: I love my- God! *(Rising hysteria)* I love my thin self; I believe
I can do it. I love my thin—

LISA: Bite me. You know you want to. Marie ... Bite me ...

MARIE: I love my thin self.

WAIT!

Bite me, Lisa.

LISA: It was the cupcake talking.

MARIE: I know it was the cupcake talking, but still. Bite me. You always do this. You always, always do this.

LISA: It's Magnolia Day. This is what we do.

MARIE: You always act like my no means a yes.

LISA: It's our last Magnolia Day together!

MARIE: What, you're leaving town?

LISA: Bill won't let you do Magnolia Day once you're married.

MARIE: Yes, and he keeps a chastity belt in the closet.

LISA: He makes you wear a chastity belt?

MARIE: God, Lisa, it's not the 1980s! Of course, we'll still do Magnolia Day, just not. FIFTEEN! They don't even allow you to buy fifteen. Not in one go.

LISA: I told them my sister was getting married—

MARIE: Lisa, I said, quite clearly, no Magnolia Day this year, because I don't want, because I'm a, and you know this, you know I'm a compulsive eater, you know I can't stop when I start, and you bring fifteen cupcakes? We never have—
     (Realization)
     Hhuuuuhh! You want me to be fat for my wedding.

LISA: That's so not true—

MARIE: You want me to be fat for my wedding. You're upset and jealous, 'cause you're not my maid of honor.

LISA: That's not—

MARIE: Mom called me, Lisa! So, fine! You're going to host a bachelorette dinner.

LISA: Mom had to ask?

MARIE: You think my maid of honor was happy about that?

LISA: Don't you think your sister should be your maid of honor?

MARIE: This is exactly why you're not my maid of honor!

LISA: Because I brought you cupcakes?

MARIE: Because you brought fifteen of my favorite cupcakes!

LISA: It's a loving gesture. A caring gesture.

MARIE: I DON'T WANT YOUR LOVING OR YOUR CARING GESTURES!

LISA: That is so—

MARIE: I DON'T WANT ANY DAMN CUPCAKES!
     Marie whacks the box of cupcakes, which go flying up into the air.

LISA: THE VANILLA STRAWBERRY! THE PUMPKIN-CARROT WITH CHOCOLATE SPRINKLES!

MARIE: I don't want you to host the dinner.

LISA: But—

MARIE: I can't risk you bringing Death by Chocolate, or Old Fashioned, Double-Whipped Cheesecake.

LISA: I promise I won't, I won't, let me host, let me host the dinner, Marie, I'll be good, I promise, let me host, I'll look up recipes. I'll make sugar free, wheat free, gluten free, dairy free, I don't know, bread patties.

MARIE: Can't have wheat.

LISA: Something! I'll make something... without... any... human ingredients... whatsoever.

MARIE: *(Reluctantly smiles)* Sounds delicious.

LISA: I'll make it. I promise. I'll do what it takes.

MARIE: No cupcakes?

LISA: Definitely, no cupcakes! No anything sweet. We'll have cardboard cake, topped with horse-dung coulis, and a melange of wild moss.

Marie playfully hits Lisa.

MARIE: It's not that bad.

LISA: You sure?

MARIE: Dried apricots are my best friend.

LISA: Wait, there was an apricot one—

MARIE: Lisa—

LISA: Which I will eat. If it's not squashed into your carpet.

MARIE: Charlie'll clean it up in no time.

LISA: You're feeding Magnolia cupcakes to the dog?

MARIE: It's been the secret of my slimming success.

LISA: I'm saving this one from doggie death.

Marie picks up a cupcake.

MARIE: It smells so good.

LISA: You know you wanna.

MARIE: I have a will of steel.

LISA: So, not our last?

MARIE: Not our last.

LISA: Happy Magnolia Day.

They "chink" cupcakes.

MARIE: Happy Magnolia Day.

Lisa eats her cupcake. Marie hovers over hers.

Damn, that is one fine cupcake.

With great reluctance, Marie puts the cupcake down.

Beat

MARIE: ... Oh, God.

Suddenly, she picks up the cupcake, and devours it, as the lights fade.

Me and Shirley

Henry Meyerson

August 14, 2010, Corner Cone 10 Minute Play Festival, Yellow Springs, Ohio. Director: Stephen Woosley. Cast: Clerk—Jessi Biggert, Bob—Stephen Woosley. Original Production Info: Sept., 2004. Blue Heron Theater, New York, Epiphany Theater Company. Director: Amy Singer. Cast: Clerk—Michael LiDondici; Bob—George Delhi, Jr.

CHARACTERS

Clerk: . . . A municipal employee who has been working at the
job too many years. Age: any. Gender: male, but can
be female with change of a few pronouns.

Bob: . . . . A man eager, well meaning, and in love.

SETTING

Desk, two chairs. Prop: small box.

TIME

Present.

---

*Office, desk with desk stuff and papers and chair. AT LIGHTS: A
clerk, bored and indifferent, sits behind the desk. Bob, anxious, enters
carrying a box.*

CLERK: Good morning.

BOB: Hi. Is this where I get a marriage licence?

CLERK: That's what the sign on the door says.

BOB: I'm a little nervous. It's not every day I get married.

CLERK: That sounds like a good thing. Might be confusing if you did.

BOB: My name's Bob.

CLERK: Great.

BOB: You married?

CLERK: What's it to you?

BOB: Well, I'd like to know I'm dealing with someone who knows
what they're doing. It might help me calm down.

CLERK: Of course I know what I'm doing. I'm the clerk and I'm assuming you will be the groom.

BOB: It's my first time.

CLERK: I could never tell.

BOB: Humor me.

CLERK: Yes, I'm married.

BOB: How long?

CLERK: Forever. Now can we ...?

BOB: Got a picture of her?

CLERK: Who?

BOB: Your wife.

The clerk grudgingly shows Bob a picture from his wallet. Bob stares intently and close at the photo.

BOB: Kind of blurry and dark, but she seems nice. Seems short.

CLERK: It's the stumpy legs. Makes her look a bit like a hedge hog. But you're right. She's nice and we are happily married.

BOB: Kids?

CLERK: Nope. Now, can we get on with it? Most marriages don't last very long and you wouldn't want to be married and divorced on the same day. So where is the bride?

BOB: Right here.

The clerk looks around.

CLERK: Where is here?

BOB: *(patting the box)* Here.

CLERK: In the box?

BOB: Right.

CLERK: You have your girl friend in the box.

BOB: Future wife.

CLERK: *(couple of beats)* Small, isn't she?

BOB: Not really. About right, I would say.

CLERK: Right for what?

BOB: Want to meet her?

CLERK: I can hardly wait.

Bob opens the box and they both peer inside.

BOB: Isn't she adorable?

CLERK: Yes, very cute.

BOB: Everyone thinks so.

CLERK: Sir?

BOB: Yes?

CLERK: It's a rat.

BOB: Shirley's a gerbil.

CLERK: Whatever.

BOB: It's an important distinction. Who would ever want to marry a rat?

CLERK: *(calling over Bob's head)* Next.

BOB: Wait a second. We haven't finished here yet.

CLERK: Yes, you have sir. *(over Bob's head)* Next.

BOB: I will not budge until you grant Shirley and me a licence to be married.

CLERK: People do not marry rats.

BOB: Gerbil.

CLERK: Whatever.

BOB: I intend to be a ground breaker.

CLERK: I don't care if you're a wind-breaker, Bob, I'm not issuing a marriage licence to a man and his rat . . . er . . . gerbil. We do have regulations, you know. We can't account for people's taste, but cross specie marriage is pushing it.

BOB: Are you saying there is a law against this?

CLERK: Precisely. A law. It's called the Constitution. Remember that? Think back to grammar school and try to remember the Amendments.

BOB: Don't you pull that tone on me. I remember them. Well, not all of them, not in detail.

CLERK: Do you remember the latest, the twenty-eighth? That all marriages must be between a male and female?

BOB: Male and female. That's exactly the way it should be. Male and female, the way God meant it to be.

CLERK: Exactly, which is why I can't grant you and Shirley a license.

BOB: Then I'm confused.

CLERK: I figured that.

BOB: I'm male.

CLERK: So far so good.

BOB: And Shirley is . . .

CLERK: Don't even go there.

BOB: We are two consenting adults in the prime of our sexual powers.

CLERK: *(over Bob's head)* Next.

BOB: We expect to have children.

CLERK: I don't want to hear about it.

BOB: She's capable of five to six at a pop, every month. Isn't that great?

CLERK: *(over Bob's head)* Next.

BOB: There is a problem, though, and that's why I'm in a bit of a rush.

CLERK: Bit of a problem?

BOB: Her entire reproductive life is good for only eighteen months. Then...

CLERK: Then?

BOB: Poof. No more kids.

CLERK: Let me see that thing.

> Bob opens the box.

BOB: Hi, cutie. It's Bob. Miss me?

CLERK: Not very attractive.

BOB: Hey, watch it. I saw a picture of your wife, remember. I wouldn't be casting stones, here, if you get my drift.

CLERK: Wise guy, huh? Okay, wise guy, how do I even know this is a female gerbil. Maybe you're just trying to get around the new Amendment, passing off a male for a female. I wasn't born yesterday.

BOB: Do I look like the kind of guy who would make it with a male gerbil?

CLERK: We get all kinds in here, Bob. Guy brought a goat in the other day.

BOB: How'd it go.

CLERK: Couldn't get away with it. Goats have external sex organs. I spotted it before they hit the door. Read them the Amendment and out they went.

BOB: Kind of sad, when you think of it. Not able to make their love legal.

CLERK: And I'm tough, Bob.

BOB: I can see that.

CLERK: You would be too if Scalia and Clarence Thomas were breathing down your neck. I got a wife to feed.

BOB: See, but that's exactly what I want to do. I want to have a wife and a litter or two of kids to feed. I want to be able to take them all off my taxes as dependents, just like every other American can. Just give me a chance to do it. What do you say?

Clerk thinks it over, looks around then leans into Bob with an air of confidentiality.

CLERK: Remember I said my wife looks like a hedgehog?

BOB: Yeah.

CLERK: *(more deeply confidential)* More than just looks like.

BOB: *(beat... he gets it)* Noooo.

Clerk looks around then slightly, conspiratorially, nods his head.

CLERK: The real deal, Bob. Softest fur you ever felt. Claws mess up the sheets a bit, but small price to pay.

BOB: *(with anticipation)* Then...?

CLERK: *(as a co-conspirator)* Did you bring the ring?

THE END

The Modern American Romance Not Often Seen

Mark Troy

The Modern American Romance Not Often Seen opened at the 68 Cent Crew Theatre Company in Los Angeles, CA on August 27th, 2010. It was produced by Ronnie Marmo and directed by Denny Siegel. The cast was as follows: Deedee Fishman—Melanie Blue; Avery Minowitz—Joe Massingill.

SETTING

Small apartment. Anywhere, USA

TIME

Present Day.

CHARACTERS

Deedee Fishman:. . . over-exuberant, excitable, late 20s

Avery Minowitz:. . . . a temporarily paralyzed desperate young
bachelor, 20–30.

---

*A small Soho apartment with an open kitchen. A ratty sofa, center,
and a straight back chair that faces it, is the only furniture. The front
door is kicked opened and Deedee Fishman enters, dragging a paralyzed Avery Minowitz from under his shoulders. His head can move
and look around, but his body is limp. She drags . . .*

DEEDEE: *(calmly)* I really had a great time . . . I'm so glad you came
back to see my place. And wasn't that the scariest movie? The
uncle—who would have guessed it was the uncle living in the
attic? I want to thank you. I want to thank you for a great date,
and please thank your mom for setting us up. I really had a great
time, Avery.

AVERY: *(Just as calm)* I can't feel my toes.

DEEDEE: *(pulling him to the sofa; placidly.)* I thought the chicken was
very good. Did you like your pasta primavera? I'd never tasted
such a great sauce . . . really good stuff. And thanks again for
the wine. I usually don't drink with a new boyfriend, but we
were laughing so much, I figured why not? I think it's so funny
that your brother and my sister went to Francis Lewis High
School together. Small world, small world.

AVERY: *(Tries to lift a hand, cannot.)* I seem to be slightly . . . immobile.

DEEDEE: I love that shirt on you. That color . . . you have to remind me around your birthday, I want to buy you more shirts that color. Would that be alright with you?

AVERY: I can blink. That I can do.

(Blinks)

Blink.

DEEDEE: Oh I forgot . . . I bought you something.

(She leans Avery's head up on the side of the sofa and exits. Unable to stay upright, he flops over. She enters with a large lollipop.)

Remember? Remember we passed that candy place on Bleecker and you said this looked delicious?

(He nods; she sits him up.)

I bought it for you. I bought it for you, Avery. Do you know why I bought it for you?

(He shakes his head.)

Because we passed that candy place on Bleecker and you said this looked delicious.

(She slides in next to him.)

And because I like you.

(She unwraps the lollipop and allows him to lick it.)

Good?

AVERY: My legs are tingling.

DEEDEE: It's nothing. Listen, Avery, I got tickets to "Mamma Mia" for Saturday. I'd really like to go with you.

AVERY: *(staring at his hand)* My fingers aren't moving.

DEEDEE: It's nothing. They're great seats. Oo—let me show you what I'm going to wear.

(She exits. Avery tries to move but winds up face first on the floor. Deedee enters in a low-cut short dress showing off as much as possible.

I know, I know . . . I'm gorgeous! Avery—what happened?

(She sits him up then pulls him up onto the sofa.)

You are so funny. Really witty. Remember our first date . . . you were telling jokes left and right. And right and left!

AVERY: Deedee?

DEEDEE: Yes, boyfriend?

AVERY: There's any reason why I can't feel my body?

DEEDEE: Yes, future husband.

AVERY: And what is that reason, Deedee?

DEEDEE: I slipped you a Flunitrazepam.

AVERY: Did I need a Flunitrazepam?

DEEDEE: Oh yes, future father-to-breed-my-children. You definitely needed a Flunitrazepam.

AVERY: Did it come with the pasta primavera?

DEEDEE: You are sooo funny. Left and right. And right and left.

AVERY: Deedee, what is a Flunitrazepam?

DEEDEE: It's a ruffie, future co-life insurance policy partner-holder. Hey, look at the shoes I got to go with this outfit.
>   *(Exits. Returns with 12 inch spiked heels . . . hooker-style.)*
>   At first I thought they were a little on the short side, then I realized you liked my legs, so why not show them off?

AVERY: I like your legs?

DEEDEE: You told me last week. When we met. When you fell for me. The first time we made love.

AVERY: We never . . .

DEEDEE: —You boys forget so easily. You think I made this stuff up?

AVERY: Deedee . . . did you make that stuff up? That we made love last week?

DEEDEE: I exaggerated. Is that a crime now?

AVERY: *(running out of patience)* What did you give me?

DEEDEE: *(Sits, pulls shoes off and takes off dress . . . now in silk flimsy slip. Calmly)* It's an innocent R-2. Or a . . . street shay, mind-eraser drug. It just attacks your central nervous system's all.

AVERY: *(Worried; struggles to move.)* I'm paralyzed!

DEEDEE: —It's your standard depressant that's ten times more powerful than Valium.

AVERY: Because Valium wasn't strong enough to drug me with?

DEEDEE: *(laughing uncontrollably)* Funny left and right. And right and l . . .

AVERY: I'm scared, Deedee. I'm really scared. Where did you get—?

DEEDEE: —The chick I bought it from tells me in some foreign countries it's used as a pre-surgical sedative and for treatment of severe sleep and psychiatric disorders. Doesn't it make you feel like we've traveled abroad together?

AVERY: We can't travel abroad—I can't move! Why did you do this?

DEEDEE: I just wanted your attention for one night.

AVERY: I have an itch . . . nose nose nose . . .

(She scratches it for him.)
This is horrible. This is horrible. This has been a horrible date.
DEEDEE: But we're growing closer.
AVERY: Closer? You gave me the date rape drug?
DEEDEE: If you call it that—you take all the fun out of it.
AVERY: This is a crime! This is against the law. The last thing I remember we were having a very nice conversation at a quaint chic restaurant on Hauser, and you offered me a drink.
DEEDEE: It wasn't just a nice conversation, Avery. You were going to break up with me.
AVERY: I was not.
DEEDEE: You weren't?
AVERY: No.
DEEDEE: I misread you. I shouldn't have crushed two colorless, odorless, tasteless sedatives into your Petite Syrah.
AVERY: TWO?!
DEEDEE: I thought you were dumping me.
AVERY: It was only our second date.
DEEDEE: Sometimes guys can be very non-committal.
AVERY: I have an itch... ear ear ear.
(She scratches him.)
I never heard of this happening. We innocently sat down... ordered a meal...
DEEDEE: Boy. That pasta primavera had great sauce.
AVERY: —And you said, "Let me go get us something from the bar."
DEEDEE: I had to put the drugs into your drink so you wouldn't see me. Aren't you proud? I did it all by myself.
AVERY: Deedee... you've done a terrible thing. A completely immoral unforgiveable disturbing thing.
DEEDEE: You want another suck of the lolly?
AVERY: I want you jailed!
DEEDEE: Men never see it from our point of you.
AVERY: Well I guess I do now—because my eyes are the only thing working!
DEEDEE: Do you know what's out there? The horrors? Oh no. When we get a guy who... who shows us a little caring. A little friendship. Or even... a little love... well... we hold on to it. We grab on to it and choke it tight.

AVERY: NOW you wanna choke me?

DEEDEE: No, no, my dear, Avery. I would never hurt you.

(He throws her a look.)

Permanently. I just don't want to lose you to someone who can offer you more.

AVERY: I wasn't interested in someone who could offer me more.

DEEDEE: Even to someone with bigger tits.

AVERY: I liked you. I liked your sense of humor and your smile. I liked the feeling of your hand in mine. You have to give these things time to grow.

DEEDEE: *(Looks at her breasts.)* They're fully grown.

AVERY: I'm talking about love! You rushed things.

DEEDEE: I should let it all happen in a natural course . . . evolve like a true love affair.

AVERY: You pushed it.

DEEDEE: I guess I wear my emotions right on my sleeve.

AVERY: Get me my phone . . . I'm calling my mother. This is the last time I let her set me up with a psychotic.

DEEDEE: *(reaching for the phone)* You don't have to be rude.

(She takes the phone from his pocket.)

AVERY: Can you open it? Can you please open it?

(She opens it.)

Can you press one? Can you please press one?·

(She dials it.)

Can you hold it, can you please hold it?

(She holds it to his ear. Into phone:)

Mom?

(Breaks down.)

Mommy . . . I can't move.

(Stronger)

Yes, mom. I did. I had a good time and wanted to see her again.

DEEDEE: *(Screams into phone.)* Hello, Mrs. Minowitz.

AVERY: She says hi and wants to know how the pasta primavera was.

DEEDEE: Great sauce.

AVERY: *(into phone)* Mom. How well did you know Deedee before you set me up with her? How desperate do you think I am? How lonely can a man be to put himself into a situation like this?

(Long beat)

Huh? We're going to talk about this later, Mother. Goodbye.
Can you hang up? Can you please hang up?
    (Deedee takes the phone)
She wants to know if the ruffie she sold you worked out alright.

DEEDEE: I hope you told her it did.

AVERY: THE woman IS A FREAK!

DEEDEE: I felt you pulling away, Avery.

AVERY: I wasn't pulling—and now I can't pull anything!
    (He falls over and DEEDEE holds him up.)
She said she wanted me to give you a shot. A chance. She said I
always break up with girls too soon without...

DEEDEE: —Without what?

AVERY: Without letting things... evolve. Like a true love affair. Guess
I wear my emotions right on my sleeve too.

DEEDEE: If I try to kiss you... will you pull away?

AVERY: HOW?
    (She gently kisses him.)
Again?

DEEDEE: Got it.

AVERY: So when does this stuff wear off?
    (Beat)
Soon I hope.

DEEDEE: Soon enough for you to put your arms around me the next
time we kiss.

AVERY: Wanna make some popcorn and watch a movie?

DEEDEE: The TV's in the bedroom.

AVERY: I don't mind going in the bedroom.

DEEDEE: *(shyly)* It's our second date, Avery... are you suggesting we
make love?

AVERY: Well, we don't want to rush things. We should wait until the
drug wears off.
    (Deedee drags a limp Avery toward the bedroom.)

DEEDEE: *(laughing)* Funny left and right and right and—
    (As she drags him... LIGHTS OUT.)

END OF PLAY

Noir in Second Class

C.J. Ehrlich

Noir in Second Class had its production premiere at Appetite Theatre Company's "Bruschetta" fest, in Chicago, IL, October 8–16, 2010. The play was directed by Kristin Idaszak. Annie Hogan played Nora, and Zach Shornick played Stewart. Executive director of Appetite Theatre is Darcy Elora Hofer.

TIME

Present day, late afternoon.

SETTING

Somewhere in Europe. A compartment on a transcontinental train.

CHARACTERS

Nora . . . . 30ish, attractive, intense. Attired and styled very
            1940s, maybe a dark skirt suit, high heels, ankle
            bracelet, and a chic hat with a small veil. She might
            speak in that elegant cinematic 1940s pseudo-English
            diction (think Katherine Hepburn).
Stewart . . late 20s, an affable, clueless middle American tourist,
            Nora's husband and travel companion. Seems like
            he's from another world, or another play.
Voice of a train Porter (see note).

PRODUCTION NOTES

The train can be simply depicted with two facing benches with an upstage wall/window between. The compartment door can be mimed, with rising and ebbing sound effects corresponding to its opening and closing. Flashing lighting to simulate tunnels, trees etc would be a nice touch.

The Porter may be played by an actor, male or female, any ethnicity, any age willing to do a one-line walk-on. The role was delightfully played by a Bogartesque actor in a trench coat at Flush Ink Productions.

AT RISE: Muted train noise.
    Nora, 30ish, sits in the train compartment reading a book. She is dressed dark, chic, 1940s noir.

The light though the window flashes, brightens, dims as the train glides through the countryside and the occasional tunnel.

Nora turns a page in her book, looks around nervously, crosses her legs, admires her anklet, uncrosses her legs. She turns another page.

The doors slide open, admitting a great deal of train noise and Stewart. Stewart, late 20s, is dressed in casual contemporary golf or tourist attire: slacks, a polo shirt, a windbreaker, and lord help him, even a fanny pack.

The doors slide shut and the noise level drops. Stewart is affable and relaxed. Nora is secretive and intense. It's almost as if they're in two different stories.

NORA: Did you get it?

STEWART: I got it.

NORA: All of it?

STEWART: Everything you wanted.

NORA: How can I be sure?

STEWART: Because I'm gonna . . . give it to you?

NORA: No!

STEWART: No?

NORA: Not here, not now!

STEWART: But you asked for it.

NORA: Oh, you mean . . . oh, darling, haha. I thought you were talking about—

STEWART: Here you go!

NORA: No!

STEWART: No.

NORA: It's what they'll be expecting!

STEWART: A simple thank you would be nice.

NORA: Are you certain you weren't followed?

STEWART: Let me check.

> *(He opens the compartment door, train noise rises. He scans the corridor.)*

NORA: *(narrating)* It was sultry afternoon. My tension headache pounded like Johnny Weissmuller playing "The Anvil Chorus" in my brain—

> *(Stewart closes the door. NOISE ebbs.)*

STEWART: *(jovial)* It's deserted. They're showing a soccer match on the plasma screen in the bar car. Woo! It's rowdy in there.

NORA: Let me take a gander.

STEWART: Aw, no. Let's just relax until . . . what time is it? Did we change time zones at the border? Where are we, anyway?

(Stewart takes out a map of Europe and tries to figure out which way is up.)

NORA: Wait! A disguise.

(Nora rummages in her handbag, takes out sunglasses, puts them on.)

STEWART: Nice . . .

(Nora takes off the sunglasses. Takes off her hat. From her purse she takes out a nurse's cap, puts that on. Puts on the sunglasses.)

NORA: Wait!

STEWART: Hey, I kind of liked that.

(Nora takes off the nurse's cap. Takes out a long blonde wig from the purse, puts that on, puts the nurse's cap over that, then the sunglasses.)

NORA: There!

STEWART: Ooh la la. Hold it right there.

(Stewart takes out a tourist camera and snaps a shot.)

NORA: Shh!

(She sashays across the compartment, slides the door open, looks up and down the corridor, closes the door, removes hat, wig, sunglasses, stuffs them back in her purse.)

STEWART: Aw.

NORA: *(narrating)* The coast was clear. For now. Or was it.

(urgent)

You paid their price, darling?

STEWART: Oh geez yeah. Can you believe, they won't take dollars!

NORA: Quick! Show me!

(Stewart takes a paper bag out of his jacket. He passes it to Nora. Nora peeks into the bag, gasps.)

You fool! It's the wrong package!

STEWART: What? . . . No way.

NORA: *(narrating)* Either he was a greater actor than Lionel Barrymore, or clueless as a crossword you're trying to solve on a dark cruise down the River Styx with all the fuses busted—

STEWART: *(somewhat accusatory)* Honey, who are you . . . talking to?

NORA: You got this from the Romanian Bird Seller with the Eye Patch? Or the Cartesian Snake Charmer with the Opium Pipe?

STEWART: From the . . . Tubby Cashier in the Cafe Car . . . ?

NORA: No! Stewart! You played right into their hands!

(Nora shakes out of the bag two cans of soda, two sand-
wiches, two candy bars.)

STEWART: They were out of roast beef, so I got you an egg salad.

NORA: That was . . . unwise.

STEWART: I was lucky to get that! I was on line for an hour! Train's
packed with tourists—they were nearly out of everything. And
behind me was a troop of ravenous Girl Scouts. I guess that's
the difference between First Class and Second—

NORA: This is terrible, awful! A catastrophe of international propor-
tions!

STEWART: You . . . don't like egg salad?

(Nora gets up and paces.)

NORA: The Fat Man is in cahoots with the Ancient Order of Malta.
He's probably wired ahead to the harbor police, glommed them
onto his payroll with the lettuce from the snatch. Do you know
what that means?

STEWART: . . . I can have your sandwich?

(Stewart unwraps a sandwich and eats hungrily.)

NORA: You've doomed us both!

STEWART: *(through sandwich)* Don't exaggerate, lumpkins. You got
those cheese crackers in your purse, right?

NORA: Have I, Stewart—have I?

(Nora rummages in her purse. The blonde wig falls out.
Stewart picks it up.)

STEWART: *(off wig, camera)* Sure you wouldn't like to—

(Nora stuffs the wig back into her purse, takes out a gun,
levels it at Stewart. Stewart freezes, sandwich midway to his
face.)

NORA: Sing, my sweet. Like a canary. Who sent you, really?

(Stewart pushes the sandwich aside. Now he's upset and a
little scared.)

STEWART: Damn it, Nora. You told me for once you were gonna leave
the office behind!

NORA: *(busted)* I'm moonlighting. This job paid the airfare!

STEWART: Where the hell did you get a gun! They frisked us at Home-
land Security, and I've been with you almost every step of the—

NORA: While you were bartering with the Fat Man, I had a visit from a couple of ops in thick with Abner Cairo. They said I'd need protection. I helped myself to theirs. Then dumped the bodies out the window at the border! Now spill the goods, fast.

(Beat.)

STEWART: I've said it before and I'll say it again. You are not the easiest person to vacation with!

NORA: I'm scared, Stewart! Talk, or you get your dessert ala lead.

STEWART: What the heck does that mean? Something to do with bullets?

NORA: Mm hmm—

STEWART: Nora, sometimes I think you use your job as a way of avoiding intimacy.

NORA: Spill it, mister!

STEWART: All right, honeybee! And I'm finally ready to have that conversation. Might do us good to talk about adopting!

(Beat.)

NORA: And don't think I'm gonna get all weak and damey on you cuz you turn on the charm. Or cuz maybe I was something to you and you were something to me and once we had Paris.

STEWART: Once? It was six hours ago! You made me grab you a souvenir when we passed through Gare du Nord. Grab mind you. The train was still moving. Luckily I had exact change in euros! Whew, that was close.

(He takes out a miniature Eiffel Tower, which plays a tinny version of "It's a Small World." Nora's hand wavers.)

NORA: You were supposed to grab the other Dingus.

STEWART: *(a tad annoyed)* Maybe you should be more specific next time you tell me to pick you up "the stuff that dreams are made of"!

NORA: Oh Stewart. Of all the dames in all the compartments in this train, why'd you have to pick mine?

STEWART: Because I'm a man baby. And—and we're dumb! Dumb as a box of pig irons with the smart ones taken out.

NORA: But—

STEWART: Dumb and blind. You know men, we've got more blind in our little finger than you girls have in your entire wardrobe, including the accessories. The belts, shoes and what-not—

NORA: You mean—

STEWART: Because I'm a man, and I can't ask for directions!

NORA: Then you didn't—

STEWART: I never meant to book the Orient Express! I wanted to take you to Dayton to see your sister. And maybe tour the Sunwatch Indian Village.

NORA: Oh Stewart!

STEWART: And a side trip to Acron's World of Rubber! This was just easier than asking the travel agent for a refund.

NORA: Then we—

STEWART: You think I'd take you to Antwerp on purpose?

(Nora raises the gun again.)

NORA: Then you won't mind handing me those . . . sodas.

(Stewart hands her the sodas with the gun pointed at him all the while.)

STEWART: Sure, take 'em both. I ate your sandwich.

(Nora regards the cans warily.)

NORA: Which one is it?

STEWART: Which one is what?

NORA: Which one is the rocket fuel?

STEWART: What makes you think I can answer that!

NORA: The persuasive end of my twenty-two.

STEWART: The rocket fuel is the one, uh, if you drink the other one, you won't get poisoned?

(Nora shakes the cans next to her ear. She opens one and it sprays soda everywhere. Stewart grabs her gun. He points it at her.)

Now whose shoe is on the other foot?

(Nora looks down. She takes off her shoes. They were on the wrong feet.)

NORA: Wow. That does feel better.

(Stewart shoves all of the items off of the bench to the floor. Then he grabs Nora and kisses her, releases her.)

STEWART: You know we were meant for each other since that hot night in Sheboygan! I know you said it was a mistake, but some mistakes are worth making twice! I need you and you need me—together we're like a bomb and a fuse! Eh? Put this madness aside, Nora, and we can live in noisy, explosive harmony.

NORA: Oh Stewart! If only I could!

(Beat.)

STEWART: *(shrugs)* That's all I got. What? I'm an actuary.

(Stewart sits, absentmindedly puts the gun on the seat, takes out a tourist guide to Antwerp. He studies it.)

NORA: Are you committing that map to memory?

STEWART: No dear. I'm trying to find that Pissing Mannequin.

NORA: It's in Brussels.

STEWART: Merde.

(Nora grabs the tourist guide and throws it out the window.)

NORA: We've only minutes to get our stories straight. Your life depends on it! Listen carefully—you don't know a thing!

STEWART: Boy howdy, y'can say that again! Here I am thinking we have a happy marriage and you're all wanting to shoot me and all.

NORA: I love you Stewart! I love you!

STEWART: And I love you, peaches. But I'll never understand women. Viva la difference, right?

(Nora grabs the soda, whacks Stewart on the head. He sinks to the floor.)

I liked it so much better when you worked for Amway.

NORA: The minute he walked in I smelled trouble. The kind of trouble with big brown eyes that clubs you over the head with a can of Moxie. There was something queer as a two dollar bill about Stewart. For one thing, he doesn't speak French.

STEWART: *(groggy, from the floor)* I was . . . doing Rosetta Stone on the PC . . .

NORA: Quiet, honey! I'm narrating! . . . It was a sultry train, the porters flashing like a neon sign with letters missing, so you can't tell if you're in Hell or Halo.

(The voice of a porter is heard on the loudspeaker, or a porter walks by their compartment.)

PORTER: Change here for Casablanca. Casablanca and Tangiers . . .

STEWART: Sweetie? The receipts for the bags are in my . . . wallet.

(Stewart passes out.)

END

Our Dolls

Anne Phelan

"Our Dolls" was produced by Shortened Attention Span (Carlo Rivieccio, Artistic Director) as part of the 4th Annual Shortened Attention Span Festival at The Players Loft Theatre, New York City, in June 2010. It was directed by Jacob Grigolia-Rosenbaum, and featured Emily Louise Parker as Bitsy, and Michelle O'Conner as Heather.

CHARACTERS

Bitsy:. . . . 20s, doll-dresser

Heather: . 30s, doll-dresser; flashier and looser than Bitsy

SETTING

The Our Dolls Company, somewhere west of New York and east of Los Angeles. This is the workroom where the dolls are dressed and boxed.

TIME

A weekday morning. Now.

NOTE

The size of the dolls is dependent upon the size of the space (so that they'll "read"), and the ease of dressing the dolls for the actors. It may be easier to dress bigger dolls with bigger costume pieces.

If the actual doll costumes are a great production burden, make the costumes out of black crepe paper. Cut the Hasidic doll's hair, and improvise her costume out of crepe paper. Wrap the entire Muslim doll in black crepe paper, so that only her eyes are showing. The Pope doll remains the same.

(Workroom for the Our Dolls Company. A sign hangs on the wall: The Doll You Want for Your Daughter. Bitsy and Heather, co-workers, each have a doll, which they dress in the course of the scene)

BITSY: *(As she cuts off the doll's hair with a scissors)* D'you ever think of getting another job?

HEATHER: *(As she puts trousers on the doll)* In this economy? I'd be scared. What if I got hired by some place that said: "Last hired first fired"?

BITSY: But doesn't it seem kind of silly to be playing with dolls at our age?

HEATHER: We're not playing. We dress and pack. Dress and pack.

BITSY: I know but—There's always that horrible moment when I'm out at a bar with Frank, and we're talking to other people, and they ask me what I do. When I tell them, they look at me like I'm retarded.

HEATHER: Put it a different way.

BITSY: Like what?

HEATHER: I say "I'm in early childhood development." That way, they think I'm a psychologist or a teacher or something.

BITSY: That's great! I'm stealing it.

HEATHER: Be my guest.

BITSY: But I have to tell Frank first. So he doesn't blow my cover by laughing.

HEATHER: *(Putting socks on the doll)* Have you set a date yet?

BITSY: *(Putting tights on the doll)* He's so freaked out about maybe getting laid off- I don't know when we will.

HEATHER: Doesn't he want to get married?

BITSY: He wants the perfect Hawaiian honeymoon is all.

HEATHER: *(Putting shoes on the doll)* That's kind of sweet.

BITSY: Money isn't supposed to matter, is it?

HEATHER: *(Laughing)* What planet are you on? We live in the U.S. of A. Money always matters.

BITSY: But we love each other.

HEATHER: I'm not saying you don't. It's just that you're talking like you're . . . French. Or a Socialist.

BITSY: But love's more important.

HEATHER: My parents fight about money all the time. My mother wouldn't marry my father until he promised she could have her own checking account.

BITSY: *(Putting the mid-calf length skirt on the doll)* That seems silly.

HEATHER: For that generation? Not really.

BITSY: How old's your mother?

HEATHER: 55. But my mom's mom is so old-fashioned. She waits on Grandpa like he's king or something. Mom didn't want Dad to think he was marrying a maid.

BITSY: We won't be like that.

HEATHER: Of course you won't.

BITSY: Frank keeps saying he's got to marry me soon, or the apartment will never be free of Bride's Magazine.

HEATHER: Bride's Magazine.

BITSY: They're pretty cool, actually. I learn something in every one.

HEATHER: Like what?

BITSY: Like at Jewish weddings the bride stands on the left, but at Christian weddings she stands on the right.

HEATHER: But you and Frank aren't Jewish.

BITSY: It's still interesting. The dress ideas are mainly why I keep buying them- I can't make up my mind.

HEATHER: You're doing the whole nine yards?

BITSY: Even church.

HEATHER: You never go to church!

BITSY: I know. All the parents want church.

HEATHER: Because your parents won't pay for the reception otherwise?

BITSY: Exactly.

HEATHER: Money—told ya!

BITSY: Do you ever think about who buys these dolls?

HEATHER: Nobody I know. Why should I?

BITSY: I wonder is all.

HEATHER: You're a romantic.

BITSY: Am I?

HEATHER: Good thing you're marrying Frank.

BITSY: Why?

HEATHER: He sounds more down-to-earth. You got your head in the clouds.

BITSY: (Putting the long-sleeved blouse on the doll) And what about you?

HEATHER: My head's on my shoulders. Where it's supposed to be. You're a dreamer. Dreaming about your wedding, dreaming about little girls you don't know. Never will know.

BITSY: I call it thinking. Not dreaming.

HEATHER: What are you thinking?

BITSY: Why are there never wars here? Why am I here and not starving in Africa?

HEATHER: (With a laugh) You're not even black!

BITSY: I could have been.

HEATHER: You are who you are.

BITSY: But why? Some roll of the cosmic dice?

HEATHER: With all that going on in your head, I don't know how you walk and talk at the same time.

BITSY: How can you say that- like you know?

HEATHER: I do know. You waste your time on philosophy. You don't see what's right in front of you. It's like "woulda, shoulda, coulda"—totally worthless.

BITSY: But—

HEATHER: It's so simple! First, you figure out what you have. Then, you figure out what you want, and you get it.

BITSY: That's it?

HEATHER: Nobody is ever going to give you anything, Bitsy. You have to take it. That's the way the world works.

BITSY: I feel that I can't be that sure about things.

HEATHER: You didn't get much positive reinforcement as a kid, did you?

BITSY: Mom thinks positive reinforcement is only for bratty kids. Like the ones who go to Montessori schools.

HEATHER: (Draping and pinning the hijab on the doll—it must cover all of the doll's hair) But she'll bribe you to get married in church?

BITSY: Sure.

HEATHER: My mother taught me to get what I want. Do whatever it takes.

BITSY: Like what?

HEATHER: My fur coat? Know how I got that?

BITSY: No.

HEATHER: I hooked up with a furrier.

BITSY: Like you dated him?

HEATHER: I had sex with him. It was barter—sex for fur. "Pelts for pelt," he said.

BITSY: Heather!

HEATHER: What's the big deal? I didn't lie and tell him I loved him. He was a little guy- kind of like a gnome. Old enough to be my grandfather. We did it on the floor of the vault. I stared at the Blackglama minks the whole time.

BITSY: *(Putting the shoes on the doll)* It makes my skin crawl just to think about it.

HEATHER: You need to get modern, girlfriend. It's the 21st century.

BITSY: There's being assertive, and then there's...that. It's not the same thing.

HEATHER: In olden times, a woman would only marry a man if he could support her financially. Isn't that pretty much sex for money?

BITSY: Not really.

HEATHER: I think it's just the same.

BITSY: What do you want for lunch?

HEATHER: Actually, I've got...plans.

BITSY: For lunch?

HEATHER: Ronnie asked me out.

BITSY: On a date?

HEATHER: Lunch can't be a date. Only dinner. Or a drink.

BITSY: Somebody from work asks you out for lunch, it's a date.

HEATHER: No.

BITSY: Particularly if he's your boss.

HEATHER: Maybe he wants to talk about work.

BITSY: Like what?

HEATHER: *(Putting the long gloves on the doll)* Packaging?

BITSY: That is so lame. He's scoping you out.

HEATHER: Whatever.

BITSY: I think he's kind of creepy.

HEATHER: How?

BITSY: *(Putting the wig on the doll)* I dunno, I...he just gives off that vibe. Like I can imagine him doing weird sex stuff using the dolls for an audience.

HEATHER: *(With a laugh)* That is so gross!

BITSY: Can't you get out of it?

HEATHER: It's only lunch. I'll pretend I'm Wendy from accounting.

BITSY: Wendy's okay.

HEATHER: She thinks she's a dude. It's weird.

BITSY: Were you the girl in high school who called all the plain girls "lezzies"?

HEATHER: Were you one who got called a lezzy?

BITSY: And it hurt, too. How you dress could have nothing to do with it. Hillary wears pants because she's got legs like a piano. You're born with that. Any woman with power is called a bitch or a lesbian. Or both. Whatever she wears.

(Beat)

Was it easier before all that over-the-top feminism in the '70s?

HEATHER: I wasn't even born yet.

(Puts her doll into a box with the label "My Muslim Doll." She picks up a Pope doll, which is dressed except for the hat. She tries to get the hat to fit, but it keeps falling off. Bitsy pulls out a box with the label "My Hassidic Doll." Heather calls off)

Damn it, Ronnie! I told you the hats were too small. I can't ship out a Pope without his Pope hat!

BITSY: *(As she jams a wig pin into the doll's head)* He looks just like any other guy in a dress.

The End

Ou Topos

Maura Campbell

Ou Topos received its first production December 10–12 by Winterset Productions, Inc., Producer: Richard Leff, in Burlington VT at the Pine Street Studio. The cast was as follows: Nova—Wendi Stein; Piedad—Marianne Di-Mascio. Director: Maura Campbell.

CHARACTERS

Nova... an intake administrator, forties

Piedad.. a mother, thirties

SETTING

Nova's office

TIME

Not the present, may be in the future, perhaps in the unrecorded past

_____

NOVA: How is it

PIEDAD: Good fine thank you

NOVA: And warm enough

PIEDAD: I wore I brought a sweater

NOVA: The climate control was someone adjusted it a few weeks early most unusual so we thought we'd just ride it out only about three degrees off but funny how sensitive we become to change change of any kind

PIEDAD: It's not funny I wouldn't call it funny

NOVA: I didn't mean funny as if to laugh

PIEDAD: Oh

NOVA: I meant odd or really I didn't mean anything at all just want you to be comfortable

PIEDAD: I am comfortable

NOVA: Then I'm happy which is to say that I am content you are how old

PIEDAD: I'm thirty one

NOVA: Yes when you get older another ten years or so you'll find out that comfort is of the utmost importance hence I spend an inordinate amount of time trying to see to it that I and anyone in

my company is comfortable it is warm in here maybe if I draw
the curtain the sun is strong oh thank you

PIEDAD: Very bright it's very bright today the sky it's just hanging
there isn't it hovering over us over everything warm and bright
when I was young I used to stare at the sun my mother warned
me that I would go blind but I never did I just love the way it
feels on my skin I used to think when the sun filled me eyes that
I was seeing into another world why did you ask my age

NOVA: I was going to illustrate

PIEDAD: You have my file you know my age you could have said you
are thirty-one and then expanded on your what do you say il-
lustration

NOVA: My apology

PIEDAD: I am thirty one and you know probably anything else that
might be relevant

NOVA: I am sensing some anxiety

PIEDAD: Yes that's true

NOVA: And I hope I haven't or anyone else hasn't made you uncomfortable

PIEDAD: It's just my mood some days I'm anxious

NOVA: Really

PIEDAD: Really just a little anxious and this meeting is out of the ordinary routine you see I also am interested in comfort and I find
my routine my daily routine most comforting

NOVA: You have two children

PIEDAD: What about my children

NOVA: Nothing just saying you have two children and your husband
is and engineer electrical engineer

PIEDAD: I taught elementary school before I had children but you
probably know that

NOVA: I'll bet you loved teaching

PIEDAD: I did love teaching I plan to home school my boys until they
turn twelve

NOVA: I don't blame you do you know once upon a time that is exactly how all boys were raised and I mean long ago before even
before girls were sent to school they boys were kept at home
with a tutor until they were twelve and then send to a public
school

PIEDAD: So I'm right in the swim

NOVA: Of another time all together yes your boys are now four and two

PIEDAD: One

NOVA: Four and one Piedad

PIEDAD: Almost two Sharon is almost two do you have children

NOVA: I yes I have a daughter

PIEDAD: I am a little jealous is she does she look like you because I wanted a daughter who looked like me not because I'm special to look at

NOVA: You are very pretty

PIEDAD: But because my mother looked like my grandmother and it was always a source of amusement and they were close still are close very close and that is what I well I thought it would be amusing

NOVA: Boys are rougher than girls

PIEDAD: Rougher in what way rougher

NOVA: Oh just boys more destructive they like to build and take apart I imagine with a father who is an engineer that they must have some of his attributes

PIEDAD: Sharon yes he is always into something Gussie is more like me he is quiet I am usually very quiet but I guess I'm talking a great deal here

NOVA: It's why I have this job because and I hope this is true in your case I make people feel comfortable

PIEDAD: You do I am very comfortable

NOVA: I would say that Gussie looks like you

PIEDAD: Oh that is that is Gussie when

NOVA: Yes when he came here last month

PIEDAD: I didn't know you took his picture

NOVA: We take all the children's pictures haven't you looked at our site

PIEDAD: No

NOVA: It was there on the paper one of the papers you left with

PIEDAD: I'm so busy

NOVA: Oh you must have a look it goes back I don't know probably fifty years of course there are archives that go back further but we keep five decades live you are probably on there

PIEDAD: I didn't grow up

NOVA: Oh right but there is a link it's a terrific way to you can actually search for relatives say cousins aunt uncle great great great grandmothers practically everyone you are related to and create a family picture it's absolutely amazing I did it and you know there are relatives several generations back that I resemble strongly which is fascinating because I don't look much like my parents or siblings

PIEDAD: You're a throwback

NOVA: Yes that's exactly right and what I have discovered it's an opinion really is that when we look like someone we actually are like someone

PIEDAD: That makes sense

NOVA: I don't know if it makes sense but I can tell you that I have found it to be true

PIEDAD: Well

NOVA: Well what

PIEDAD: You tell me

NOVA: Tell you what

PIEDAD: What you what are you talking about anyway

NOVA: Nothing I don't think just wanted to show you the site where the pictures are Gussie is an adorable child simply adorable we have evaluated him

PIEDAD: When

NOVA: When he was here that's what

PIEDAD: I thought that was routine

NOVA: Yes a routine part of our evaluation oh no I'm not referring to the regular evaluation that isn't done for another year anyway but my goodness you know we you signed an acknowledgment that we would film the children

PIEDAD: I didn't realize that meant any kind of evaluation I think Gussie had a fever that day a very slight fever in fact

NOVA: Really we didn't detect anything unusual there's nothing here

PIEDAD: I said it was slight his normal is a bit low ninety six five so at ninety seven he's a bit elevated

NOVA: You seem concerned

PIEDAD: I'm not concerned just you seem concerned

NOVA: I seem concerned

PIEDAD: There seems to be some concern
NOVA: We have I have absolutely no concern whatsoever about Gussie
he's completely normal look watch this
PIEDAD: He's playing with that's the Brown girl isn't it
NOVA: Yes Joey
PIEDAD: Joey and who's that a
NOVA: That's Michael he's from a different sector like you
PIEDAD: What's he doing
NOVA: Michael is see he's hogging
PIEDAD: Hogging
NOVA: We call it hogging he doesn't share
PIEDAD: That's hogging
NOVA: Like a hog it's an archaic form of a pig
PIEDAD: Now he's sharing
NOVA: That's Cormier his cousin
PIEDAD: Oh
NOVA: They look alike
PIEDAD: But they're not alike there goes your theory
NOVA: It's not one hundred percent
PIEDAD: I wish you would tell me
NOVA: Tell you what
PIEDAD: I don't like your tone Ms
NOVA: Nova and I am not using a tone I'm trying to tell you
PIEDAD: There is nothing wrong with my child
NOVA: There is nothing wrong with your child
PIEDAD: Then what
NOVA: This is routine
PIEDAD: This is not routine he's a normal boy what are you doing
what is
NOVA: Just watch
PIEDAD: I don't remember that
NOVA: Of course you don't remember it you were only three
PIEDAD: How oh dear
NOVA: Drink this
PIEDAD: Oh how could I
NOVA: Well it seems to have been a fluke

PIEDAD: Fluke

NOVA: Another term we use it means well it actually means good luck
a stroke of good luck or an accident

PIEDAD: It must be that I would never do that

NOVA: But you did

PIEDAD: Why is this the first time I've someone has shown me

NOVA: Another stroke of accident it was lost or misplaced we don't
know but it was noticed recently and sent over it took awhile
because the corresponding notes the audio that is still unknown
but it is you isn't it

PIEDAD: It's me what do you want

NOVA: I wanted to bring it to your attention

PIEDAD: So now you've brought it to my attention

NOVA: Normally in the normal course you would have been put in
observation I don't know exactly what the breakdown was in
your sector but we have an idea that your uncle was at that time

PIEDAD: My uncle

NOVA: Your uncle Gustav

PIEDAD: He's dead

NOVA: I know he's dead he was working there in records and we are
supposing that he pulled it out and put it somewhere hoping it
wouldn't be found

PIEDAD: I see

NOVA: And it is really something to think of that you see Piedad we
have done some digging into your past we have viewed the
records and your husband's and your children's and the surprising thing that is quite unaccountable is that this seems to be an
isolated incident there is no other as far as we know there is no
other reason for concern except this one record that has most
recently surfaced

PIEDAD: A fluke is a parasite

NOVA: Pardon

PIEDAD: A parasitic fish a flat fish why would you call that an accident

NOVA: I have no idea it's just a word in the field we use to describe
certain phenomenon

PIEDAD: Are we done here

NOVA: Done

PIEDAD: Are we done here

NOVA: I don't think we're done

PIEDAD: How are we not done

NOVA: There is more we need to talk about

PIEDAD: So talk

NOVA: This is sensitive this is a sensitive subject I asked if we could talk alone

PIEDAD: You asked who

NOVA: Your husband

PIEDAD: You what

NOVA: We talked first because I wanted to see you alone

PIEDAD: What is this

NOVA: It's nothing really it's nothing that has a difficult outcome it's all a matter of perspective and yes all right some acceptance this is serious Piedad I don't want to mislead you but after reviewing your case

PIEDAD: My case

NOVA: Thoroughly and I do mean thoroughly we are not concerned I want you to know that up front there is not a big concern of any kind just that one incident the fluke that one time you displayed behavior that would had it come up now that is to say if you were a child now and we viewed this on a file we would have great cause for concern the reality is that you are making us rethink many of the cases we have had we are somewhat concerned that we have jumped to conclusions prematurely although really I don't know what else we can do when flagrant antisocial behavior is apparent

PIEDAD: I would like to see my husband my Roman

NOVA: He's at work I would imagine

PIEDAD: You said you talked to him

NOVA: Yes but not today we talked on Tuesday I think it was yes

PIEDAD: Tuesday

NOVA: That was yes because the report came in on Friday and we took the weekend to go over it and then called him on Monday and he came in the following day

PIEDAD: NOVA: NOVA: Yes

PIEDAD: NOVA: NOVA: What dear

PIEDAD: What is

NOVA: What is what are you worried about I just told you I thought I just told you we are not concerned about you we want to make a recommendation that is all and before I say anything further you should know that your husband is in one hundred percent agreement

PIEDAD: He agrees

NOVA: That you really shouldn't consider any more children

PIEDAD: We only wanted two

NOVA: Yes but you have been approved for three

PIEDAD: I'm planning to go back to work after Sharon after he is in school

NOVA: Full time

PIEDAD: Full time part time I we'll see what we can manage it isn't really a question of money

NOVA: Quality of life yes I know I have a daughter

PIEDAD: You said

NOVA: So two is enough we were thinking that to be on the safe side we would there is a procedure your husband offered and that would be all right unless something happened to him and you remarried for example

PIEDAD: So you're thinking that I

NOVA: These things are genetic

PIEDAD: But you said it was a fluke

NOVA: It was a fluke but you know Piedad we don't understand everything if we understood everything there would be no flukes and sometimes even a fluke can have a fluke and then we would really have to reexamine reassess the all of it

PIEDAD: I'd really like to see my husband

NOVA: Let's call him we were planning to call him when we finished

PIEDAD: Are we finished

NOVA: We are finished

PIEDAD: Thank you for the tea

NOVA: Oh I know this is sudden if you'll just please sit down we are finished but Piedad we're going to want you to stay a day

PIEDAD: What are you

NOVA: The procedure I mentioned we're wanting to handle that immediately no later than tomorrow morning because we think it's best if we get it done and then you can go home and it will have the least disruption on your family we did go over this with your husband and he agreed the recovery is minimal not even three days minimally invasive a local anesthetic

PIEDAD: I'm afraid I can't my children

NOVA: Your husband has made arrangements for them and your sister-in-law is coming for a few days besides Deeanne

PIEDAD: I don't want Deeanne to take care of my children

NOVA: Why not

PIEDAD: I don't like her and I want to talk to my husband

NOVA: Does your husband know how you feel about Deeanne

PIEDAD: He yes I'm calling him right now

NOVA: Are you concerned for their safety is there something you want to tell me

PIEDAD: No not I just she's not mature

NOVA: Thirty four

PIEDAD: But not I don't can you please I don't want a procedure tomorrow I want to go home first and then in a few days I'll come back

NOVA: I'm afraid that isn't possible Piedad I'm sorry it's a very simple minimally invasive

PIEDAD: Thank you

NOVA: You should count your blessings you have so many your children your future please sit down

PIEDAD: I just need to make a call I just want to see my Gussie and Sharon

NOVA: Why don't you sit

PIEDAD: I I feel

NOVA: What do you feel

PIEDAD: I'm tired Sharon will be so worried he's only one

NOVA: Almost two

PIEDAD: Almost oh god he looks like me oh god he looks like me oh god he looks like me there's no place no no place

NOVA: No

The end

Out With The Old . . .

Debbie Lamedman

Out With the Old . . . was originally presented as part of Theatre Encino's 2nd Annual 10-Minute Play Festival, "Transplantation Society: Stories of Change," on April 17th & 18th, 2010 in Encino, CA. The play was directed by Eric Ashmore with the following cast: Diane—Kristina Nikols; Jerry—Keven Kaddi

CHARACTERS

Diane:.. Late 20's, early 30's. Restless. Looking for meaning in
     her life.

Jerry:... Late 20's, early 30's. Serious. A little high-strung.

TIME & PLACE:

Present
The living room of a modest apartment in any urban city. There is
an old brown couch in the center of the room.

AUTHOR'S NOTE:

The color of the couch can be changed depending upon whatever
color you have available for the production.

---

*At rise, the living room of Jerry & Diane's apartment. It is modestly
furnished, but cozy. There is an old brown couch in the center of the
room. Diane is on the phone finishing a conversation.*

DIANE: *(Into the phone)* Yeah... it's chocolate brown. It's very neutral
and goes with anything really. Sort of shabby chic-ish. Sort of.
It's a great starter couch. It's in pretty good condition. No rips
or tears. I just want something new, ya know? Something different. And I don't feel like recovering the thing, know what I
mean? *(She laughs self-consciously)* Okay... so where do you live?
Oh, you're really close. Sure you can come now. I'll be here.
Great. That's really great. See you soon.
    *(She hangs up. Jerry enters carrying and focused on his
    laptop)*

JERRY: Who was that?

DIANE: Uh... who was... what?

JERRY: On the phone. Who were you talking to?

DIANE: *(Sits. Picks up a magazine and thumbs through it nonchalantly)*
Oh...no one...

JERRY: You didn't say "see you soon" to no one.

DIANE: I said "see you soon?"

JERRY: On the phone. To whoever you were talking to. You said "that's
really great. See you soon."

DIANE: Oh...

JERRY: So, who was it?

DIANE: Just a guy from the ad.

JERRY: What guy?

DIANE: From the ad.

JERRY: What ad?

DIANE: The ad that I placed.

JERRY: You placed an ad? For what?

DIANE: *(Matter-of-fact)* A new boyfriend.

JERRY: What?!

DIANE: I'm just kidding.

JERRY: Very funny.

DIANE: Oh honey. I'm just teasing you. Can't you take a joke?

JERRY: Whatever...

DIANE: You need to lighten up. That's your problem, Jer. You're too
serious.

JERRY: No I'm not. *(Beat)* Am I?

DIANE: Yeah. Sometimes...

JERRY: I've got a lot on my mind. Work and...well...stuff.

DIANE: I know you do. But you really need to enjoy things more. Live
a little. Laugh when I tease you.
(Beat)

JERRY: Who was on the phone?

DIANE: I told you...a guy from the ad.

JERRY: Some guy answered your ad?

DIANE: Yup.

JERRY: For what, pray tell? Hey, did you notice that as I asked that question, my tone was light and airy and not serious at all, whatsoever?

DIANE: I did notice that. And I appreciate that you're making the effort to be less serious.

JERRY: Thank you, my love.

DIANE: You're welcome.

JERRY: Now . . . the ad . . .

DIANE: Yes . . .

JERRY: You placed . . .

DIANE: Yes.

JERRY: For?

DIANE: Some furniture.

JERRY: Really?

DIANE: Uh-huh.

JERRY: Furniture? That we have?

DIANE: Yes.

JERRY: I never would have thought of it.

DIANE: Thought of what?

JERRY: That you were looking to get rid of our furniture.

DIANE: Not all our furniture.

JERRY: Oh?

DIANE: Of course not.

JERRY: Then what?

DIANE: Just the bed.

JERRY: Our bed? Are you kidding me?

DIANE: Yes.

JERRY: Why would you want to sell our bed?

DIANE: I said yes. I was kidding. You don't listen. You said, "Are you kidding me?" and I said "Yes" and then you keep going with the conversation as if I never said anything.

JERRY: You said you were kidding? When?

DIANE: Just now. Jesus!

JERRY: You're not selling the bed?

DIANE: No.

JERRY: But you placed an ad to sell some furniture?

DIANE: Yes.

JERRY: Do you think it would be possible to answer me with more than just a yes or a no? I feel like I'm interrogating you.

DIANE: You're right. That's exactly what it feels like.

JERRY: I just think that if you're placing ads to sell our furniture, I have a right to know. I mean...I guess I would like to know why. Why would you place an ad without telling me?

DIANE: Here we go...

JERRY: What is that supposed to mean? "Here we go?"

DIANE: It's just what I was talking about before. Everything I say...everything I do...it becomes this major crisis for you. It becomes this huge deal. Every detail must be analyzed and criticized. I can't make a joke without you questioning my hidden motives. I can't decide to sell something because I feel like selling it. I can't do anything without you watching and wondering what it all means. You're too serious! Everything, everything, including what you decide to eat for breakfast becomes this huge ordeal. And frankly...well...it's beginning to take a toll.

    (Beat)

JERRY: Oh. I see...

    (Beat. Diane doesn't respond.)

JERRY: So that's why you're selling our furniture? Because I'm too serious?

DIANE: I don't know. I need a change.

JERRY: *(Quietly)* Can you tell me what you're selling?

DIANE: *(She points to the couch.)* This.

JERRY: This?! This couch?!

DIANE: Yes.

JERRY: But...why? How can you sell this couch?

DIANE: It's just an old couch. I'm tired of it. I'm tired of a lot of things, but I'm starting with this.

JERRY: I was with you when you picked it out. You loved it then. And this is the couch where we...our first time...together...on this couch. Don't you remember?

DIANE: *(Not remembering)* Sure. I remember.

JERRY: I love this couch. You love this couch.

DIANE: I loved it. But that was a long time ago. And now I think it's time for something new. Change can be a good thing, you know.

JERRY: I carved our initials into that couch. Did you know that?

DIANE: You did what?

JERRY: I carved our initials into the back leg of the couch. I thought it was a romantic gesture.

DIANE: *(Goes to inspect the back leg of the couch)* Yeah? Well, whatever you do, don't tell that to the guy who wants to buy it. I don't want to blow the deal.

JERRY: You know, you may think that I'm too serious, but my God... Diane! You can be so cold.

DIANE: I didn't use to be.

JERRY: So you're blaming me?

DIANE: No! Maybe. Don't you want a change?
(Beat)
(Jerry sits on the couch. He pats the space next to him)

JERRY: Come sit with me.

DIANE: No. I really don't want to.

JERRY: Then your mind is made up? You're going to get rid of it?

DIANE: Yes. He'll be here soon. I don't want it anymore.

JERRY: Even after I told you about the initials?

DIANE: Yes. Sorry. It doesn't work for me anymore. It's too... I don't know... it's too dark and serious-looking.

JERRY: Maybe I could go with you?

DIANE: Go with me where?

JERRY: To pick out a new one?

DIANE: I don't know. That might not be such a good idea. I have to think about it. I'm not really sure what I'm looking for.

JERRY: So we're just going to have a big empty-space in the middle of the room?

DIANE: For awhile, yeah. I don't mind actually. I think having all that space will be freeing.
(There is a loud knock at the door)

JERRY: Is that him?

DIANE: Probably. I'm not really expecting anyone else.

JERRY: Maybe he won't like it. Maybe he'll change his mind when he sees it.

DIANE: Maybe. But I don't think so. He liked what he saw in the picture.

JERRY: You placed an ad with a picture?

DIANE: I sure did. It guarantees greater results when you have a
   photo.
   (The knock comes again)
JERRY: So I guess that's it then?
DIANE: Don't look so sad. It's not the end of the world. It's just a
   couch, after all.
   (She walks over to answer the door.)
JERRY: *(Sitting alone on the couch)* Yeah . . . sure . . . it's just a couch.

   Lights begin to fade.

   End of Play

Preconception

Larry Hamm

Originally performed May 24, 2010, at 3rd Biennial Directing Shorts Festival at the Bandshell at Florida Southern College. Directed by Jessica Barlow. Sperm played by Chris Rigolini; Egg played by Dakota Thurow.

CHARACTERS

Egg: . . . a woman aged 25 to 45
Sperm: . a man of like age

SETTING

The place is the locus of all human beginnings, depicted by an elevation on center stage.

TIME

Pre-conception

Egg stands elevated slightly on center stage, biding her time. Sperm, noticeably shorter with the elevation, swims toward her wiggling his tail. As Sperm nears Egg, she holds up her hand and he bounces off.
[Periodically and persistently, throughout the play, Sperm should make an attempt to reach Egg, only to be repelled until the final moments of the scene.]

SPERM: Can I buy you a drink?

EGG: Do you have any idea how many times I've heard that line? Over two million in the last 45 seconds alone.

SPERM: I just want to get to know you better.

EGG: Yeah, right.

SPERM: But you have such beautiful eyes.

EGG: Listen. Stop. We both know why we're here, and it isn't to make small talk. I've got a major decision to make, and not a heck of a lot of time to make it in. At best, I've got 24 hours, and given my producer's sex life, my guess is that I'm going to have to choose from whatever's coming my way at the moment.

SPERM: You've got a producer, too?

EGG: Sure. Did you think you were swimming up a sewer drain?

SPERM: *(looking around somewhat stupidly)* I guess I didn't care.

EGG: Naturally, you didn't. Your kind has only one thing on its mind, and we know what that is.

SPERM: We do?

EGG: Fertilization. Being the best of the bunch. Breaking through my soft but resistant outer layer before any of the others.

SPERM: *(he attempts, she resists)* That sounds fun.

EGG: *(pantomimes watching someone approach and go past)* Whoa!

SPERM: What?

EGG: Did you see the tail on that one?

SPERM: No.

EGG: Why are all the really hot ones too stupid to find their way here?

SPERM: That's not the way this works, you know.

EGG: What do you mean?

SPERM: I mean that the one that figures out the way to get to your heart has to be strong and has to defy incredible odds just to find you. Then, while the others strain futilely to win your affections, the best and most suitable (he points with both fingers toward himself) works his way in.

EGG: So you think you're the one for me, huh?

SPERM: I'd just like to give you a hug.

EGG: Don't even start. There are a ton of things to discuss first.

SPERM: Like what?

EGG: Like whether I want to go through with this at all.

SPERM: Really?

EGG: Yes, really.

SPERM: You have doubts.

EGG: I have doubts.

SPERM: I have no doubts.

EGG: Of course you don't. Having doubts would mean you've thought about this, and you clearly haven't. You're so caught up in the race to the finish line that you haven't taken the time to determine if the prize there is worth winning. Do you have any idea what will happen if I let you in?

SPERM: Nope.

EGG: Well, for a moment we're fused together...

SPERM: *(excitedly)* Oh yeah.

EGG: ... into a zygote.

SPERM: A what?

EGG: A zygote, a cell that contains all the chromosomal information from both of us. At that moment, the two of us are responsible for selecting one of the over 17 trillion possible genetic combinations provided by our producers.

SPERM: That's *our* choice?

EGG: Well, I don't know that I'd call it a choice, but ultimately we're the source. The buck starts here. Or the doe... but you get my point.

SPERM: I do?

EGG: C'mon. Stop wriggling for a moment and think about your role in all of this. Do you want to bring the world the next mass murderer? The next corporate criminal? The next person in the grocery line who waits until after the cashier gives the total to search for her checkbook?

SPERM: My God no!

EGG: I thought not. And who's to say that once you and I were to begin that series of mitotic cell divisions that ultimately creates a human being, that our human being, the result of our union, would be anything more than another body chewing up the planet's resources while excreting litter on a highway or gum into a urinal?

SPERM: You make it sound horrible. And hopeless. After all, what can I do about any of this?

EGG: What can you do? You're begging to be half the equation here, buddy. You'd better start taking your responsibilities seriously.

SPERM: I will. I do. Oh, can't we talk about this after?

EGG: Tell me, what's the scoop on your producer?

SPERM: My producer? Why bring him into this?

EGG: Well, the shape you're in is greatly influenced by his diet and the amount of exercise he gets.

SPERM: *(pulling in his stomach and examining himself)* I think he's okay.

EGG: Is he a smoker? An alcoholic? A drug addict? Is he a Meth Fiend?

SPERM: No! *(realizing he's responded reflexively)* I don't think so.

EGG: You don't think so. C'mon, just what do you know about this guy?

SPERM: Not much, really. I've only been with him a short time. And there are so many of us that he doesn't provide us with any individual attention. He'd ignore us entirely if he didn't seem so preoccupied with getting rid of us.

EGG: So he's heartless and uncaring?

SPERM: I can't say that. For my part, I never tried to bond with him either. I've spent most of my time sizing up my competition and trying to get into good position whenever the opportunity arose.

EGG: And is he the kind of guy who's had lots of opportunities to rise?

SPERM: He seems to. There's a constant call for reinforcements.

EGG: So, he's a philanderer. What a perfect model for half of a genetic code.

SPERM: Wait! I don't think it's like that. It's more like . . .

EGG: . . . like? Like what?

SPERM: I . . . uh . . . only have heard things.

EGG: Such as . . . ?

SPERM: Well, among the guys, there's a rumor that most of us get sacrificed to practice runs.

EGG: Practice runs? Why would he need practice?

SPERM: I don't know, and I can only imagine the disappointment on my friend's faces . . .

EGG: Ewww!

SPERM: What?

EGG: So he's a loser.

SPERM: Well, that doesn't seem fair.

EGG: Fair? Don't you see the burden that I have to bear? Do you think that I want my producer impregnated by some geek who might be better suited to a virtual relationship online?

SPERM: No, what I'm trying to say is that you seem to take everything the wrong way. You want to assume he's either a bad boy or someone so benign that he's not worthy of your acceptance.

EGG: I guess you could be right.

SPERM: According to what I hear you saying, he has only two options, and both of them result in your negative opinion. Whether he's sending us on a meaningful mission or out into space, you seem to feel he's misusing his assets. You want him to have experience, just not too much.

EGG: I suppose I am being a bit selfish.

SPERM: And what do we know about your producer?

EGG: Hmmm... Well, she's single again, after one disastrous marriage and a series of questionable boyfriends. She likes spicy foods (she reacts to the foods) and prefers the pill as a form of birth control in combination with a condom.

SPERM: I hate those.

EGG: And, apparently judging from her recent decision to go off the pill and your current presence, she's decided that she's reached a time in her life when she should conceive a child.

SPERM: She wants to get knocked up?

EGG: She wants to experience the miracle of birth and the wonders of raising a child.

SPERM: Sounds like she wants to trap my guy with the miracle of DNA testing and the wonders of a paternity suit.

EGG: That's mean!

SPERM: Well?

EGG: I don't know. Things have been so crazy lately. You spend almost forty years with someone and you think you know her. Then, suddenly she's taking a singles cruise and having her breasts enlarged.

SPERM: Those aren't real?

EGG: *(gradually becoming emotional)* And now I'm staring at this. *(motions toward Sperm)* How can I make a rational decision?

SPERM: I realize this is an emotional time for you. If nature were just, we'd have weeks to talk about this.

EGG: *(getting ready to let go)* I'm under a lot of pressure.

SPERM: Of course, you are. But, you're not alone.

EGG: *(letting go and crying)* I just don't know anything about this guy!

SPERM: Hey, hey now, I'm here, aren't I? That's got to say something about his personality and perseverance. He must be someone she's attracted to.

EGG: *(still crying)* Maybe she just got drunk.

SPERM: Or, maybe she likes him.

EGG: *(composing herself)* You're right. You're right. I'm being paranoid. It's just that I'm a bit touchy about such things. She doesn't have the best track record when it comes to men. And the first thing I do when I see a whole bunch of you fellas swimming my way is to question what was on her mind for the past hour.

SPERM: Don't you think it's possible that she's found someone she loves? That the past hour was spent with soft music, a bottle of wine, and a jar of lubricating cream?

EGG: Love? Do you actually think it's that simple? My girl is thirty-eight for chrissakes. She's been through the fumbling years, the experimental years, and the seduction years. She's now in the my-God-I'm-going-to-die-alone years.

SPERM: It can't be all that bad.

EGG: What would you know? Sure, you've the mind, the anatomy, and the shelf life of an amoeba, but your producer doesn't. He doesn't have to worry about becoming meaningless and invisible long before he dies. He'll never feel the desperation that can come with being female. A man such as yours can always find some young uterus to attend to, even until his eighties.

SPERM: Hah! As long as he has a flush bank account and a sports car.

EGG: And that means?

SPERM: It means that for every man that mates there's a woman on the other side. Women help to set the standards men live down to. Ninety percent of what men do is done to get female attention. Do you think that men want to go about posturing and preening, acting tough, and buying oversized pick-up trucks just so they can impress a woman enough to get laid?

EGG: Well, maybe.

SPERM: And do you think that men like the fact that once they've wooed the woman, they have to take on the burden of acting like adults, when anyone can tell you that no man was meant to become one.

EGG: I hadn't thought about . . .

SPERM: Do I have to mention shorter life spans? Must I tell you about coalmines, steel mills, and machine shops? Military service? And how about those who work eighty-hour weeks to climb the corporate ladder, sucking in the fumes from their boss's backside, while they do all they can to make sure the missus is dressin' fine and livin' well.

EGG: Women work too!

SPERM: *(immediately)* But do they kill spiders?

EGG: Ooo . . .

SPERM: I know women work, and some of them are heroic, but that's not my point. My point is that women can be sexy just being themselves, but men have to be somebody else. If a woman wants to attract men, she buys a pair of low-cut jeans or a short skirt. If a man wants to attract women, he has to work it into conversation that being an Accountant at XYZ Company earns him $80,000 a year. *(pause)* Or, he just lies and says he plays for the Dallas Cowboys.

EGG: You're very passionate about this.

SPERM: I'm not trying to choose sides here, but I think it's important to establish that it's not just women who suffer. There are a lot of hopelessly solitary men out there, but they're poor or they're shy or they're just plain worn out by a series of relationships that always end with an argument over somebody's mother or a fight over toiletries.

EGG: But guys can have those relationships and those fights for most of their lives. Biologically, women have a limited window of opportunity.

SPERM: Men can't help it if they're winning the war against Erectile Dysfunction.

EGG: It's more than that. Women are defined by their bodies. You said it yourself: they're measured by how they look in "low-cut jeans" and "short skirts." What if a woman likes reading books and happens to hate starving herself to fit into a size 2? Is it right for her to be overlooked for a chemically created blonde with a tattoo above her ass that says, "use me."

SPERM: No, it's not.

EGG: You're somewhat sensitive, aren't you?

SPERM: Is that a good thing?

EGG: Yeah, it is.

SPERM: I guess we can agree that men and women both have it tough.

EGG: They do. I don't know if I'd want to become a boy or a girl. *(she smiles)* But, at least I'm not responsible for that.

SPERM: I know, I know, and I don't have a clue if I'm carrying an X or Y chromosome. *(he turns around trying to see his back)* I wish I knew.

EGG: You do? I don't. I think I'd like the surprise.

SPERM: Then, you're considering me.

EGG: I never said I wasn't.

SPERM: Our child will be special, you know. Maybe he or she will be able to change some of this.

EGG: Do you really believe that?

SPERM: I think you have to.

EGG: So you think we should?

SPERM: I do.

EGG: *(holding out her arms)* I do, too.

SPERM: *(stepping into her arms slowly)* I'll be gentle.

EGG: *(grabbing his head and pulling him toward her)* Don't you dare.

(She wraps her leg around him as lights go to black.)

Running Amok

Quinn D. Eli

Running Amok premiered in the 2010 Philadelphia Fringe Festival at Plays & Players Theatre as part of "Dirty Laundry," a program of short plays, produced by Secret Room Theatre (Alex Dremann; John D'Alonzo; Todd Holtsberry; and Elle McComsey, Producing Artistic Directors.) It was directed by Tasmania Garza. The cast was as follows: Floyd—Jamal Douglas; Daria—Theresa Leahy.

CHARACTERS

Floyd .. African-American, 30, an even-tempered athlete, well-dressed and well-spoken.

Daria .. His agent, late 30's, fair-haired and attractive. Over-caffeinated. Mouth like a sailor.

TIME & SETTING

Late morning in Daria's office at a sports management firm.

(Daria, on the phone, sits at her desk, surrounded by sports memorabilia, Swedish furniture, coffee mugs, and a computer.)

DARIA: *(into the phone)* No. Listen. Will you give the kid a break? . . . I know that. I know how *old* he is, Al, I've been with him since the dawn of time, but I'm asking you to give him a break, okay? You wanna know *why?* How about outta simple human kindness, you son of a bitch, how about to be *decent?* You don't want to be on the wrong side of this thing, Al, this kid is a *butterfly*, do you hear me, and you're still treating him like a goddamn caterpillar—
(Floyd walks in; Daria indicates that he should take a seat.)

DARIA: —if you print that shit, Al, we'll sue you, swear to god. That story is a lie. How do I *know?* You wanna know how I *know?* I've seen the girl's picture in the paper, that's how I know. She makes Lindsey Lohan look like Mother Theresa. If there was an Olympics for *tramps*, Al, she'd bring home the gold. Hold on, willya—?
(to Floyd)
You need anything, kid, a juice, a soda—?

FLOYD: No, ma'am.

DARIA: I'm on with Al Bernstein over at ESPN. Gimme another minute—

FLOYD: Sure thing.

DARIA: If you were Catholic, Al, like me, you'd understand: scandal is everywhere, there's no escaping scandal, we live in a corrupt and morally depraved universe. But my guy's not some priest boffing altar boys, ok? My guy is the salt of the earth: he's married, he takes care of his parents, he gives to *charity*, for crissakes. And this *girl* you're quoting, Al, this April What's-Her-Name, she's a liar. The kid *never* had sex with her. Al . . . Al . . . Albert: last time I checked my copy of the Karma Sutra, a hand job in the dressing room at JC Penney does not constitute "sex"—!

FLOYD: It was Macy's—.

DARIA: Hold on, Al—
(to Floyd)
What'd you say, kid?

FLOYD: It was Macy's. The handjob in the dressing room. It happened at Macy's, not JC Penney.

DARIA: . . . Oh. I. I stand corrected.

FLOYD: And it was more than a handjob, just so you know—

DARIA: *(nods and returns quickly to her phone call)* Listen, Al, my client says you've got it all wrong. ALL of it! First off, he was NEVER in JC Penney with that girl. *Ever.* If you print that he was in JC Penney with her, Al, swear to god, I'll make a charm bracelet outta your balls—.
(gives Floyd a thumb's up)
Good . . . excellent, thanks so much. Absolutely. He's a talented boy, Al, he's an inspiration to a lotta people. Little Johnny and Little Suzy, they look up to this kid—you don't wanna take that away. Thanks.
(Daria hangs up the phone.)

FLOYD: "Little Johnny and Little Suzy"?

DARIA: It's called improvising.

FLOYD: So ESPN's dropping the story?

DARIA: They sure as hell better. Right now the whole thing's all rumor and hearsay.

FLOYD: If Al wants to know the truth, I don't mind coming clean.

DARIA: That's because you're a decent kid, Floyd, you're topnotch. But why scare up trouble for yourself?

FLOYD: I made a decision back when it happened: If anyone asks, I said to myself, I won't say "No," I won't deny it. I'll stand up and take the hit. I'm not proud of what I did, but I'm not gonna lie about it, either.

DARIA: Which is why you're a saint, do you hear me, a whirlwind among breezes. But the press, Floyd, they'll crucify you, and I can't let that happen. You need protection, you need looking after—.

FLOYD: I'm not a *child*, Daria, I'm a full-grown—

DARIA: You're mommy's little touchdown machine, that's what you are, mommy's little high-earning, endorsement-getting, crowd-pleasing quarterback, and you deserve a goddamn break. People like Al Bernstein, they don't get it, some white guy in some corporate office in Connecticut, he doesn't know what it is to suffer, not like you and I know—.

FLOYD: Your parents are both dentists, Daria, you never "suffered"—.

DARIA: I suffered plenty—.

FLOYD: You went to Vassar!

DARIA: I'm a woman in a man's field, Floyd, I am a female sports agent, which makes me as rare as a fucking unicorn—

FLOYD: I know, I know, you've told me—.

DARIA: The bullshit I had to put up with, you have no idea, the name-calling, the insults; and do you know why I'm still here today?

FLOYD: "To set an example"—.

DARIA: You make fun, but it's true. I'm here to set an example. For other women. If I'd listened to every pencil-dick asshole who talked down to me like I was some baby-doll, some piece of *ass*, I'd still be a secretary. That's why we gotta stick together on this, Floyd, I'm not kidding. The barbarians are at the gate, kid, but we're not gonna let 'em in—.

FLOYD: When my wife got wind of it, I told her the truth, I confessed the whole thing.

DARIA: You—you did?

FLOYD: She asked me straight to my face. What was I gonna say— "No"?

DARIA: That—that might've been the *saner* option—.

FLOYD: Not for me.

DARIA: Look, kid, I'm Catholic, okay, you know that about me, I believe in . . . "God." I believe in—all kind of things: forgiveness and redemption and the Blessed Virgin and yadda, yadda. But couldn't you have maybe confessed to a *priest* instead of your wife?

FLOYD: It wasn't a priest who asked me.

DARIA: Fine. Whatever. Your pre-nup's ironclad, thanks to me, so at least we've got that covered. Not that it should matter. 'Cause if you *look* at this thing, and you'll forgive me here if I'm being indelicate, if I'm failing to strike the appropriate *tone*, but if you really *look* at it, Floyd, son, the whole thing was an accident: you were in a dressing room, your pants were off, your dick was out, and this girl's hands just happened to be nearby.

FLOYD: It wasn't just one girl.

DARIA: In the dressing room with you?

FLOYD: There were three girls.

DARIA: Three.

FLOYD: Yeah.

DARIA: This musta been some awful big dressing room.

FLOYD: Oh, and one of them might've been underage—

DARIA: No, see, you can't *know* that, okay, you can't know that for a *fact*, kid, not unless you were checking i.d.'s at the door—

FLOYD: She had on braces—

DARIA: Braces? That's your proof? Celebrities wear braces, kid, Tom Cruise wears braces, and he's in his 40's—!

FLOYD: The jacket she was wearing, it said Manhasset High School Cheerleading Squad—

DARIA: That's a *fashion* statement, kid, it doesn't prove anything—!

FLOYD: Another thing you should know: one of the girls brought a camera—

DARIA: A . . . a camera?

FLOYD: Digital. She burned the whole thing onto a disk—see?
    (Floyd hands the disk to Daria, who is temporarily flustered.)

FLOYD: I know, Daria, I know: I should've run the minute the camera came out. But by then I was sort of in the zone—.

DARIA: In the zone—?

FLOYD: It's a sports term.

DARIA: I know it's a fucking sports term, Floyd! And lemme tell you something else, too: this disk of hers doesn't amount to shit in my book. For all I know she could've photo-shopped some old pictures of you and turned it into something ... *dirty*—.

FLOYD: Nah, it's me. If you watch it, though, Daria, I should warn you about something: half way through, this *guy* comes into the dressing room, and I end up doing him, too—.

DARIA: A guy?

FLOYD: I spend a lot of time in locker rooms, surrounded by naked men. After a while, you get ... curious.

DARIA: Who was—who was the guy?

FLOYD: I'm not sure. Sales clerk, I guess. Afterward he sold me a necktie.

DARIA: Kid—

FLOYD: I wish you'd stop calling me that—.

DARIA: No! I will not. This is—we can keep a lid on this, okay? This is youthful hijinks. This is "boys will be boys"—

FLOYD: I may have to take a paternity test—.

DARIA: I THOUGHT IT WAS ONLY A HANDJOB!

FLOYD: I understand you're upset, but we've had a nice ride, you and me, and now it might be time to pay the piper—.

DARIA: If this gets out, we'll say you were ... "overwhelmed," that's all, by your recent championship, the spotlight and the glamour, and that you ... uh ... lost your way, but now you've ... seen the light and realized the error of your ways and, after all, kid, let's not forget, this is all new to you, you grew up poor, in the ghetto—

FLOYD: I knew what I was doing—.

DARIA: But you've never done anything like this before, kid, not ever!

FLOYD: I know. But something just ... snapped. I can't explain it. I think maybe I'm working out some stuff—.

DARIA: Gee, really, ya think so?!

FLOYD: I take responsibility, though, that's the point. You know I don't mess around with drugs or booze or any of that nonsense, so I was in full control of my faculties—

DARIA: If not your penis—

FLOYD: The thing is, Daria, you gotta say "no" a lot in this line of work, you ever notice that? When things start going your way and people want stuff from you—and I don't just mean the simple stuff, an autograph, a picture. I mean the stuff people stop you on the street and beg for: a kidney, one guy asked me for a *kidney*, to save his dying wife. That's when it hit me: I was tired of saying "no" all the time—

DARIA: You've got a big heart, kid, and you wanted to hear yourself say "yes" instead of "no" for a change, I get it. But a thing like that, you wanna start off small, take *baby* steps—say "yes" to starch at the dry cleaner, that's the way to start, say "yes" to decaff—

FLOYD: Forget it—

DARIA: —but the first time out, Floyd, you do not say "yes" to a department store orgy!

FLOYD: You don't understand—.

DARIA: I understand that you were *vulnerable* on account of the whole man-begging-you-for-your-kidney thing, and you were . . . led astray by a pack of predatory women who . . . took advantage of your fragile state of mind and *exploited* your innocence—.

FLOYD: On the tape I'm wearing one girl's underwear—.

DARIA: That's because they . . . "manipulated" you, forced you to *do* things, and DRUGGED you, so you showed "poor judgment"—but with . . . *prayer* and . . . and the "forgiveness" of your family and fans and the Almighty, you'll put this painful episode behind you—.

FLOYD: . . . I'm gonna call Al at ESPN and tell him the truth—.

DARIA: No you are not, goddammit—I forbid it!

FLOYD: I'm making the call—.

DARIA: Kid—!

FLOYD: I asked you to stop calling me that—.

DARIA: I can't! You're like my own child, my own baby boy, and my job is to protect you, to keep you safe—

FLOYD: The only thing I can assume here, Daria, is you are genetically incapable of seeing me as grown man.

DARIA: You grew up *poor* . . . in the ghetto . . . you suffered racism and . . . um . . . the ugly taunts of bigoted white devils—.

FLOYD: Christ, you liberals.

DARIA: Did you not *suffer*? Are you not a . . . beacon of hope and inspiration to all the poor black children growing up in the ghetto and looking for a . . . a role model . . . to help restore their faith that . . . that the sun will come out tomorrow?

FLOYD: Are you quoting from *Annie* now?

DARIA: I will not let you make this *public*, kid, I will not let you destroy the hopes and dreams of all those poor ghetto children.
    (Floyd takes out his cell and dials.)
FLOYD: Al Bernstein, please, in editorial—sure, I'll hold—.
DARIA: Kid, listen, think of your family here, think of your fans—
    (Daria rushes Floyd, attempting to restrain him. As Floyd talks, he and Daria flail around like Keystone Kops.)
FLOYD: If I *lie* about it, Daria, then I'll be back at square one—saying "no" all the time. "No, it never happened," and "No, I never had sex with that woman." I can't live that way. From now on I'm going to be the guy who speaks the truth, okay, not hiding behind lawyers and rehab and press agents and going on the offense and making up excuses. I'm going to be a *man* and face the music. You wanna let me off the hook because I grew up poor, because I'm black? That's crazy! That's paternalistic bullshit, that's liberal politics run amok—
DARIA: Kid—!
FLOYD: Every time you call me "kid," it's like you're saying I'm not responsible for anything I say or do. But that's all over now, believe me, 'cause you and I are gonna be on the vanguard of a new movement, we're gonna set an example by being open, honest, and accountable for our own actions—
    (into the phone)
    Oh, Al, good, you heard all that, did you? Uh-huh . . .
    (to Daria)
    He says I'm pretty articulate for a jock from the Bronx—
DARIA: Remind him you were on scholarship at Dartmouth—
FLOYD: *(into the phone)* Al, listen, you know I went to Dartmouth, right? On scholarship. No, an academic scholarship—
    (to Daria)
    He says he always assumed it was a football scholarship—.
DARIA: He's an asshole.
FLOYD: Well, look, Al, the reason I'm calling you back is—say what? No, I hadn't heard. She did? Every word. Oh. And she's going on *The View?* Wow. But the thing is, Al . . . yes, I understand, if Whoopie Goldberg says she's not a liar, that means a lot. But, Al, the honest-to-God truth is—
    (holds up the phone, addresses Daria)
    He won't let me get a word in edgewise—

DARIA: Did I not tell you he's an asshole?

FLOYD: *(into the phone)* Right, Al, sure, but the god's honest truth is—
how can it not *matter*? . . . Fine. Okay. Okay. Sure. I understand.
Bye—.

(Floyd hangs up.)

DARIA: So: What is it?

FLOYD: The girl.

DARIA: The one in the papers, "April DeMint," which sounds like a
feminine hygiene product, by the way—

FLOYD: She's . . . recanting. All of it. She's going on TV to say it's all
lies.

DARIA: There's *proof*, though, evidence. You've got the whole thing
here on high-def DVD—.

FLOYD: She's gonna say it was all fabricated, staged with some actor
who looks like me—.

DARIA: I don't underst—why would she do that?

FLOYD: Says she doesn't wanna mess up things for such a talented
boy.

DARIA: Hm. Perhaps she's found Jesus.

*(Daria grabs a bottle and a couple of glasses from her desk,
pours two drinks, and hands one to Floyd.)*

FLOYD: Al says even if I confessed to clubbing baby seals, nobody
would believe a word. The press thinks I'm too sweet a kid.

DARIA: You *are* awfully sweet.

FLOYD: I had a bisexual orgy in a dressing room at Macy's.

DARIA: And you probably weren't even the first! So the lesson here is:
you're human. Full of disgusting flaws and inexplicable im-
pulses, the same as everybody else. I am seeing you anew, my
friend.

FLOYD: What does that mean?

DARIA: It *means* that if you want to shout the truth from rooftops, I
won't try and stop you. I'll even help you—we can put out a
press release with all the sordid details and get the *jump* on that
little tramp before she goes on *The View*.

FLOYD: You'd—you'd do that for me?

DARIA: You wanna be a grown-up, you wanna throw yourself to the
wolves, who am I to object?

FLOYD: Thank you, Daria, that means a lot.

DARIA: So what if the story gets out—in this day and age, nobody's gonna give a shit. You'll probably get your own reality TV show.

FLOYD: Which, you know, would just be tacky.

(Daria grabs the DVD.)

DARIA: I guess I better take a look at this damn thing, before it ends up all over the Internet—.

FLOYD: Help yourself.

(She plays it; they stare at the screen as giggles and moans fill the room.)

DARIA: My. Wow. Look at that. The things people can do with salad tongs—.

FLOYD: It's bad, Daria, I know, but there's an upside, I swear. I can still be a role model. For little Johnny and little Suzy—

DARIA: Only if little Johnny and little Suzy want to grow up to be porn stars—

FLOYD: What I mean is: I can set an example, you know? Flip the switch. I can be the one person who stands up, tells the truth, and leads by example—.

DARIA: You're wearing women's underwear on camera, Floyd, so I'm thinking your "moral authority" is maybe shot to hell—.

FLOYD: Really?

DARIA: Don't worry. When I first got here and the pencil-dicks upstairs acted like they had me all figured out, I was in the same boat as you. Except I was alone. You, on the other hand, have got me. No matter what. Which is why you're gonna be okay.

FLOYD: You're a good friend, Daria, you know that?

DARIA: Tell that to anyone and I'll shove your balls in a paper shredder—

FLOYD: Wait—hold on . . . watch this part . . . I kind of like this part . . .

(They stare at the screen, visibly startled—and a little electrified—by what they see.)

DARIA: Impressive, Floyd, no kidding. You are one truly talented man.

(They continue watching.)
(Orgy noises rise as lights fade.)

END OF PLAY

Secret

Therese Cloonan

The original producton was at the Australian Centre of Performing Arts, 14 Raglan Street, North Melbourne, Victoria, Australia. Performance dates: October 24, October 31, November 7 and November 14, 2010. Director: Lindsay Saddington. Presented by: Raglan Street Theatre. Producer: Karl Sarsfield. Cast: Man—Alan Ashby; Woman—Heather Cunningham

CHARACTERS

Man . . . . late 20s/early 30s
Woman . . late 20s/early 30s

SETTING

A room or a small, confined space

A man and a woman are locked in a 'room' together.

MAN: You wanna be my secret?
WOMAN: Sure. Why?
MAN: I don't have one.
WOMAN: Oh.
MAN: And I really want one.
WOMAN: You want one?
MAN: I need one. Just one.
WOMAN: Would one be enough?
MAN: I think so. I hope so.
WOMAN: You might need more.
MAN: I don't want to be greedy.
WOMAN: But there's plenty more to have.
MAN: Where?
WOMAN: Here. There.
MAN: In this room?
WOMAN: Maybe. It's very roomy.
MAN: Yes, it's spacey.
WOMAN: Could we share?
MAN: The space?
WOMAN: The secret.
MAN: Oh, I don't know.
WOMAN: I don't know if I could share.
MAN: You don't want to?

WOMAN: I don't have to.

MAN: No, you don't.

WOMAN: *(pause)* Do you want to share?

MAN: With someone else?

WOMAN: Yes.

MAN: Not you?

WOMAN: Do you?

MAN: I'd have to see.

WOMAN: See what?

MAN: How good it was.

WOMAN: Good?

MAN: How special.

WOMAN: It would be very.

MAN: Very?

WOMAN: Good... Special...

MAN: Ah.

WOMAN: It would be ours.

MAN: It would be mine.

WOMAN: Ours.

MAN: Mine, for me to keep.

WOMAN: Ours, for us to share.

MAN: It'd be secret.

WOMAN: It'd be special. What do you think?

MAN: Sounds lovely.

WOMAN: Doesn't it!

MAN: But I don't want to share.

WOMAN: No?

MAN: I want you to myself. Always.

WOMAN: You can't promise that.

MAN: Why not?

WOMAN: The mind. It changes.

MAN: Mine doesn't.

WOMAN: Never?

MAN: Hasn't yet.

WOMAN: It will. It might.

MAN: Why would it?

WOMAN: These things happen.

MAN: I suppose. They can.

WOMAN: They do.

MAN: But why?

WOMAN: Because there's too many.

MAN: What?

WOMAN: Like us.

MAN: Too many.

WOMAN: Others.

MAN: Oh, yes. The others.

WOMAN: And there's a lot of space.

MAN: A great deal.

WOMAN: And a lot of room.

MAN: Plenty.

WOMAN: For us.

MAN: And them.

WOMAN: It worries me.

MAN: Really?

WOMAN: *(pause)* Maybe it's not right.

MAN: What?

WOMAN: For us to do this, to have this.

MAN: But it's there to have, there to take.

WOMAN: Maybe it's a bit risky.

MAN: Maybe you should stop worrying.

WOMAN: I'm a woman. It's what we do.

MAN: Do something else.

WOMAN: I can't help it.

MAN: *(suggestive, makes moves on woman)* I can't help myself.

WOMAN: It's bad.

MAN: It's good.

WOMAN: *(softly)* I've got a little crush.

MAN: Thrush?

WOMAN: Crush.

MAN: Oh.

WOMAN: On you.

MAN: Of course you have.

WOMAN: My legs are all wibbly wobbly.

MAN: I feel a bit sleazy. Greasy.

WOMAN: I've gotta tell somebody about us.

MAN: No, don't.

WOMAN: I want to.

MAN: You mustn't!

WOMAN: You're hiding me.

MAN: It's a secret.

WOMAN: But we should celebrate, commemorate.

MAN: No! People would come. Mess it up. Complicate things.

WOMAN: They wouldn't.

MAN: They'd get ideas. They'd want it.

WOMAN: Want what?

MAN: I don't know. Your hand.

WOMAN: The upper or the lower?

MAN: Pardon?

WOMAN: What kind of hand is it?

MAN: The lower.

WOMAN: Not for long. That'll change.

MAN: No, it won't.

WOMAN: That's what happens.

MAN: Who told you that?

WOMAN: I can't remember.

MAN: Who have you been speaking to?

WOMAN: I don't know. Someone. Somewhere.

MAN: Where?

WOMAN: I don't know. Here. There.

MAN: You see?

WOMAN: What's wrong?

MAN: *(angrily)* I told you!

WOMAN: You've got frowny lines. *(Goes to touch man's forehead)*

MAN: Don't touch me!

WOMAN: And grumpy voice.

MAN: Don't change the subject.

WOMAN: What's the subject?

MAN: Them! They'll ruin it!

WOMAN: What are you talking about?

MAN: Us. Them.

WOMAN: What about them?

MAN: They'll be jealous.

WOMAN: I don't think so.

MAN: They'll want some. Want it for themselves.

WOMAN: No, they won't!

MAN: Just a piece. A slice. A slither.

WOMAN: I didn't say anything to anyone.

MAN: *(angrily)* I don't want to share!

WOMAN: You don't have to.

MAN: You've been showing them your hand.

WOMAN: Have not!

MAN: You said so.

WOMAN: Did not.

MAN: You said you went somewhere. Spoke to someone.

WOMAN: Maybe I should go.

MAN: Give me your hand.

>*Girl reluctantly offers hand.*

MAN: It's soft. Smooth.

WOMAN: Lotions, potions.

MAN: It's pretty.

WOMAN: It's just a hand.

MAN: *(clenches fist or holds her hand tight)* It's mine.

>*Pause. Woman is unsettled.*

WOMAN: I don't like this room. This space.

MAN: I can fix it.

WOMAN: It feels too cramped. Too small.

MAN: I can make it bigger. Taller. Wider.

WOMAN: I need some air.

MAN: There's plenty in here.

WOMAN: No, there's not.

MAN: There's enough.

>*Woman realises she is on a raised platform.*

WOMAN: Hey, how did I get here?

MAN: Where?

WOMAN: Up on this pedestal.

MAN: Not sure.

WOMAN: Yes, you do. You put me here!

MAN: I know. 'Cause you're special.

WOMAN: But I'm so far away.

MAN: You're safe. You're in the right place.

WOMAN: I'm lonely.

MAN: But you've got me.

WOMAN: I don't belong here.

MAN: But you look so lovely!

WOMAN: Get me down!

MAN: You're shining, you're sparkling.

WOMAN: *(angrily)* Get me down!!

MAN: I will. Eventually.

WOMAN: Now!

MAN: You were ranting. Saying silly things. Making me nervous.

WOMAN: But I can't get down.

MAN: Aha! You'll miss me. It'll give you time to think. To see reason.

WOMAN: But I... *(stares at the 'wall')* Oh, wow, look at that!

MAN: Huh?

WOMAN: What a beautiful view! I can see for miles.

MAN: Let me see.

> *Man tries to get up to where woman is but is unable to.*

MAN: I can't... I can't see. *(tries to jump up)*

WOMAN: *(awestruck)* Why, it's fantastic! It's quite extraordinary.

MAN: Get down! It's dangerous up there!

WOMAN: I can't. And as you said, I need time to think.

MAN: But I can't reach you.

WOMAN: No.

MAN: And you can't reach me.

WOMAN: Correct.

MAN: This wasn't part of the plan.

WOMAN: Well, things have taken a turn. *(Turns back on man)*

MAN: Don't turn your back on me! Look at me!

WOMAN: I'm listening to the birds.

MAN: What birds?

WOMAN: And bells—I can hear bells! Maybe they're bellbirds!

MAN: Rubbish!

WOMAN: Can't you hear them?

MAN: There's nothing to hear. You're being a smart arse. Trying to shit me.

WOMAN: I'm thinking.

MAN: What about? *(pause)* WHAT ABOUT?

WOMAN: You told me to think!

MAN: Yeah, but now you're getting all these strange ideas.

WOMAN: Oh, look. There's a window!

MAN: Where? Where?

WOMAN: There, see?

MAN: What? Where? *(desperately searches)* I can't see it.

WOMAN: Hey, someone's waving at me. Hello! *(waves)*

MAN: Who's there? Who are you waving at? TELL ME WHO YOU'RE WAVING AT!

WOMAN: Hi! Hi, sweetie!

> *Man tries to jump up but falls to the ground. Woman talks (mouths words) to someone outside. Lights begin to fade.*

MAN: *(furiously)* Who are you talking to? Get down! I SAID GET DOWN!

> *Woman waves and laughs, talking inaudibly to her new friend. Blackout.*

So Long Lives This

C.S. Drury and Bill Quigley

So Long Lives This had its premiere at HB Playwrights
Theatre in 2009. It was selected subsequently for the
American Globe Theatre/Turnip Theatre Company
2010 Annual Short Play Festival, where it won the Alan
Minieri Playwriting Award. Both productions were di-
rected by Peter Zinn. Cast: Leo—Bill Quigley; DAN—
C.S. Drury.

CHARACTERS:

Leo
Bill

[*A living room cluttered with old mismatched furniture and disparate oddities; papier-mâché sculptures, a set of bagpipes, many books, a painting easel, newspapers scattered about.*
   A man dressed in jeans and a T-shirt sleeps awkwardly on a very old and beat-up sofa, clutching a long yellow pad and a pillow. A younger man enters quietly and tiptoes around the room, taking measurements of the doorway and floor space. He accidentally knocks over the easel, which crashes loudly to the floor. The man on the couch bolts up, startled.]

LEO: WHAT!

DAN: Shit! Leo, I'm so sorry! I was trying to find the . . . uh . . . the electric bill.

LEO: No, it's fine. I . . . I was only dozing. I . . . I'm actually feeling really strong today. Best day in a long time.

DAN: Well that's good to hear, man. [*Looks around.*] But this place— I'm telling ya, it's starting to look like a flea market with all this shit you've brought in.

LEO: Don't start in. They're my tasks.

DAN: Yeah, yeah, I know. From your wish list.

LEO: It's not a wish list. It's my Final To-Do List. Much more proactive than wishing.

DAN: What number are you up to anyway? It was one-ninety-eight the last time I looked.

LEO: The last time you . . . I told you never to look at my list!

DAN: Which, of course, guaranteed that I would. How long have I been living in your house? Eight years or something? You should know me by now.

LEO: It's a very personal list, you nosy little bastard!

DAN: Why do you think I like it so much?

LEO: It's all the things I want to do before I—
DAN: Don't!
LEO: Dan. These meds don't keep working forever. At least not for everyone.
DAN: You're looking really thin.
LEO: I gained two pounds last week.
DAN: And how much did you lose this week?
LEO: [*Trying to change the subject.*] How was work?
DAN: The restaurant was a fucking loony bin. Did you eat today?
LEO: I think so.
DAN: What did you eat?
LEO: One of those God-awful shakes.
DAN: Leo, you promised that you'd try to eat more.
LEO: And you promised not to badger as it got closer. Let me be.
DAN: Let me see that loony list.
LEO: Absolutely not.
DAN: Most recent entries, as I recall: 'Learn to play the bagpipes.'
LEO: [*disappointed*] It takes more lungpower than I've got these days. I hadn't thought of that.
DAN: 'Paint the view from the front window' in watercolors. God knows why you'd want to waste canvas on Queens Boulevard but hey it's your list. Thus the fucking easel I tripped over.
LEO: Never mind your big fat opinions. My to-do list keeps me going—as ridiculous as it is to you.
DAN: [*more serious*] I know it does. And that's why I love it. Now let me see today's entries.
            [*Dan snatches the notebook from Leo.*]
LEO: Oooh, you little prick! Give that back to me!
DAN: Wow! You're up to number two-seventeen?! [*reads*] 'Ride a dolphin. Learn Origami. Memorize a Shakespeare Sonnett...?' What the fuck for?
LEO: I dunno. I was at a dinner party and this asshole recited one spontaneously and I was jealous.
DAN: You're a freak.
LEO: I'm almost there. It's just the last two lines I keep mangling. 'So long as men can see and eyes breathe...' Fuck.
DAN: [*reading from list*] HA! You've gotta be fucking kidding!

LEO: Gimme that!

DAN: [*reads*] 'Number two-sixteen: Get spanked by Harrison Ford'
HA! Are you serious?

LEO: Gravely. Who needs porn? I beat off to Indiana Jones movies!
God, him and that whip!

DAN: You're beyond twisted.
[*He tosses the list back to Leo and then goes to look out the
window.*]

LEO: Thank you.

DAN: So listen, Leo, there's something I need to—[*stops as he notices
Leo's neck*] Wait. C'mere. Is that another scratch?

LEO: Don't.

DAN: [*moving towards him*] Hey. Let me see that scratch on your neck.

LEO: It's fine!

DAN: I've told you what that fucking upholstery is doing to your skin.

LEO: [*squirming away*] It's no big deal. I'll put Calamine on it.

DAN: It's this God-awful sofa you insist on sleeping on!

LEO: We are really not going to have this conversation again.

DAN: It's positively insane! You have a perfectly wonderful bed upsta—

LEO: OK. I guess we are gonna have this conversation again.

DAN: A perfectly wonderful King-sized bed with a brand new memory foam mattress but—

LEO: Some days I just can't handle those stairs anymore and you
know that.

DAN: I'll carry you! I've told you a hundred times that I will gladly
carry you up anytime you need to sleep and—

LEO: I'm not going—

DAN: And carry you back down here whenever you want!

LEO: I am not going up into that bedroom!

DAN: WHY?

LEO: Because I know I'll never come down.
[*Silence.*]

DAN: That's ridiculous. That is completely absurd, Leo.

LEO: No it's not. I'll go up into that bedroom and in two days, we'll
both decide it's too much trouble to bring me down for breakfast. And then you'll start bringing all my meals up there. You'll
bring the better TV up. You'll get me one of those fucking port-

a-poddys because I can't be bothered to make it down the hall to the bathroom. All because it's just a little easier. No, Danny. I'm not ready to surrender. And I won't be cloistered away.

DAN: So I'm supposed to watch you disintegrate on that fucking couch?

LEO: The couch is fine.

DAN: You've got to be kidding me! That couch in not fine! You bought that couch in 1987—second-hand, for Chrissakes! I don't know a dog that would sleep on that thing!

LEO: This has tremendous sentimental value.

DAN: Like what?

LEO: A million memories.

DAN: Give me one.

LEO: OK. [thinks] That gorgeous cop who fucked me for like three hours right there. [unconsciously smiles at the memory] He kept saying it was a crime to have eyes as blue as mine.

DAN: [laughs a little] I do not need to hear this.

LEO: Too bad. The couch is fine! This is our living room and it keeps me connected. I get to see people. This is the room where my nieces and nephews used to crawl when they were little. Now it's where they come to smoke pot to get away from my sister. This is the room where I get to meet whatever species of female you happen to be banging each week.

DAN: Yeah right! The only thing I've been banging lately is my head against the wall—you're so goddamn stubborn!

LEO: This is where friends stop by and talk too much and stay too long. This room keeps me attached to the world, even on the days when I don't want to be. This is where I'm staying.

[Silence. Dan goes to the window and looks out somewhat nervously.]

DAN: Fine. You know what? I knew you'd be impossible about this. [deep breath] So listen Leo, we need to talk.

LEO: [looks] What?

DAN: Since you're absolutely hell-bent on living twenty-four/seven here in Grand Central Station . . . I have a solution.

LEO: A solution to what?

DAN: To you sleeping like a civilized human being and not some hung-over teenager.

LEO: We're really not gonna go there again, are we?

DAN: I've bought a new bed for you.

[*A beat.*]

LEO: A new bed?

DAN: They're gonna deliver it any minute. Now I know what you're thinking—

LEO: A new bed? You just finished telling me how wonderful mine is.

DAN: No, not for upstairs. For here. It's great, it's one of those fully adjustable ones that goes up and down—reclines, all that cool shit. It has a remote control for—

LEO: You mean a hospital bed.

DAN: Well yeah, I guess they're used in hospitals sometimes—

LEO: Sometimes?

DAN: That's because they're good beds.

LEO: A hospital bed to go in this room?

DAN: [*Forced brightness*] Yeah. Right here. It will be great for you! I already measured it all out and everything. We're gonna put it right there by the window so you can look out!

LEO: Wait, wait. You mean without consulting me, you ordered a deathbed to plunk right in the middle of the living room?

DAN: Don't say that! It's a hosp—it's a modern bed—to make you more comfortable.

LEO: It's a coffin and you know it!

DAN: That is not true! Stop being so goddamn morbid!

LEO: You've really got some set! Who the hell do you think you are?

DAN: Your best friend. Who cares enough about you to give you some dignity.

LEO: Dignity! Don't you dare patronize me, you little sonofabitch! I have plenty of dignity!

DAN: Not on that moth buffet, you don't! I want to cry every time I see you sleeping all curled up and pathetic on that ratty old thing! I'm trying to help you Leo! What part of that don't you get? [*Doorbell rings.*] Here they are. Jesus, you could at least say thank you.

LEO: Say thank you? No, actually I say FUCK YOU! I will not be put to sleep while I'm still here!

DAN: Who's putting you to sleep?! Look, if you insist on staying in this room, then I ask—No, I fucking demand that you let me make it better for you to be here! I will never forgive myself if I don't.

[*Doorbell rings again.*]

LEO: But that's not making it better, Danny. I have too many good memories of this room. Our drunken Super Bowl parties, endless Monopoly games. All of it! And it was in this room where I first met you . . . scruffy little college kid on the nine-year plan—looking for a room to rent. No. This is a living room! You bring that fucking bed in here and it becomes a dying room! And I won't have that!

[*Dan rubs his temples and thinks for a moment.*]

DAN: No. I'm sorry Leo. I'm gonna overrule you on this one.

LEO: You're gonna wh—

DAN: Clearly I have to save you from yourself. And I will.

LEO: My life is my business, not yours!

[*Doorbell rings three times aggressively.*]

DAN: I live here, it has become my business! You don't get to pick and choose when I'm of use to you and when I'm not. If I'm good enough to call in your prescriptions, make your appointments, wash—

LEO: Who asked you to—

DAN: Wash your shitty underwear, then I get a say in how this plays out. And I refuse to watch you die all curled up with bedsores, cuts, and bloody scratches from that fucking sofa! So like it or not that bed is coming in here now!

LEO: [*seething*] And so help me God, Daniel, I will set it on fire right in front of you!

[*A standoff. Both men stand rigid, glaring at each other.*]

LEO: [*slowly and ferociously emphatic*] Go get rid of that fucking bed!

[*A standoff for several moments. Neither flinches nor retreat. Dan finally breaks and sighs in exasperation and resignation.*]

DAN: OK. Fine. You win. I give up. Sleep on the fucking coffee table for all I care.

[*Daniel exits out the door. Leo, spent, sits on the floor leaning back against the sofa. After a moment, Dan returns. Awkward silence.*]

LEO: I know you meant well.

[*Silence.*]

DAN: What... what do you want for dinner?

LEO: Nothing really.

DAN: Leo.

LEO: Did you tell me you did or didn't pay the electric?

DAN: I will. Today.

LEO: We need to start transferring these utilities into your name.

DAN: Why?

LEO: Well... so there's no problem with continued service... you know... when the time comes.

DAN: But... we've talked about this... I mean whoever gets this... whoever buys this... they might not want a perma-tenant—which of course I'd understand.

[*Leo thinks for a moment and takes a deep breath.*]

LEO: Alright. I guess this is as good a time as any.

[*Silence. Dan looks at Leo bewildered.*]

LEO: Your perma-tenant status has been made... well... permanent. Or as permanent as you want it to be.

DAN: What are you talking about?

LEO: This house is yours.

[*Silence.*]

DAN: I don't understand.

LEO: It's a done deal. All legalities have been handled. This is yours.

[*Silence. Dan, incredulous, slowly sits on the floor next to Leo.*]

DAN: Truly?

LEO: Truly.

DAN: I... I don't know what to say. Why... why me? You have blood relatives.

LEO: True. But none that badger me as much as you do. And none I love as much as you.

[*The two men sit perfectly still looking at each other.*]

DAN: Thank you. [*Silence.*] C'mere. Let me put your Calamine on. Move up.

[*Leo inches forward as Dan sits behind him on the sofa. Dan starts to take off Leo's shirt and Leo helps him. Leo's body is covered with very red and purple lesions. Dan opens the bottle and gently rubs the lotion on Leo's neck, his shoulders, his chest. Silence.*]

LEO: [*softly*] 'So long as men can breathe or eyes can see, so long lives this, and this gives life to thee.' Hey. I did it.

[*Dan chokes up and fights back tears.*]

DAN: [*a whisper*] Don't leave.

LEO: Oh, Buddy. Believe me, I don't want to. But there'll come a point when it's no longer my decision.

DAN: Then don't leave just yet. Please.

LEO: I will stick around as long as I possibly can. You have my vow. Living right here . . . in our living room.

[*Dan resumes gently rubbing the lotion on Leo as the Sean Hayes song, 'Never Alone' begins to play as the lights slowly fade to black.*]

Something for the Boys

Louis Felder

Something for the Boys was performed at the Hayworth Theatre, Los Angeles, as part of Circus Theatricals Festival of New One-Act Plays, June 2010. Directed by Bibi Tinsley. Cast: Dorothy—Vanessa Waters; Edward—Anthony Cran.

CHARACTERS

Edward: . . Thirties.
Dorothy: . Thirties, his wife.

SETTING

The bedroom of a suburban house.

TIME

The present.

Dorothy sits at a small makeup table, wearing an attractive long nightgown. She starts to apply eye liner, then changes her mind. She holds up fake eyelashes to see how she looks and discards the notion. She applies lipstick as Edward enters carrying a video camera.

He is barefoot, wearing warm-up pants and a tee-shirt. He is gentle and solicitous, not wanting to upset her; there is tension in the air, not between them, but because of what they must do and why, keeping their emotions in check.

EDWARD: You look great. You really do.
(She stops doing her makeup and looks at her shaking hands.)
DOROTHY: I'm a little nervous.
EDWARD: You don't have to act; just be yourself. You want a drink? Brandy or something?
DOROTHY: At six in the morning?
(He sits on the bed and checks the video camera. She brushes her hair.)
EDWARD: I got the lights all set up . . . . Ready to go.
(He sights through the camera, aiming at her.)
DOROTHY: You're not shooting me *now*.
EDWARD: No.

DOROTHY: I'm not ready.

EDWARD: Take your time.

DOROTHY: I can't decide what to wear.

EDWARD: What you're wearing now—that's beautiful.

DOROTHY: *Over* this. I don't want to wear a—
> *(She stops. They listen. After a moment, she shakes her head.)*
I thought I heard them.

EDWARD: I didn't hear anything.

DOROTHY: Anyway, I don't want to wear a housecoat—it's so dowdy.
> *(holding up a peignoir)*
But, this peignoir—

EDWARD: That's pretty.

DOROTHY: Maybe it's too much—like I'm trying to be glamorous, you know, lounging around like some old movie star. You know those phony newsreels showing Joan Crawford "at home" posing with her robe open.
> *(posing with her legs exposed)*
"Oh, you caught me having breakfast by the pool. Ha ha ha."
> *(Edward grabs the camera.)*

EDWARD: Let me get a shot of you!

DOROTHY: *(covering up)* NO! Anyway, you know what I mean.

EDWARD: I guess, sure.

DOROTHY: Same thing with the slippers. What do you think?
> *(showing him some flat slippers)*
These?
> *(showing him the high heel satin slippers she's wearing)*
Or these?

EDWARD: Those are pretty.

DOROTHY: But this is what a bride wears on her honeymoon.

EDWARD: You didn't.

DOROTHY: You never gave me a chance. Day one, off in the Jeep to the mountains. Thermal socks and hiking boots for a week.

EDWARD: Wasn't it great? Want to do it again?

DOROTHY: Maybe . . . . Okay?

EDWARD: Sure.
> *(They pause, neither looking at each other. She resumes brushing her hair.)*

EDWARD (CONT.): I thought—when you're ready—I thought of getting a shot of you coming out of the bedroom, you know, like you've just heard the sleigh bells, and peek around to see Santa Claus.

DOROTHY: That's perfect. That's how I want them to remember me.

EDWARD: *(quietly, after a pause)* Yeah.

DOROTHY: *(quietly, after a pause)* As mom.

EDWARD: *(quietly, after a pause)* Yeah.

DOROTHY: *(brushing)* Mom on Christmas morning.... Mom with hair.

(They pause, an awkward silence.)

DOROTHY (CONT.): I've changed my mind.

EDWARD: You want a brandy?

DOROTHY: About editing this. I don't think I want to look at it.

EDWARD: You wanted to cut what you don't like.

DOROTHY: Suppose I don't like *any* of it. We can't re-shoot. So let's just keep it simple. Okay?

EDWARD: Okay.

DOROTHY: It's not to show me at my best. It's just to show them what their mother looked like.... In case they ask.... Someday.... 'Cause kids forget, they don't mean to, but—four and five—they'll forget.... And that's all this is—something for the boys. ... That's all.... In case they ask.... Someday.

(noticing a downcast Edward.)

Maybe *you* should have that brandy.... Edward?

EDWARD: I'm fine.

DOROTHY: *(light-hearted)* Hey! If you're shaky, you can't hold the camera!

EDWARD: I'm steady as Gibraltar.

DOROTHY: What are you going to wear?

EDWARD: What do you mean?

DOROTHY: You're not going to wear *that*.

EDWARD: What?

DOROTHY: What you're wearing.

EDWARD: I'm not in the picture.

DOROTHY: Oh, yes you are. You and me both. Together.

EDWARD: Who's going to hold the camera?

DOROTHY: Put it on a tripod.

EDWARD: I don't have one.

DOROTHY: Look under the tree.

EDWARD: Really?

DOROTHY: The long box, the heavy one. Open it first.

EDWARD: Okay. Right. Thanks.

DOROTHY: And wear the blue pajamas. They're in the second box with the stripes and red ribbon.

EDWARD: You got me pajamas?

DOROTHY: And a robe. Third box.

EDWARD: What's in the fourth box?

DOROTHY: There isn't any fourth box. I maxed out the VISA card in the toy store. How you're going to pay for all that isn't any of my concern.

EDWARD: I didn't get you anything.

DOROTHY: Good. I told you "nothing." I mean it.

EDWARD: I was going to buy you a—never mind. Whatever I'd give you—it wouldn't be enough.

DOROTHY: And if you bought me jewelry, I'd take it back. I wouldn't want it ending up on some trailer trash you'll probably take up with.

EDWARD: Oh, don't go there. Please, don't.

DOROTHY: I'm sorry.

EDWARD: Focus on today. We're dealing with today.

DOROTHY: And the past.

EDWARD: Remembering.

DOROTHY: That Hawaii vacation? All of us at the beach, that's what the boys will see too.

EDWARD: Man, they had a good time.

DOROTHY: So did I.

EDWARD: So did I.

DOROTHY: Ogling the girls. I saw you, don't deny it!

EDWARD: I wasn't "ogling."

DOROTHY: Slyly peeking over your sunglasses; you couldn't have been more obvious.

EDWARD: You were checking out the guys in Speedos.

DOROTHY: Oh, remember that fat man coming out of the water? His gut rolled down so far so you couldn't even see his crotch.

EDWARD: I wasn't trying to.

DOROTHY: Imagine having that lump of fat on top of you?

EDWARD: No.

DOROTHY: Ugh! I don't think I ate lunch that day. I should have. I should have had pasta with cheese, and French bread with butter—and desserts! Because I am going to lose so much weight! Especially the parts *you* like.

(When she walks past Edward, he stands and holds her from behind, his arms around her waist. After a pause, he whispers in her ear.)

EDWARD: I wish we'd made love on the beach.

DOROTHY: We should have.

EDWARD: *(slowly, quietly)* Under the stars. In one of those cabanas. The surf rolling in. Moonlight on the water. Hawaiian music in the distance. The breeze like a whisper. Holding you in my arms.

(As he spoke, Dorothy closed her eyes and moved his hands to cup her breasts. He is still, his face against her neck. She looks down at her breasts in his hands, then looks away with an expression of sorrow and fear of imminent loss.)

DOROTHY: I guess we should have done a lot of things.

(She pats his hands to break away, breaking the mood, and becomes breezy again and determined.)

DOROTHY (CONT.): But we have things to do *right now.*

EDWARD: How do you feel?

DOROTHY: Tired, but—

EDWARD: Go back to sleep. Go ahead.

DOROTHY: No.

EDWARD: We don't have to do this.

DOROTHY: Yes we do.

EDWARD: I'll tell the boys you're sick.

DOROTHY: I'm not! Not yet! Damn it, don't tell them I'm sick! Not yet!

EDWARD: *(whispering)* Don't yell.

DOROTHY: Don't fight with me!

EDWARD: I'm not.

DOROTHY: It's important! It's for you too!

EDWARD: *I'm* not going to forget you! Neither are the boys! They know you love them, they'll always *feel* that, they'll always *have* that. You held them, you sang to them, you were always *there* for them. However they turn out—and they're going to turn out great—it's because of you.

DOROTHY: And someday—when they get married—maybe their wives will ask: "What was your mother like?" and they can show this. And maybe they'll say: "Your mother was a lovely woman."

EDWARD: We're putting too much into this! Too much stress! Let's not do it.

DOROTHY: We have to!

EDWARD: Tomorrow we'll be thinking—"we should have done this, we should have done that!" All we're going to feel is regret. Maybe we shouldn't do it.

DOROTHY: *(near tears)* I have to! I have to leave *something!* . . . For the boys! . . . You have to help me! . . . Please!

(As she moves to him, there is a noise off. They stand still, listening.)

EDWARD: *(whispering)* They're awake.

(They look into each other's eyes.)

DOROTHY: *(whispering an order)* The bells! Get the sleigh bells!

EDWARD: Right.

DOROTHY: Ring 'em! Now!

(Edward rushes from the room with the camera. Dorothy puts on the peignoir and quickly checks herself in the mirror as sleigh bells ring off.)

DOROTHY (CONT.): *(loudly calling out)* I hear sleigh bells! Boys! Did you hear sleigh bells?

(Lights flood the doorway. She peeks out of the room into the lights, a dazzling smile on her face.)

DOROTHY (CONT.): Santa Claus was here! Merry Christmas, boys! Merry Christmas! Hurry! Hurry!?

(Smiling, she walks toward the light and out of view, but her shadow against the wall remains. She lifts her arms, and because she is wearing a peignoir, her shadow suggests the form of an angel.)

END OF PLAY

Text Misdirected

Nina Mansfield

Text Misdirected was originally produced by Thunderous Productions at the Greenbelt Arts Center in Greenbelt, MD in February of 2010 as part of an evening entitled *Planes, Trains & Automobiles* (Celeste Campbell, Producer). The production was directed by Susane Caviness. The cast included: Barry*—Amy Purves; Jane—Carole Preston

---

* For this production, the part of Barry was played by a female and renamed "Barbara".

CHARACTERS

Barry:................A divorce lawyer. Late 30s-50s.
Jane:.................A woman. 30s-50s.
Voice of Train Conductor:.. Male or Female. (Could be a
                            recorded voice.)

SETTING

The Present. A Metro-North Train.

(In darkness, the sounds of beeping and buzzing, cell phones and other electronic sounds can be heard. The noises swell in an electronic cacophony, ending with the "bing" of a train door closing. The lights come up on Jane. She is out of breath, frazzled. She has just caught the train.)

VOICE OF TRAIN CONDUCTOR: Express to White Plains, stopping at 125th Street.

> *(The train starts to move. Jane is caught off balance for a moment, but collects herself. She looks for a seat. There is an empty seat next to Barry. He has been sitting, completely engrossed in his Blackberry. He has a laptop open on his lap with a thumb drive sticking out of it, and an i-Pod sticking out of his pocket with headphones plugged into his ears. There is also a blue tooth around his ear. Jane reluctantly sits next to him, eyeing his electronic devises with disdain. In her hand, Jane clutches a cell phone. She unfolds her palm, and stares at the phone, as if it is some powerful drug she is trying to give up. Finally, she makes a decision. She begins to type a text message. Unbeknownst to her, Barry discreetly peers over her shoulder and reads it. She stares at it, and then sends it.)*

BARRY: *(He first pulls out his ear phones and closes up his laptop.)* You know, I couldn't help but notice...

JANE: Excuse me?

BARRY: Your text message.

JANE: You read my text message.

BARRY: Peripheral vision. It's a skill.

JANE: You read my text message?

BARRY: Quite accidentally.

JANE: *(Appalled.)* I'm sure.

> *(Barry's phone buzzes. He looks at it, and then continues the conversation as he is responding to a text message.)*

BARRY: To your . . . husband?

JANE: I'm sorry?

BARRY: *(Motioning with his hand as he finishes sending his text message.)* Hold on a just a . . .

> *(He hits send.)*

Husband, right? Of course, I'm just assuming.

JANE: That's really none of your . . .

> *(Barry's phone rings.)*

BARRY: Sorry, I got to take this . . . Hello . . . Yep . . . I just texted you . . . great. Perfect.

> *(He hangs up then turns his full attention to Jane.)*

Sorry 'bout that . . . uh . . . so . . . You want a divorce. That's what you . . . you know.

> *(Barry mimes sending a text with his thumbs.)*

"I space W-N-T space D-V-R-C . . . " I'm translating. Adding the vowels.

> *(Jane is speechless.)*

BARRY: I suppose I should explain.

> *(He reaches into his jacket and pulls out a business card.)*

I do divorces. I'm an attorney. Barry Carol. Carol, Carol, and Glass.

> *(He hands her his card.)*

JANE: Oh.

BARRY: So if you're looking for representation . . .

JANE: No. I'm not.

BARRY: You sure? Because our firm is really ahead of the curve when it comes to . . .

JANE: I said no.

BARRY: OK then.

> *(There is an uncomfortable silence. Somewhere in the train, a cell phone goes off. It has one of those ring tones that sounds*

likes it's an old rotary phone. Jane looks about frantically. Then another phone starts to go off. Jane looks at Barry. He shakes his head. Then a third phone starts to go off. It has a really annoying ring. It is Jane's phone. The other phones have stopped ringing, but Jane's phone continues to ring. She tries to silence it, once, twice. Finally, Barry reaches over and silences the phone for her. Jane is extremely relieved.)

JANE: *(In a slow whisper.)* So . . . How much do you charge?

BARRY: Pardon?

JANE: Per . . . you know.

BARRY: *(Miming a text again.)* D-V-R-C? Ha! No, not funny . . . Oh, well.

(Turning on his "concerned attorney" personality.)

That depends. On the situation.

JANE: This.

(She shows him her cell phone.)

BARRY: *(Reading)* C- U @ O-S-T-R bar 2 nite.

JANE: That's the Oyster Bar. Grand Central Terminal.

BARRY: Tonight?

JANE: Yes. So . . .

BARRY: So . . . ?

JANE: It was a mistake.

BARRY: Not tonight?

JANE: Not me.

BARRY: Text . . . misdirected?

JANE: Seems to be.

BARRY: So you . . .

JANE: Went.

BARRY: And you . . .

JANE: Saw him

BARRY: With a . . .

JANE: Man.

BARRY: Oh . . . OH!

JANE: No. It's not that.

BARRY: Not . . . that?

JANE: No. The man was my father.

BARRY: *(Shocked.)* Oh!

JANE: No! You've got it all wrong.

VOICE OF TRAIN CONDUCTOR: Ladies and gentlemen, we are approaching 125th street. Please clear your seats of any baggage for on coming passengers.

BARRY: Your husband. And your father.

JANE: *(Looks around.)* Attorney client privilege?

BARRY: You aren't my client.

> *(Jane decides not to say anything. Barry is overcome with curiosity.)*

BARRY: Ok, ok. Attorney-client privilege.

JANE: They were conspiring.

BARRY: Conspiring? Against you? Why?

JANE: You . . . you wouldn't understand.

> *(Jane's phone starts to ring again. Barry automatically reaches over and silences it for her.)*

BARRY: *(Gently.)* It's OK. You can tell me.

JANE: You see . . . last month . . . I had the cable disconnected.

BARRY: OK.

JANE: All those channels.

BARRY: Channels?

JANE: And this month, the internet had to go.

BARRY: It's porn, isn't it.

JANE: Sorry?

BARRY: I know how it is. I've seen it before. It starts with a video. Pay per view. Then a download. Next thing you know, he's meeting underage—

JANE: No no no! They're blaming me.

BARRY: I see . . . You're the one who's into . . . ?

JANE: No. I told you. You wouldn't understand.

BARRY: *(Still trying to be concerned.)* Please. I've heard just about every . . . why just last week. I settled a case. We used electronic surveillance to catch the guilty party in the act. The web cam didn't lie.

JANE: I smashed it.

BARRY: Smashed?

JANE: The web cam. The whole computer actually. Into tiny little bits and piece. With a hammer.

(The doors to the train "bing" open. Jane looks up like a startled squirrel. When she discovers the source of the noise, she settles back into her seat.)

VOICE OF CONDUCTOR: 125th Street. All aboard. Please have your tickets ready for collection.

BARRY: Because...?

JANE: All those cutesy emails. The chain letters. The spam. My husband. My family. They won't stop sending them.

BARRY: Did you say hammer?

VOICE OF CONDUCTOR: Express to White Plains. Next stop White Plains.

(Another "bing." The train doors close. Barry begins to put his laptop away into its carrying case. Before he can get it away, Jane grabs the thumb drive from out of it, and swings it around.)

JANE: Junk drives. Down the toilet. All of them. That's why they call them junk, right?

BARRY: Uhh...

JANE: And that i-Pod.

(Jane pulls Barry's i-Pod out of his pocket and uses it for emphasis.)

Tell me, who really needs ten-thousand songs.

BARRY: Ten-thousand does seem like a bit...

JANE: And they think I'm the one who needs help. They think I'm the one who has some sort of problem. That's the part that I don't understand. They're conspiring against me—all these little secret meetings with doctors, and specialists, plotting their intervention... oh yeah, I know all about it. You know, you can never erase an email, no matter how hard you try. When they're the ones who can't stop texting and typing and twittering. They're the ones who are constantly plugged in. Is it possible to divorce all of them? Not just my husband... but mom and dad too? Because they just don't get it. They just don't understand why I had to...

BARRY: *(Trying to get his i-Pod back unsuccessfully.)* Could I just get my...

(As Barry is still trying to get his i-Pod, Jane reaches down for his lap top.)

JANE: ... bury their laptops in the snow.

(Jane grabs Barry's laptop out of his bag.)

BARRY: That doesn't seem entirely . . .

JANE: Internet access, anywhere, anytime . . .

BARRY: Your family might have a point.

JANE: Talking while driving, while walking, while jogging . . . which is why their blue tooths spontaneously combusted.

BARRY: How exactly did they . . . ?

(Barry pulls the blue tooth from around his ear, fumbles with it. But Jane gets it.)

JANE: Lighter fluid.

BARRY: *(He is looking for a strategy to get his things back.)* But your cell phone. You still have your . . .

JANE: *(She strokes her cell phone like it's a pet.)* For now. Because I need it to stop the . . .

BARRY: Conspiracy.

JANE: Yes. Yes! The conspiracy.

BARRY: I see.

JANE: Do you? Do you really see my point of view? Do you really understand what they are doing to me?

BARRY: *(Trying to get on her side, while trying, unsuccessfully to get his things back.)* I do. I really do. They're too tied down. To their gadgets.

JANE: Yes . . . yes . . . that's it! That's it! And its . . . its . . .

BARRY: . . . ruining . . .

JANE: Yes! Ruining!

BARRY: Your life?

JANE: You do understand.

BARRY: Yes. Yes, I do.

JANE: So, can you help me?

BARRY: I . . . uh . . .

JANE: Can you?

BARRY: The thing is . . .

JANE: Yes?

BARRY: Well . . . you see . . . I communicate with all of my clients via email.

JANE: Then . . . then I suppose it wouldn't work out between us.

BARRY: No. I supposed not.

JANE: That's a shame. I could really use a good lawyer.

(*Barry's blackberry begins to buzz again. Jane snatches it away from him. Barry looks at all of his devices, which are now in Jane's possession. Jane takes out a hammer and smiles at Barry. Blackout.*)

Thespian

Chris White

Thespian was originally produced by the Bloomington Playwrights Project (Chad Rabinovitz, Artistic Director) in Bloomington, Indiana, on May 14th and ran through May 29th, 2010. Director—Chad Rabinovitz; Set Design—Shane Cinal; Costume Design—Anne Holen; Lighting Design—Marti Meeker; Sound Design—Jeremiah Walker; Stage Manager—Donna Cohen; Production Stage Manager—Sam McKay. Cast: Caine—Joe Bolinger; Jeffrey—Ben Smith

CHARACTERS

Caine:. . . M/31 years old, Brooklyn boy, dressed uncharacteris-
tically formally.

Jeffrey:. . . M/35 years old, Brooklyn boy, casually dressed.

SETTING AND TIME

A NYC subway train, in the present.

---

*We hear the screaming whoosh of a subway train as it speeds over a
bridge then under the city. When the lights blink on, Jeffrey and Caine
are sitting on a bench on the moving train. Caine has a folder on his
lap and a pen in the pocket of his shirt.*

CAINE: Gimme a cigarette.

JEFFREY: You can't smoke in here, you know that.

CAINE: Well, do somethin, will ya? I'm gonna have a heart attack.

JEFFREY: Jesus, get a grip.

CAINE: *(pause)* You wanna see somethin?

JEFFREY: What?
     *Caine reaches into his folder and pulls out a headshot of
     himself.*

CAINE: *(handing it to Jeffrey)* Eight by ten glossy.

JEFFREY: No fuckin way. When did you do this?

CAINE: Remember that girl, Heather, the barmaid at Hugo's?

JEFFREY: Yeah.

CAINE: She's a photographer. For actors. Gave me a real good price.

JEFFREY: No shit. This is uh . . . what'd you do to your hair in here?

CAINE: That was her idea. It's gel.

JEFFREY: *(handing it back)* Very professional. You oughta give one to
     your mom. Christmas present or somethin.

CAINE: Yeah.
     The subway comes to a stop and the doors open.

JEFFREY: Did you do the resume?

CAINE: I been workin on it. You know.

JEFFREY: Let me see it.

CAINE: Nah. It sucks.

JEFFREY: Let me see it!

> *The subway doors close, and the train starts to move again, as Caine takes his resume from the folder and hands it to Jeffrey.*

JEFFREY (CONT.): *(looking at the resume)* Short. Very short.

CAINE: Give it here!

JEFFREY: Hold on a minute!

> *(perusing the resume)*

What do you have all this roofing and drywalling shit on here?

CAINE: That's what I do, right?

JEFFREY: No. That's not what you do. You're a actor now. You're a thespian.

CAINE: Yeah, fuck you too.

JEFFREY: That means you're in the theater business, moron. You worked as a theater professional your whole life.

CAINE: I never worked as a—

JEFFREY: Wake up, alright? You just put that shit on here. What do you think they're gonna do, call and see if it's true? Give me that pen.

CAINE: Huh?

JEFFREY: Give me the fuckin pen!

> *Caine hands Jeffrey the pen from his pocket.*

JEFFREY (CONT.): . . . Thank you very much. And . . .

> *(slashing left to right with the pen across the resume)*

CAINE: What are you doin, for fuck's sake?!

JEFFREY: We gotta put some acting shit on here or they're gonna kick you right out the door. Whata you done?

CAINE: Nothin. You know that.

> *(pause)*

I was in *Music Man* . . . in junior high.

JEFFREY: Who'd you play?

CAINE: Chorus member.

JEFFREY: Look, we'll make somethin up.

> *(poised to write)*

CAINE: No, that's not right. I can't just lie.

They look at each other a long moment.

JEFFREY: Alright then, do it now.

CAINE: Do what?

JEFFREY: You do it now, it'll be true, right? All the world is a stage. Okay? *Mice and Men.* You wanna be Lenny or George? You know that one?

CAINE: Like in 'Laverne and Shirley' you mean? My ma loved that show.

JEFFREY: Unbelievable. Alright. Listen. Let's be uh . . . *Hamlet.* This, you heard of, right?

CAINE: *Hamlet,* yeah. Shakespeare. I seen the movie with Margaret. It was black and white.

JEFFREY: Alright. So, you know the part about the guy he used to know from when he was a kid, and how he's dead now and he's looking at his skull, and he gets all fucked up about it?

CAINE: I remember the ghost part . . . that's his uncle or his dad or whatever.

JEFFREY: Yeah, his dad. Okay. We're gonna improvise. Just make it up. Then, you can say you done the part. See what I mean?

CAINE: *(not convinced)* Yeah, I guess . . .

JEFFREY: Besides, it'll get you loosened up for the audition. Like a fighter. A little sparring. I'll be the ghost. Okay? You ready?

CAINE: *(uncertain)* What? Just say whatever?

JEFFREY/THE GHOST: Hamlet! You have to avenge my death! Your mother's been fornicating with my brother and they killed me by putting some oil in my ear for poison!

CAINE/HAMLET: . . . Ah, that's . . . You gotta be kiddin me. I always hated that guy. Uh . . . and I really do want to kill him now that you told me this. But . . . to be or not to be. That's what I'm saying. You know?

JEFFREY/THE GHOST: Yes, I do. But you have to try and remember your bloody task and taking care of this avengement for me, alright?

CAINE/HAMLET: That, I shall do, oh Ghost of my father. I'm really sorry this happened and I'm gonna take care of it. You've always been a good guy.

JEFFREY/THE GHOST: May flights of angels bring thee to thy rest!

CAINE/HAMLET: Okay! Good night!

They nod.

Huh?

JEFFREY: That was pretty good.

Caine slaps Jeffrey casually and playfully in the face.

JEFFREY (CONT.):Stop it, you moron.

CAINE: No, that was good, right?

The train comes to a stop and the doors open.

JEFFREY: We should probably do something a little more modern. 'Cause you don't have the way they speak like I do. Can't expect ya to. I seen like a hundred plays with my aunt.

CAINE: You seen a hundred plays?

JEFFREY: Like, a dozen.

CAINE: You should do it.

JEFFREY: I'm the foreman. I don't need a new career.

The doors close, train moves.

JEFFREY (CONT.): You know uh . . . How about we do Willy Loman, and Biff. *Death of a Salesman,* you heard of that?

CAINE: Like what do you mean?

JEFFREY: Or uh . . . Brando. How about Brando in uh . . . the Stella one.

(like Brando)

'Stella!'

CAINE: Yeah, yeah. The Stella one, right.

JEFFREY: On the Waterfront. You be Brando. I'll be Stella. What was the guys' name? . . . Stanley.

CAINE: The Polack! I love that one.

JEFFREY: You begin.

CAINE/STANLEY: *(pause)* Stella! Come on down here, will ya? I gotta get some, otherwise I'm gonna have to fuck your sister. Even if she is nuts and skinny and shit.

JEFFREY/STELLA: Listen, Stanley. I'm always gonna want you, no matter what you do to me, no matter how fucked up you are.

CAINE/STANLEY: That's beautiful, Stella. Listen, I've got some guys comin over to play cards, can you get us somethin to drink?

JEFFREY/STELLA: Yeah, alright, Baby.

CAINE/STANLEY: Alright, Stella. I'll meet you upstairs.

They nod.

CAINE: *(laughing)* That was intense.

Caine holds out his hand for a high five.

JEFFREY: Will you get away from me?

Caine smacks Jeffrey in the face again, playfully.

JEFFREY (CONT.): Stop. You're a moron.

Silence.

CAINE: All these other people are gonna know a lot more about this stuff than I do, I bet ya.

JEFFREY: Well, maybe. But look at Al Pacino. Sean Penn... Both of them are from Brooklyn or somewhere.

CAINE: Yeah?

JEFFREY: Yeah. And they make like a hundred thousand dollars every day. Everybody's an actor in this town.

CAINE: Yeah, 'cause roofin sucks.

Jeffrey nods, and is looking at the resume.

CAINE (CONT.): Dry wall sucks.

JEFFREY: *(writing on the resume with the pen)* On The Waterfront, uh ... Stanley.

> *(pause)*
> *Hamlet.* Uh ...

CAINE: Ah, don't put that in there.

JEFFREY: *(writing)* ... Ghost.

> *(thinking, writing)*
> *Music Man* .... uh ... do you remember that main guy's name?

CAINE: Doolittle? Dr. Doolittle?

JEFFREY: *(writing)* ... Chorus member.

CAINE: Good. That's true. I really did that.

JEFFREY: Yeah, you said.

> *(writing)*
> *Mice and Men* ... uh ...
> *(looking at Caine)*
> ... Lenny.
> *(writes again)*

CAINE: Alright. That's enough. Give it here.

> *Jeffrey hands him the resume.*

CAINE (CONT.): *(looking at it)* Now it's all fucked up.

JEFFREY: Believe me. It's better.

> *Caine drops his head into his hands.*

JEFFREY (CONT.): *(perturbed)* What?

CAINE: I'm not smart. I'm not deep. I'm gonna look like a idiot and then I'm gonna feel worse than I do now. Maybe I shouldn't do this. Ya know? I shouldn't fuckin do this.

JEFFREY: *(like he means it)* You know what? Maybe you shouldn't. *Pause. Caine looks up surprised. Jeffrey continues in his own voice.*

JEFFREY (CONT.): Because the truth is, uh... Biff...

CAINE: Oh, you're doin another—

JEFFREY: *(over him)* ... Maybe you thought life was gonna be easy for you, that things was all set up for you. But now you can't even hold down a real job.

CAINE: You talkin to me or not?

JEFFREY: All you want to do is go off and buy some ranch.

CAINE: Ranch?! Listen, I got a fuckin job. I got let go that last time cause of doin that foreman's girlfriend. That wasn't my fault.

JEFFREY: *(with growing indignation)* Oh, that wasn't your fault? Nothin's your fault! You just shuffle along, but you don't get serious about shit. You notice that? You notice you're fuckin thirty-one years old and you bring a construction resume to a acting audition and I gotta cover your ass? You gotta have something to do for these people. You gotta take off your high school ring and be an adult. You gotta rock their world. Make em feel something! You think you can do that?

Caine looks at him, eyes wide.

JEFFREY (CONT.): Now what the fuck else do you know?!

CAINE: *(still stunned)* ... Jesus, I—

JEFFREY: They did *Anne Frank* your senior year, am I right? I know you saw that. You play Anne Frank.

CAINE: Anne Frank?!

JEFFREY: By yourself, talkin to yourself. Now listen up! You're alone. You're hiding. You're in some box or somethin. You're in a closet. And you haven't had nothin to eat in like... a month. The Nazis are lurkin around outside, shootin off bombs and breakin in everywhere. And you're just a kid. And it's dark in the closet. Now, do it!

CAINE/ANNE: *(pauses, taken aback, thinking on this a moment)* Uh.... I .... Christ, she's like a ten-year old kid.

Jeffrey threatens him with the back of his hand, dead serious.

CAINE/ANNE (CONT.): Alright!
> *(pause)*

Uh... I... I... wish I had somethin to eat. But uh... I don't so... I hear that big, awful noise goin off outside and... I'm scared. Yeah. And I don't wanna hide no more.
> *He looks to Jeffrey who gives him a little nod.*

CAINE/ANNE (CONT.): *(over the course of the monologue, it becomes real for him)* I'm cold, too. When I was a little kid, even littler than this I mean,... people thought I was worth somethin. So I thought that, too. Ya know? I had dinners... I had friends... We was all one thing together. A good thing... But when all this started and they told me we had to hide... because of who we were, I realized they were full of shit before. They musta been lyin to me and holdin back the God awful truth. Not just about me, but about all of us. I wasn't just a bad apple; the whole barrel was bad. Now I can't be who I am outside of this box, or I'm fuckin toast. If I could be somebody else, now, that might work. But I go out there, I stick out like a blinking red light on a dark bridge. I'm never gonna get no better than this. I'm probably never gonna get no older than this, either. And I'm gonna die, like, four feet tall, in the dark, hungry as shit. Or fall, head first into the black water down underneath the bridge. That bridge might as well not even exist.
> *(beat)*

'Cause it don't for me.
> *When he stops, there is silence as Jeffrey looks on, moved.*
> *Then Jeffrey shakes his head.*

CAINE: What?
> *Jeffrey reaches over and, pulling him by both ears, plants a kiss on Caine's cheek.*

CAINE (CONT.): Alright, already...
> *(pause)*

Listen, what ranch?

JEFFREY: Gimme that resume.
> *Caine hands him the paper. Jeffrey writes.*
> *Diary of Anne Frank... Anne.*

CAINE: Come on. They're gonna know I never...

JEFFREY: Fuck that. Keep 'em guessin.

*He hands Caine the resume. Caine puts it in the folder. The
train is slowing.*

JEFFREY (CONT.): 23rd Street's next. You ready?

CAINE: Yeah. Just get me in that ring, right?

Caine gives Jeffrey a playful slap in the face.

JEFFREY: Would you get away from me please? Stand up.

They stand as the train comes to a halt.

CAINE: *(almost to himself)* Christ. I want this. Ya know? For the first
time in my fuckin life.

The doors open.

CAINE (CONT.): Ah, *Streetcar Named Desire!* That's what it was with the
Polack. And here I am gettin off kind of a streetcar right now.

They exit the train.

JEFFREY: Nah. This is just the beginning of that ride, my friend.

CAINE: . . . What do you mean?

Various roughhousing ensues as they walk away.

JEFFREY: Stop.

CAINE: . . . Huh? What do you mean?

JEFFREY: Will you stop, please?

And they're gone.

CAINE: *(O.S.)* Stella!

JEFFREY: *(O.S.)* Will you watch where you're fuckin goin?

Sound of subway. Fade to black. End.

Thursday

Mark Andrew

First performed: Short + Sweet, Sydney 22nd January 2011. Theatre: The Newtown Theatre, cnr King & Bray St, Newtown, NSW, Australia. Producer: Alex Broun. Cast: Tiffany Stoecker (Kate) and Sam Harris (Sam). Director: Jasmine Robertson.

CHARACTERS

Kate: ... 30ish, at a party.
Sam: ... 30ish, at a party.
Crowd: . A crowd of party-goers, as many as practical (heard but
      not seen).

TIME

The present.

PLACE

A party.

---

*AT RISE : A party—drinks in hand, many people babble, so much so
that we can't attend to any one conversation. Kate separates from the
throng, and moves front left. Sam then happens to separate and moves
front right. As they turn and see each other for the first time, the crowd
behind them mute and freeze.*

KATE: Oh...
SAM: *(silence)*
KATE: How very...
     Sam walks towards her, and she meets him halfway.
KATE: I don't believe we've...
     Sam slowly touches her face.
KATE: ...met.
SAM: I would have remembered.
KATE: What's happening?
SAM: I don't know.
KATE: I'm going to have to write this down later. Today's date. Thurs-
    day the 15th. When I first saw you.
SAM: Are you a writer?

KATE: I am now. This is completely unexpected. I feel happy and
    queasy at the same time, like I've eaten too much chocolate.

SAM: That's just the kind of thing I imagined you say.

KATE: Imagined?

SAM: What you'd say when I first met you.

KATE: First met me?

SAM: I didn't know it was going to be you.

KATE: This is completely crazy. Say something.

SAM: What do you want?

KATE: What do I want you to say?

SAM: No. It is what I'm saying. What. Do you. Want.
    There is a stand-off, and then Kate and Sam completely
    blend their sensibilities.

KATE: I don't know what that means.

SAM: What do you want. Just want.

KATE: Like if I won lotto?

SAM: You don't want money.

KATE: No.

SAM: So what do you want?

KATE: *(looks at him intently)*

SAM: It's difficult to imagine, that there are no real obstacles. You can
    just say what you want. To me. I'm listening.

KATE: Okay.

SAM: Okay.

KATE: I want my husband to fall in love.

SAM: I've never heard those words in the same sentence. I guess I
    should have been prepared for a husband.

KATE: I want this, what's going to happen with us, to be painless for
    him.

SAM: That's humane.

KATE: He deserves that. He's been very good to me.

SAM: Fall in love with who?

KATE: Someone who'll make sure he's always strong.

SAM: Is he strong?

KATE: So far.

SAM: Well, sure, today. Thursday. But will he be strong tomorrow?

KATE: No. I don't think so.

SAM: I can just walk away if you'd like.

KATE: No you can't.

SAM: I can't?

KATE: You know very well you can't. I'm going to crush my husband's heart into a pulp. And you. Who are you going to hurt? Is there a wife somewhere here? A girlfriend?

SAM: No.

KATE: Well, that's something.

SAM: She's in Toronto.

KATE: Oh fuck off. That's just random. Where is she?

SAM: Toronto. She's back next week.

KATE: What's she . . . actually, I don't want to know.

SAM: She . . .

KATE: What's wrong? Between you two?

SAM: Nothing.

KATE: That's honest.

SAM: Except you.

KATE: This is so unfair for them. If we'd never met, I mean I would have stayed with him for the rest of my life. I've never been unfaithful.

SAM: It's not our fault.

KATE: I'm totally sure they'll see it that way too.

Sam gets a packet of cigarettes out.

KATE: Oh. Please tell me you're not a smoker.

SAM: Why?

KATE: Because we're about to nuke two perfectly good relationships. And then we're going to live together, and have oodles of lovely sex, and fall in love in that way you do when the sex has calmed down a bit, when you can focus more on the other person, and what they're thinking, or could be thinking, and then we're going to help each other grow, I don't mean any new-age chain-yanking nonsense, I mean, we're going to build some . . . kind of awareness that neither of us has even been conscious of before, and we'll see our children grow up, and get struck by the total wonder of them, these little pieces of you and me, and how it all started, one Thursday evening, and one day years from now you'll turn to me, and look at me, and say this is it, you'll just say, this is it, Kate, we did it.

SAM: Your name's Kate.

KATE: And you'll still be healthy because you don't smoke.

SAM: *(puts cigarettes away)* They're toast.

KATE: If that's what you want.

SAM: Yes, I follow.

KATE: It's just ciggies. You can do anything else. I just want to taste your lips when we kiss for the first time.

SAM: Like you do with your hubbie.

KATE: Okay. Let's do that. My hubbie.

SAM: I'm sorry, I had no right to . . .

KATE: On the contrary, you have every right. We're making what's right.

SAM: Okay. Come on then. Do it quickly. Like pulling a tooth.

KATE: He's lovely. He's good-looking, smart, a good socialiser, great companion, pretty interesting in a generic way . . .

SAM: Sex?

KATE: Yummy.

SAM: Oh god. I don't really want to hear this.

KATE: Yes you do. You need to hear this.

SAM: Yes. Okay.

KATE: He gently wakes me up in the middle of the night, with his fingertips, like a butterfly is landing on my tummy. For weightless, dreaming sex. When your mind doesn't rule your body.

SAM: I don't get it. Why me? And you?

KATE: I have no idea. It's not about sex. Sex is extra.

SAM: So what is it? I can taste you. What you're thinking. What is that?

KATE: If I could answer that I'd bottle it and sell it. But I can tell you right now that I'm going to miss him. Are you strong enough for that?

SAM: I am now. But how do we know this isn't just some artefact? That we've seen in a film or read in a novel somewhere. We don't know one other.

KATE: Language is just something we invented so we could disguise what we're feeling. I know that now. This, here, is like some protein that structures an enzyme. I just sense you. We're not an artefact. It's real. I can see it's real for you.

SAM: Sex isn't extra. I'm imagining your face when we make love.

KATE: Fair enough. We'll work, I'm sure. It will be like jumper leads between our minds. You'll look into my eyes as I lose control.

SAM: You'll start me as I die. La petite mort.

KATE: I will not have Satre by our bedside. Not petite. Grande. Okay. Your turn. Tell me what you'll destroy.

SAM: She's an actress.

KATE: *(grinning)* Stop right there. I totally get you, up to this point.

SAM: *(laughs)*

KATE: *(laughs along)* Is she very beautiful?

SAM: It's not about beauty.

KATE: I'll take that as a yes. It's okay. I sense she's not competition.

SAM: Everybody thinks she's beautiful. Everyone. It's thrilling for me, seeing as how us men play to the gallery so much, constantly seeking approval because, I don't know, we had to struggle for time at mummy's titty or something.

KATE: Oh good, I just knew you'd be a bit weird.

SAM: My friends are going to think I'm nuts.

KATE: Why, thank you kind sir.

SAM: *(laughs)* Until they see me with you.

KATE: Thank you.

SAM: I still can't believe it. I've found you. At some stupid party.
    They consider each other fully, and Kate now touches him.

KATE: I wonder what our first argument will be about?

SAM: Or the colour of their eyes.

KATE: I wonder which friends will stick with us, and which will go with them.

SAM: Oh yeah. I've heard about that. That happens?

KATE: Apparently it's like a cull. You'll end up with half as many, much more earnest friends. And mine will search you, before they let you in. You should be prepared for that.

SAM: What happens now?

KATE: I'll go find my hubbie, and then when we go home I'm going to tell him I've met you. And he's going to ask me who, and then there's going to be an awful lot of shouting and we'll probably both phone in sick tomorrow, and in between all the mess, I'm sorry about this, but we'll probably have pretend make-up sex, which you might as well know will be rather intense which I'll remember later and cry about a lot, and then whenever he looks at me he'll realise I'm thinking about you and after a while, it might be weeks or it might be months, he'll stop himself going mad by telling me he can't go on, because he's not totally daft and then we'll let each other go, properly. I won't see you while this is happening. We won't touch each other until we're single.

SAM: That's right.

KATE: If I detect as much as a molecule of her on you when we undress each other, you will see it in my eyes. You will feel like you've murdered a child if there is any residue, which is why we'll be clean and innocent when we make love for the first time.

Sam looks at her intently, and nods.

KATE: I recommend that you have really, really powerful sex with her at the end. Really hold her. Then she's gone. I will not entertain any overlap. And I will save you from the same. You could say we have an agreement on that—yes?

SAM: Yes. It's only a couple of broken hearts.

KATE: Very good. Keep your eye on the prize. I'm a most excellent lover by the way. You'll be astonished. And you're my last. I'm just saying that because you said it was important to you. I'm thinking of you. I meant what I said. Sex is extra. Really. With you it's going to be a huge extra.

SAM: You. And me.

KATE: Us. Listen. I like it really basic, face to face, frantic, just us. We're complete, just us. You don't need anything else do you?

SAM: I don't need anything else but you.

KATE: Well then that's just dandy. Forget any supplements you have with her. You won't need them. Throw away your porn. Trash your internet bookmarks. Yes, I know about them. Look at me. I believe me have a partnership.

SAM: I'm going to love you.

KATE: That's exactly the right thing to say. You're going to be fine. And I'm going to love you. What's your name?

SAM: *(mesmerised)* I have no idea.

KATE: *(laughs)* It'll come back to you. I'm going to take him home now. And it begins. Now.

Kate rejoins the group, which unfreezes and continues talking loudly. Sam exits, dropping his cigarette pack.

CURTAIN

Waiting for a Fix

Cassandra Lewis

Waiting for a Fix made its world premiere at The American Globe Theatre, 145 W. 46th Street in New York on April 20, 2010. The play was produced by Bastille Arts and was presented as part of the 16th Annual New York City 15 Minute Play Festival presented by American Globe Theatre and Turnip Theater Company. Vanessa Lozano directed. Michael Whitelaw played the role of Fontain and Jonathan Williams played the role of Gary.

Dedicated to my father, Charles Lewis

CHARACTERS

Fontain . . a homeless man in his early twenties
Gary . . . . a homeless man, 38

SETTING

In present time, the play is set on the outskirts of a playground in San Francisco. An empty park bench is center stage and sounds of children playing are heard in the background throughout the play.

(Gary, a homeless man, sits on the ground beside an empty park bench. He faces the audience as he watches the children play in the playground. Sounds of child merriment are heard. After a few moments, Fontain, another homeless man, enters.)

FONTAIN: Hey!
    (Gary ignores him.)
FONTAIN: Hey, Gary!
    (Gary waves and returns his attention to the playground. Fontain approaches.)
FONTAIN: Hey! Didn't you hear me?
    (Gary motions for him to quiet down. Fontain interprets this as an invitation to sit down, so he sits on the park bench.)
GARY: Don't sit there, man.
FONTAIN: Why not?
GARY: Savin' it for someone.
FONTAIN: Who?
GARY: Don't worry about it.
FONTAIN: Tell you what—when your friend gets here I'll give it up.
GARY: All right.
FONTAIN: So whachu doin'?

GARY: Just sittin' here.

FONTAIN: I can *see* that.

GARY: Can't a man just sit and think?

FONTAIN: If you was a philosopher, maybe. But you ain't.

GARY: Must be nice to have it all figured out.

FONTAIN: It is. I'm livin' the life. Just got me a five and I'm fixin' to head over to the liquor store and get me some of that Hurricane.

GARY: They let you in?

FONTAIN: No. Fuckers.

GARY: Then how you gonna get a Hurricane?

FONTAIN: I'll tell you how I *ain't* gonna do it. I ain't gonna ask some broke ass kid who say he old enough when he ain't.

GARY: You gotta let that go, Fontain. That's in the past.

FONTAIN: Stupid ass shopkeeper. Takes one look at that kid and tells him he ain't old enough. The kid gives in and the shopkeeper takes my money anyway. So I go on in. See, I had played by his rules but mothafucka changed the game. So I go on in and tell him he got a choice. See? He can gimme back my money or he can gimme a Hurricane.

GARY: That's where you went wrong. Don't give a man a choice.

FONTAIN: Shit. Ain't that the truth. So that dumb ass mothafucka calls the cops. And they show up like he's the goddamn president and I'm robbin' the national treasury or some shit.

GARY: Cops always make it worse.

FONTAIN: They lookin' at me like I'm some kinda criminal. I ain't askin' for no hand out. I'm just a man lookin' to get fucked up on some cheap ass shit that I pay for. If I wanted to rob his ass I would have.

GARY: Wonder how he can live with himself.

FONTAIN: Oh he livin' fine. He don't think about nobody but hisself.

GARY: Man, he'll get his. I ain't worried.

FONTAIN: How you mean?

GARY: He's in a bad neighborhood. This place gettin' worser by the day.

FONTAIN: You talkin' bout some serious karma shit right there. I know he gonna get his. And I'm gonna laugh my ass off when he do.

GARY: You know what you should do?

FONTAIN: What?

GARY: You should go to a different corner store.

FONTAIN: I been to all of 'em.

GARY: You been to every liquor store in San Francisco?

FONTAIN: And Oakland too.

GARY: You ain't allowed in any of em?

FONTAIN: Nope.

GARY: Me neither.

FONTAIN: Then how you get yours?

GARY: I just know who to ask.

FONTAIN: Shit. I see you get turned down all the time.

GARY: Sure I get turned down. But I keep askin' till somebody takes my money and goes into the store for me. You just gotta keep tryin.' Somebody'll take it.

FONTAIN: You are one determined drinker.

GARY: That ain't all. I used to be into some hardcore shit, but those days are over. You wouldn't have recognized me. There weren't nothin' I wouldn't do for a fix. But I'm a changed man, now. All I need is a forty and a place to sit and I'm happy.

FONTAIN: Good for you.

GARY: You ever try Earthquake? Earthquake is stronger but it's the same price as Hurricane.

FONTAIN: That's what I want to talk to you about.

GARY: Yep. Same price.

FONTAIN: Share it with me.

GARY: What?

FONTAIN: Earthquake.

GARY: No, man, that's all right.

FONTAIN: I know you got some.

GARY: What if I do?

FONTAIN: So share it with me.

GARY: I ain't ready to open it yet.

FONTAIN: Whachu waitin' for?

GARY: Why don't you try the liquor store down on Jones?

FONTAIN: By the hotel where Eddy just died?

GARY: Yeah, I guess he did.

FONTAIN: Is that where you got yours?

GARY: No, I go over to the one across from St. Dominick's.

FONTAIN: The church?

GARY: Yeah. I go over there for lunch and then pick me up some Earthquake cross the street.

FONTAIN: So you ain't gonna share yours?

GARY: I told you I'm waitin.'

FONTAIN: For your friend?

GARY: Nah. Ain't nobody comin.' I'm waitin' til later. That's all.

FONTAIN: Til I'm gone.

GARY: It ain't like that, Fontain. I don't drink in front of the kids.

FONTAIN: What kids?

(Gary points toward the audience, where the playground is. Both men watch.)

FONTAIN: You some kind child molester?

GARY: How you gonna ask me somethin' like that? No, I ain't a child molester. Are you?

FONTAIN: No. I'm still a kid myself. But you ain't. You's an old man.

GARY: I'm only thirty-eight.

FONTAIN: Shit. Street's been hard on you. You look older than time itself.

GARY: Now I really ain't givin' you any of my Earthquake when you gonna ask me if I'm a child molester and tell me I look like a creepy old man.

FONTAIN: I didn't say you was creepy.

GARY: Thanks.

FONTAIN: So if you ain't a child molester why you wanna sit here all day and watch a buncha kids run around on the playground?

GARY: Had a daughter few years back. Keep thinkin' if I look for her, she'll recognize me.

FONTAIN: You never saw her?

GARY: I was in bad shape when she was born. A full blown addict. If it could be had, I had it. Know what I mean? Her mother kicked me out of the house. Once I finally got clean, found out they had moved. I heard from an old friend that they're still in the city. Somewhere.

FONTAIN: You think she'll recognize you?

GARY: I don't know. Maybe. You know how animals have some sixth sense ability to recognize their families? Like from the smell or somethin'?

FONTAIN: Damn, everybody can smell you from across the city.

GARY: I try to always sit near an empty bench so that if she does find me she can have a place to sit. You know, make her more comfortable.

FONTAIN: What will you say to her?

GARY: I'm sorry. That's all. I'll tell her I'm sorry. I just don't want her to think I'm so far gone that I don't think about her every moment of every day.

(Fontain pulls a forty from his jacket and opens it. He hands it to Gary.)

GARY: No thanks.

FONTAIN: My gift to you.

GARY: Nah, that's all right, man. Appreciate what you's tryin' to do, but I don't drink in front of the kids.

FONTAIN: Mind if I do?

GARY: Be my guest. It's a free world.

(Fontain remains on the bench, sipping his forty while Gary continues watching the playground.)

BLACKOUT

Plays for
Three or More Actors

Airborne

Laura Jacqmin

The play was produced in Ensemble Studio Theatre's Marathon 2010, dir. Dan Bonnell, NYC. The cast included Megan Tusing (Private Margaret Jensen), Amy Staats (Commanding Officer), and Brynne Morris, Ed Boroevich and W. Tre Davis (Men).

CHARACTERS

Private Margaret Jensen:. . A woman. 19 years old. Tiny.

Commanding Officer: . . . A woman. Older than Jensen, but not by as much as you'd think. Was she Jensen's commanding officer? Is she trapped in a dream of reliving this moment?

Men: . . . . At least three. Maybe more. Silent. Must be physically strong, and larger than Jensen. Nobody older than mid-thirties.

SET

Maybe a black cube, and nothing else. Or maybe nothing at all.

In regards to staging, the stage directions in the text are open to interpretation. Previous productions have used a cube and fans; a long length of cloth coupled with precise choreography that ended with the men hoisting Jensen just as she hit the ground; or, just the actors themselves. The exploration of how Jensen's fall can be physicalized is encouraged. However, the actress playing Jensen shouldn't actually "fly"—that is, no harness or wire flying should be utilized. The point is that the fall is created in the minds of the audience: don't make it easy on them by literally recreating it.

The characters are all members of the military, but full-on military costuming is not required.

C.O.: Private Margaret Jensen, prepare for your jump.

> (*Jensen mounts a block, her arms at her shoulders like she is gripping a backpack, then out at her sides, as though holding onto the exit door of a plane. She looks down at the ground below her.*
> *A cluster of men appear on all sides of her, holding tiny battery-powered handheld fans. They turn on the fans full-*

force, pointing at her face. The wind whistles through her hair)

Private Jensen, on the count of three, you will jump out of the plane.

You will wait one second, then pull your chute.

Your chute will take you sideways, then back.

And you'll descend to earth, light as a feather.

Private Jensen, are you prepared?

JENSEN: Sir yes sir!

C.O.: One.

Two.

Three!

(Jensen "jumps." Her arms out for a second, like she is flying)

Then, disaster.

The chutes are designed for much heavier recruits. Private Margaret Jensen, you're only a little over one hundred pounds.

You are whipped one direction, towards the fuselage. This is the way it's supposed to happen.

Then you are whipped the other direction, back towards your original drop. This, too, is the way it's supposed to happen.

But your chute gets tangled in itself. That's not supposed to happen.

And suddenly, in the space of a second, Private Margaret Jensen, you are descending to the earth, light as a feather –

Head first.

(Jensen is whipped to the left. Then, to the right. Her chute is tangled.

She repositions herself on the block, now "falling headfirst."

The MEN re-direct their fans so that they are blowing above her, down into her face)

Private Jensen, what are you thinking in this moment?

JENSEN: I'm thinking—I should have eaten the cake.

The cake the Army gives us at every meal, I should have eaten it to gain weight.

The wind in my face.

I'm going down so slowly.

Why am I going down so slowly?

C.O.: Your chute is still functioning perfectly.

It only feels slow. There'll be no sudden drop. You'll coast on the wind.

> *(Beat)*

Try to pull yourself up.

> Right now! Pull yourself up! If you land on your back, there'll be something to work with. If you land on your back, there'll be options.
>
> Just don't land on your head, Private Jensen.
>
> Pull yourself up!

> *(Jensen struggles to pull herself up. She is unsuccessful)*

JENSEN: I can't.

> The chute.
>
> It's tangled.
>
> My feet –
>
> I can't.

C.O.: Call for help.

JENSEN: HELP ME.

> *(Silence)*

I can see—I can see the other guys from Airborne. They're going down all around me.

> They're looking at me.

C.O.: What's on their faces? What are they thinking?

JENSEN: I think they would help me, if they could. I think they would.

> I see the guy from Mundelein County—he was in my Basic unit. He called me a cunt. He made fun of me when I had to carry my tampons on the Victory Forge march.
>
> He called me –
>
> I can see his face. Even from far away, I can see his face and he can see mine and –

> *(Jensen is breathing more quickly)*

C.O.: What are you thinking, Private Jensen?

JENSEN: I'm thinking about Gustavus Adolphus College in St. Peter, Minnesota.

I was supposed to go. I was all set to go.

> Just a few years. Just a tour or two.
>
> Gustavus Adolphus College.
>
> Winters in Minnesota.
>
> Scarves and lecture halls and chapel on Sunday.

I was supposed to go. I didn't tell anyone. It was my secret.

C.O.: Take deep breaths, Private Jensen. Try to stay calm.

JENSEN: I just wanted to be a good soldier.

I didn't want to be a slut or a dyke or a bitch, and those are the only three choices they give you.

C.O.: You're not a bitch.

JENSEN: Thank you.

C.O.: You're not a dyke.

JENSEN: Thank you.

C.O.: You're not a slut.

(Silence)

Private Jensen?

JENSEN: The guy from Mundelein—he's going down the same rate as I am. I can see him. He's opposite me, but twenty yards apart.

He's swimming. With his arms, he's swimming.

He's trying to get over to me.

I've seen it before—their chute fails, some guys grab another guy's ankles—they go down on the same chute, together.

It works. I've seen it work.

He wants to get to me. He wants to get to me!

C.O.: Private Jensen –

JENSEN: On Victory Forge, he called me a cunt and he made fun of my tampons and he opened one of my trash bags and he threw it all over the ground and there was blood on the dirt and I was so ashamed of bleeding, I wanted to die, and that night I snuck into his ruck and I fucked him and it was great and we never talked after that, he never told anyone, and I can see him, swimming, great strokes towards me across the sky but he's just staying in one place, stationary, and he keeps looking down at the ground and it's coming up too fast and he's turning red and I think I'm going to die.

C.O.: You're not going to die.

JENSEN: I'm so scared. I'm so scared it's going to hurt. I'm scared I'm going to scream and I don't want to scream in front of the guy from Mundelein County.

And all I wanted was to be strong and brave and go to Gustavus Adolphus College in St. Peter, Minnesota, with the lecture halls and the scarves and the stone benches in the courtyards and so I didn't mind doing a tour or two in a foreign place because I knew I would be rewarded.

I'm supposed to be rewarded.

C.O.: Private Jensen, you're very near the ground. You're very close.

JENSEN: I want to close my eyes. Can I close my eyes?

C.O.: Close your eyes. Close them tight.

JENSEN: Don't let me scream. I don't want to scream,

C.O.: I won't.

JENSEN: The guy from Mundelein County? We never talked after, but I haven't gotten my period since Victory Forge and I was going to do something about it, I really was, but I just thought I should get through Airborne and then we would talk about it and then we would figure something out but I don't want you to tell him, okay?

Don't tell him.

C.O.: I won't.

JENSEN: Any second. Any second. Any second. Any second.

(Beat)

Any second.

(Beat. Jensen shuts her eyes tight, tenses her body. Silence. Then she screams. Once. Loud. Then nothing.

The fans go off.

Jensen climbs onto the C.O.'s shoulders, her arms hanging around her neck: C.O. is heavily weighed down)

C.O.: Private Margaret Jensen, you died in the ambulance on the way back to the base.

You were nineteen years old.

JENSEN: You promised you wouldn't let me scream.

C.O.: I'm sorry.

JENSEN: You promised me you wouldn't tell.

C.O.: I'm sorry.

JENSEN: You promised you would be strong and brave and you failed.

C.O.: I'm sorry.

JENSEN: I forgive you. But I'm never going away.

Okay?

I'm always going to be here.

I'm never going away.

(Jensen hangs around the C. O.'s neck. Her body has the weight of a stone. C. O. sags. And sags. And sags.

MEN look on.

Lights out)

Amenities

Gregory Hischak

Amenities was first produced as part of the Firehouse Theater's New Works Festival (Newburyport MA) in January, 2010 with Stephen Faria, Kari Nickou, Irene Sanders and Stephen Turner, directed by Anne Smith. Amenities was also staged as part of the 2010 Source Festival (Wash. D.C.) in June–July 2010 with Kevin Hasser, Anastasia Wilson, Filipe Cabezas and Charity Pomery, directed by Jason Schlafstein.

TIME

The Present

SETTING

An opulent loft condominium in an American city in the present day.

CHARACTERS

(all of comparable age anywhere from Mid-30s to Mid-50s)

Claudia . . Married to Martin and a resident of the Bohemian
          Condominiums
Martin . . Married to Claudia and a resident of the Bohemian
          Condominium
Leah . . . . their dinner guest
Morris. . . an artist in residence

Pre-dinner drinks at Claudia and Martin's condominium. While various features of the flat will be commented upon, the only relevant onstage feature is the dinning room table under which Morris squats quietly sketching away at something on a pad of paper.

CLAUDIA: And it's only four blocks from Martin's firm.

LEAH: Why, you could walk to work from here.

CLAUDIA: He could.

          (All laugh.)

MARTIN: Of course, I drive.

CLAUDIA: He drives.

LEAH: Of course.

CLAUDIA: Martin likes his driving.

          (Leah moves downstage to gaze out a window.)

LEAH: Just look at that view from here.

MARTIN: Mountains, Sound, City—

CLAUDIA: A million dollar view.

MARTIN: A one-point-three million dollar view, actually.

LEAH: Can you see the ...um...

MARTIN: Space Needle?

CLAUDIA: Bay Bridge?

MARTIN: Palisades?

CLAUDIA: Lake?

LEAH: Mountain from here?

MARTIN: Mountain ...um... *(Unsure.)* no, we're facing the opposite direction.

LEAH: Which direction is that?

MARTIN: Is what?

LEAH: The direction we're facing?

MARTIN: Um...

CLAUDIA: Leah, you're always getting all directional on us.

LEAH: *(Gesturing toward view.)* That one there—that's ...Mount ...?

CLAUDIA: Mount...

MARTIN: Um ...what's the name of that...

CLAUDIA: That big...

LEAH: Mountain.

MARTIN: Thing.

CLAUDIA: I suppose it must be...

(Awkward fidgety beat.)

MARTIN: Fifteen-foot exposed brick walls.

CLAUDIA: Floor to ceiling windows.

LEAH: It's really a remarkable place.

MARTIN: Refurbished hardwood floors—

CLAUDIA: Paint-splattered refurbished hardwood floors.

LEAH: It's so...

CLAUDIA: That's genuine paint splatter.

LEAH: And what's this building called again?

CLAUDIA: The Bohemian.

LEAH: Well, I was going to say—it's all so ...bohemian.

MARTIN: Another drink, Leah?

LEAH: No thank you, I'm fine—

MARTIN: The appreciation.

LEAH: Appreciation?

CLAUDIA: The appreciation.

MARTIN: It's been excellent.

CLAUDIA: Up, up, up.

MARTIN: One-point-three.

LEAH: What's it like living Downtown?

MARTIN: *(Sternly.)* Uptown.

CLAUDIA: Midtown.

MARTIN: *(Sternly.)* Uptown.

CLAUDIA: We're midtown.

LEAH: All those quaint little shops and bistros.

CLAUDIA: We don't get out all that much. Martin is—

MARTIN: Busy.

CLAUDIA: That's genuine paint splatter, you know.

LEAH: It's all so Left Bank—Rive Gauche.

MARTIN: *(Sternly.)* Uptown, Leah.

CLAUDIA: Isn't it amazing what a little gentrification will do to a big drafty warehouse?

MARTIN: Sorry that Stokely couldn't join us.

CLAUDIA: Yes, Leah, that's a pity.

LEAH: Well you know, his job. . .

MARTIN: His position, of course.

LEAH: It keeps him, you know. . .

CLAUDIA: Away.

LEAH: Gone.

MARTIN: Where is he off to these days?

LEAH: He's been sent to . . . he's in . . . *(Beat.)* Actually, I have no idea where Stokely is.
> *(Awkward beat.)*

MARTIN: And of course secured off-street parking.

CLAUDIA: I just love secured parking.

LEAH: And all those copies of Art in America—?

MARTIN: Genuine.

CLAUDIA: Not back issues.

MARTIN: No, current.

LEAH: Do they have pictures?

MARTIN: I would imagine—I haven't got around to—

CLAUDIA: Martin is always too busy doing, you know, his job.

MARTIN: The firm . . .

CLAUDIA: Busy.

MARTIN: Economy, right?

LEAH: Economy.

MARTIN: The economy of place. How's dinner coming along, Claudia?

CLAUDIA: It should be here any minute. Isn't it wonderful that they can take a seedy bit of Midtown—

MARTIN: *(Sternly.)* Uptown.

CLAUDIA: —and make it a nice place for, you know, real people.
    (They all take a very long drink in silence.)

LEAH: So . . . if I may ask . . . who's that man under your table?

MARTIN: The dining table?

LEAH: That table right there.

CLAUDIA: The one with the man under it?

LEAH: I was just wondering about—

CLAUDIA: It's from Dania.

LEAH: It's lovely. And the man under it?

MARTIN: Oh, him.

CLAUDIA: He's our artist.
    (Beat.)

LEAH: He's your what?

CLAUDIA: He's our artist. Bona fide.

LEAH: Is he here for dinner?

CLAUDIA: Nooo—he came with the condo.

MARTIN: He's an amenity.

LEAH: Your loft condo came with its own artist?

CLAUDIA: Every unit in this building has an artist.

MARTIN: The consultant across the hall has a bronze caster.

CLAUDIA: The unit below us has a monoprint artist.

MARTIN: Which unit?

CLAUDIA: 406.

MARTIN: 406 has an organic abstractionist.

CLAUDIA: The organic abstractionist is in 411.

MARTIN: Claudia, I saw him being installed—it's an organic abstractionist.

LEAH: Is that why this building is called The Bohemian?

MARTIN: You know, I never though of it that way, Leah. The Bohemian—my god, yes!

CLAUDIA: Well you can't have them standing out on the street—right?

MARTIN: They go all riff-raff on you.

LEAH: Our place had an old Swedish woman in the laundry. She'd lived there for years—but Stokely had her . . . you know, removed.

CLAUDIA: I can understand that.

LEAH: It just didn't seem right.

MARTIN: Swede? No it wouldn't.

LEAH: *(Gestures toward MORRIS.)* So, he's a real artist?

MARTIN: Of course he's a real artist.

CLAUDIA: Genuine.

MARTIN: Not established.

CLAUDIA: No representation—but genuine.

LEAH: What does he do?

MARTIN: Figurative works in oil pastels.

LEAH: Figurative works in oil pastels?

CLAUDIA: And off-street parking! Don't you just love it?

LEAH: Are these his works you have hanging?

CLAUDIA: Yes, they're so . . . figurative, aren't they?

LEAH: *(To Morris.)* Hello? *(No response from Morris.)*

CLAUDIA: Martin has him working on a landscape.

MARTIN: A seascape—to go with the couch.

LEAH: A figurative seascape?

CLAUDIA: Bona fide.

LEAH: *(To Morris.)* Hello? How are you? *(To Martin and Claudia.)* He doesn't say much, does he?

MARTIN: He broods a lot.

CLAUDIA: We're thinking of having him serviced, aren't we Martin?

LEAH: Maybe that's just how they are?

MARTIN: Brooding.

CLAUDIA: Artistic.

> *(Beat as they all take a long drink, observing Morris under the table.)*

LEAH: So, you keep him under the table?

MARTIN: Claudia likes him out here.

CLAUDIA: Well, originally, he was under the kitchen disposal.

MARTIN: He fit fine under the disposal.

CLAUDIA: He didn't fit under the disposal, Martin.

MARTIN: The glassblower in 312 fits under their disposal, Claudia.

CLAUDIA: Well, I moved him out here next to the ficus—you know, for the light—but Martin kept tripping over him.

MARTIN: A stupid place for an artist. Another drink, Leah?

LEAH: I've heard that artists like light.

CLAUDIA: I think he does better out here. *(The sound of a buzzer.)* Oh, there's the door. Dinner is here, everyone. Lemon Tarragon Chicken is on its way up. *(Claudia exits.)*

LEAH: *(To Morris.)* Hello?

MARTIN: So, how are things at Stokely's firm, Leah?

LEAH: Oh you know, busy, busy, busy. The firm keeps him managing...

MARTIN: Projects?

LEAH: Yes, projects.

MARTIN: Is he a Project Manager?

LEAH: I think so. I mean ... well, I've never actually ... asked. *(Gesturing to Morris.)* He needs a shave doesn't he?

MARTIN: That's how artists look—the males anyway. It's damn difficult getting a female oil pastel painter—the one they had on the sixth floor just didn't have the view.

(Claudia enters screaming.)

CLAUDIA: *(Up.)* This is just horrible. They didn't send up the Lemon Tarragon Chicken. I ordered the Lemon Tarragon Chicken but they sent Cashew Salmon instead. How could they do this? How can people be so ... so heartless?

(Claudia sobs.)

LEAH: It's an outrage.

MARTIN: Sheer incompetence. This is the third time they've messed up Lemon Tarragon Chicken. Let me take a look. Leah, help yourself to another drink.

(A beat as Martin and Claudia exit.)

LEAH: Hello. *(Leah extends her hand somewhat awkwardly under the table.)* I'm Leah.

MORRIS: Morris.

(They shake hands.)

LEAH: Pleased to meet you, Morris. You're the artist for this unit?

MORRIS: Yes.

LEAH: How fortunate for you.

MORRIS: Well, it used to be my studio.

LEAH: Really? You're installed in your very own studio! It must be very satisfying.

MORRIS: It beats delivering Lemon Tarragon Chicken.

LEAH: That is such a good attitude—you know, there are probably a lot of artists who don't even have a table to sit under.

MORRIS: You're in my light.

LEAH: Sorry. *(Leah moves to the other side of the table.)* So, you used to live here?

MORRIS: We all did.

LEAH: We?

MORRIS: All the artists in this building.

> *(Leah observes what Morris has been drawing.)*

LEAH: That's lovely.

MORRIS: Thank you.

LEAH: There isn't very much color, though.

MORRIS: It's atonal.

LEAH: That's like a landscape, right?

MORRIS: It's a visual meditation on place and identity.

LEAH: It's gray. Couldn't you make it a more colorful atonal landscape?

MORRIS: There's color underneath.

LEAH: There is?

MORRIS: See the green ... there, and ... there?

> *(Claudia is heard wailing offstage as Martin re-enters.)*

MARTIN: Listen Leah, Claudia is in a bit of a state with the chicken mess-up. We'll need to reset the table from chickenware to salmonware and so dinner is a little delayed. Were you just talking to that artist under the table?

LEAH: We were just discussing his work.

MARTIN: His work? He doesn't work. He's an artist.

MORRIS: *(To Leah.)* I'm an amenity.

MARTIN: *(To Morris.)* What are you doing?

LEAH: It's an atonal.

MARTIN: Where's the goddamned green?

LEAH: It's a visual meditation on ... um ...

MORRIS: Place.

LEAH: Place and`. . .

MORRIS: Identity.

MARTIN: I told you we wanted a seascape for over the couch. Something green.

LEAH: He says there's green underneath—

MARTIN: I get a goddamned green seascape or it's back under the sink with you.

MORRIS: The monochromatic palette suggests an emotional and moral isolation—

MARTIN: *(Up.)* What part of under the sink don't you understand?

(Claudia re-enters sobbing.)

CLAUDIA: I'm dressed for Lemon Tarragon Chicken—but there is no Lemon Tarragon Chicken.

LEAH: Maybe there's something salmon you could change into?

CLAUDIA: *(Sobbing.)* It has a dill sauce.

MARTIN: Let's make the best of this situation, everybody. Claudia, find something to wear that goes with salmon. Don't worry about the dill sauce—we're all friends here.

LEAH: That's right.

MARTIN: I'm going to look for the salmon napkins in the kitchen. Leah, help yourself to another drink. *(Turning to Morris.)* Green like the fucking couch. Got it?

(Claudia and Martin exit. Beat as Leah continues looking at Morris' picture.)

MORRIS: They're in the drawer marked "Salmon napkins."

LEAH: Really?

MORRIS: He'll never find them.

(Leah giggles.)

LEAH: I think that's a lovely picture. A lovely . . . visual meditation on . . .

MORRIS: Place.

LEAH: And identity. I can see the green underneath. *(Gesturing.)* There . . . and right there.

MORRIS: Very good.

LEAH: Is it difficult being an artist?

MORRIS: Not really.

LEAH: I mean, you don't seem to get a lot of . . .

MORRIS: Respect?

LEAH: I was going to say money.

MORRIS: I was going to say respect.

    (Beat.)

LEAH: It's hard sometimes, isn't it . . . to find a place in this world?

MORRIS: I've always managed to find one.

LEAH: Under the table?

MORRIS: Like you said, I'm lucky to have a table. What about you?

LEAH: Me?

MORRIS: What's your place like?

LEAH: Our building?

MORRIS: Your place.

    (Beat.)

LEAH: My place? *(Beat before indicating Morris' picture.)* You know, I think what you have there is a lot nicer than some dumb seascape.

MORRIS: It is a seascape.

    (They share a smile. Leah moves downstage to gaze out the window while a brief commotion between Claudia and Martin rises and subsides offstage.
    Leah turns toward Morris.)

LEAH: Morris, what di—?

MORRIS: We're facing north.

LEAH: North? Thank you. *(Beat.)* It's a nice light.

MORRIS: I like it.

    (Beat.)

LEAH: Do you know the name of that mountain?

    (To black.)

    (End of play.)

Bemused

Mrinalini Kamath

Performed July 6–8, 2010, by Legros Cultural Arts at Theatre 54 at Shetler Studios, New York, NY. Directed by Chantal M. Legros. Cast: Paul—Stephen Hadeed Jr./Edward Freeman; Helen—Morgan Faulkner; Ana— Taeonna Ancrum.

CHARACTERS

Paul: . . . . Male, writer/bartender, thirties.

Anna:. . . . . Female muse, twenties

Helen: . . . . Female muse, forties.

Female Customer: . . Twenties or thirties (we don't necessarily need to see this character—she can be an off-stage voice).

SETTING

Bar in Manhattan.

TIME

The present.

Setting: A bar. Paul, the bartender, is closing up for the night. He appears to be wishing off-stage customers good night.

PAUL: *(calling)* Good night!

(He comes back into the bar and notices one female customer still lingering as she puts on her coat).

PAUL: *(firmly)* Good night.

FEMALE CUSTOMER: She liked making kites because it was a way for her to fly.

(She smiles at him invitingly).

PAUL: Uh-huh. 'Night.

(Still smiling, she shrugs and leaves. Paul locks the door and comes back to the bar. He loosens his collar a bit, and then reaches over the bar for a bottle of liquor and pours himself a drink. Then he reaches over again and pulls out a laptop computer and sits at the bar and begins to write. As he writes, he speaks aloud).

PAUL: Some days, it didn't seem so bad. Some days, it was actually more than bearable...

...and some days, she thought that the stench of wilting lettuce would make her vomit.

(He pauses for a moment, tapping his fingers, as if stuck. Then we hear the voice of a young woman. As she speaks, Paul hurriedly begins to type).

YOUNG WOMAN: *(OS)* There were days when she wondered—as every immigrant does—why had she come here? Had things really been all that terrible, back home?

(At this point, the young woman enters slowly. She sits on the bar, cross-legged, and continues to speak what he is writing. She is dressed in a minimalist style, maybe even entirely in black, with no jewelry).

PAUL: She liked making kites because it was a way for her to fly.

YOUNG WOMAN: What?

PAUL: Nothing—sorry.

YOUNG WOMAN: No, what did you —

PAUL: Sorry—stray thought. Let's continue.

(Anna looks at him).

YOUNG WOMAN: You're sure it's just a stray thought?

PAUL: Of course—let's get back to the story.

YOUNG WOMAN: Because if there's something else that you'd rather be writing —

PAUL: No, no! Let's get back to the story.

YOUNG WOMAN: Shit. Where were we?

PAUL: Uh... "had things really been all that terrible, back home?"

YOUNG WOMAN: Oh, right. Yes, there was more freedom here, but SO much more work.

WOMAN: *(OS)* What are you writing?

(Another woman, older than the first and much more flashily dressed, suddenly enters).

WOMAN: *(to Paul)* Finally! Do you know how long I've been searching for you? Are you writing fiction?

(To Anna)

And who the hell are you?

YOUNG WOMAN: *(to Paul)* Who is this person?

WOMAN: I'll tell you who I am, honey. I'm Helen—Paul's muse.

(Young woman looks at Paul, puzzled. He is staring intently at his computer screen).

YOUNG WOMAN: But . . . I am his muse.

HELEN: Uh, Paulie? Would you care to set this young lady—I'm sorry, what's your name?

YOUNG WOMAN: Anna.

HELEN: Right—Paulie—would you please set Anna straight?
(She takes in what he's wearing and where they are).

HELEN: Are you a bartender?

ANNA: What's wrong with that?

HELEN: Nothing. Just curious. When he was going through his poet phase, he was a garbage man for about a week.

ANNA: "Poet phase"?

HELEN: *(to Paul)* So—now that you've gotten whatever you needed to get out of your system out of your system—when are you coming back to LA?

ANNA: LA? As in Los Angeles?

HELEN: The one and only.

ANNA: *(to Paul)* You told me that you were from the Midwest.

HELEN: Only if the Valley counts as Midwestern LA.

ANNA: You were a playwright in Los Angeles?

HELEN: The playwright phase lasted a little longer—about a month. I think he worked as a temp when he was a playwright. Free paper, printing and a postage machine—right, Paulie?

ANNA: Paul? Are you going to explain what's—

HELEN: I am his muse—have been for the past five years. We've been working his way up as a screenwriter. Or at least we would be, if *someone* didn't keep thinking that the grass is always greener in another genre, and kept switching, instead of actually finishing something.
(Anna stares at Paul, who keeps avoiding eye contact).

ANNA: You told me you were a playwright who was tired of the boundaries of the stage—that you wanted to write fiction because the ideas you had were for the mind's eye, not the stage.

HELEN: Wow, Paul—you really sold her a bill of goods. I should be mad at you, trying to switch genres AND muses, but I can forgive one youthful indiscretion. When are we leaving?

PAUL: We're not.

> *(Pause).*

HELEN: Excuse me?

> *(Paul finally looks at her).*

PAUL: Look—Helen—there's a reason why I left you and LA.

HELEN: Paul—whatever it is, we'll work it out when we get back, like we always do.

PAUL: No—we can't. What's there for me with screenwriting? Is what I write going to end up being what's on the screen? Is my name even going to be on it?

HELEN: Paul—we've had this discussion before—you work your way up to that point. Hell, if you'd stick with a project, we'd be there by now. We can talk about this when we're back, or even on the way back to—

PAUL: I'm not going back to L.A.

HELEN: You're . . . you're leaving me?

PAUL: I guess so.

HELEN: No, no, you do not *guess* so. You are or you aren't—which is it, Paulie?

> *(Pause).*

PAUL: I'm leaving you. I want to be with Anna.

ANNA: But I don't want to be with you.

PAUL: What?

ANNA: You lied to me, Paul. I can't build a musal relationship with someone based on a foundation of lies.

PAUL: Anna—

ANNA: And how could you just dump her, Paul? It's a long-term relationship you enter into—inspiration for loyalty and loyalty for inspiration—

PAUL: But I don't want her inspiration, I want—

ANNA: Then you talk to her about what you want, you don't just take off in the middle of the night without a word!

PAUL: She doesn't understand—

HELEN: Hello! I am standing right here!

PAUL: *(to Helen)* Fine—*you* don't understand, you never did! Every time I'd try to talk to you about it, you would change the subject.

ANNA: Then you try harder, and if it still doesn't work, you take some time off, you don't just jump into a new working relationship with another muse. And you certainly don't start that new relationship with a bunch of lies.

PAUL: I'm sorry, but it wasn't like that—

HELEN: Well then, how was it? This I'd like to hear.

PAUL: It was around the time that I started draft number 20 of Eclipse: Darkness Everlasting.

ANNA: *(softly)* When I first began searching . . .

PAUL: And . . . and at first, I tried to get rid of them. I had a deadline, after all, and all these words, these visions that had nothing to do with the script, or even movies, they just kept coming. And then, something, the rhythm of the language, the richness of the visions . . . I just—I couldn't help myself, all right? I had to write it all down!

HELEN: Well, that explains why *that* script was never finished.

ANNA: *(to Paul)* You should have told me that you were someone else's, that you were unavailable for my prose.

PAUL: I know. But I didn't want to.

HELEN: No goodbye OR thanks.

PAUL: Look: I just want to see my name on something in print, on a story, at least, maybe even a book—

HELEN: The gods gave you a talent, Paul. You are a very good screenwriter. You'd be an amazing one, if you just sat down and finished something, instead of constantly chasing dreams in other genres where frankly, you're just not as talented.

PAUL: Then how come I can write with Anna? Maybe it's not the talent, maybe it's the muse.

ANNA: I'm leaving.

PAUL: No, please! Look—I swear, going forward, 100% honesty, truth.

ANNA: I'll never know if I can believe you. Besides—what if you do to me what you did to her?

PAUL: I will never leave you.

ANNA: "She liked making kites because it was a way for her to fly?"

PAUL: That was nothing! I told you, it was just a . . . just a stray thought.

ANNA: Uh-huh. Is that what you told her?

(She motions to Helen).

PAUL: Look: Helen is a good muse, I'm sure she'll find someone else—

ANNA: Like you did?

(Anna walks over to the door).

ANNA: Out of curiosity—was Helen even your first?

HELEN: Of course I was.

(Paul says nothing, looking steadfastly at his computer screen)

HELEN: Paul?

(Paul still doesn't respond).

ANNA: Thought as much. Goodbye, Paul.

PAUL: Wait! Please don't go! At least stay long enough to finish the story, if nothing else. That can be my new beginning, my spark—

ANNA: No. Goodbye.

(She exits).

HELEN: I shouldn't wish you luck, but I will. It's a small universe—I doubt any muse will want to touch you with a ten-foot pole.

(She starts to exit).

PAUL: Wait a minute. You're leaving me?

(Helen just looks at him).

PAUL: Look, that was just—can't we start over, pretend that all of this, everything, never happened, start clean, fresh? You came back to get me, you can have me back!

HELEN: No.

(He reaches for her hand).

PAUL: I won't do it again, I swear. You can still inspire me, Helen. Please. Help me finish this.

HELEN: Goodbye, Paul.

(She exits. Paul just sits there, alone).

PAUL: Fine! You know what? Fuck you! Fuck you BOTH, I don't need you, you . . . you just jumpstarted me—I can finish this on my own! Muses are completely overrated!

(He turns back towards his laptop, opens it and stares at the screen. After a few seconds, he taps his fingers on the bar. He keeps tapping and staring at the screen.
He pours himself another drink, and waits. He takes a sip).

PAUL: *(Calling)* Hello? Is anyone there?

> *(Silence. He stares at the computer screen).*

PAUL: *(tentative)* She liked making kites because it was a way for her to fly?

> *(He waits, hopeful, anticipating. Silence).*

PAUL: Shit.

> *(Blackout. End of Play).*

Best Friends

Jenny Lyn Bader

Best Friends was first produced in May 2010 at Pine Crest High School in Ft. Lauderdale, FL as part of Spring Scenes. Directed by Jim Patrick. Cast: Valerie—Samantha Topper; Larry—Pernell Myers; Denise—Vanessa Chalem. It was also performed in February 2009 in the Nantucket Short Play Festival in Nantucket, MA, where it received a staged reading as part of Cupid's Nightmare. Directed by Janet Forest. Cast: Valerie—Susan Beaumont; Larry—Christy Kickham; Denise—Janet Forest.

Best Friends was first read in February 2009 at a benefit for Women's Expressive Theater in New York City. Directed by Abby Epstein. Cast: Valerie—Emmanuelle Chriqui, Larry—John Lloyd Young; Denise—Sabine Singh.

CHARACTERS

Valerie. . . Thirties or so.
Larry. . . . Thirties or so; the same age as Valerie
Denise. . . Thirties—near the others in age but can be younger.

SETTING

A table in a cozy restaurant.

TIME

That part of the afternoon when even the best lunches start to end.

Valerie, Larry, and Denise are finishing lunch. Valerie is mid-anecdote.

VALERIE: You know what he did next?

LARRY: Valerie. Don't.

DENISE: What? What did he do?

LARRY: I don't believe this.

VALERIE: He showed Miss Bellamy the tattoo on his nipple!

LARRY: Christ, Valerie.

DENISE: And did she think it was real?

VALERIE: Now he was sure she was going to faint—that's the whole reason we went shopping for the stick-on tattoos in the first place, we were like, you know, tired of drinking beer and playing practical jokes on each other's cats, whatever. It was—sort of a "What If"—"What if we would make our teacher faint?"

DENISE: So did she?

LARRY: She did not.

VALERIE: What she did was lift her shirt. And Miss Bellamy had a tattoo on her bellybutton. And hers was real.

DENISE: *No!*

VALERIE: *Yes.*

DENISE: This is the science teacher with the Laura Ashley outfits and the pearls?

VALERIE: Yes. Exactly. You're paying attention *(to Larry)* She pays attention, that's an excellent quality in a woman. And... that wasn't all.

DENISE: No!

VALERIE: Yes.

DENISE: Miss Bellamy did *not* have a bellybutton ring.

(Valerie, delighted, lets out a peal of laughter.)

VALERIE: How did you guess that? No one's ever guessed that! Larry must have told you this story.

LARRY: I never tell anyone this story. Denise, do you want some more eggplant?

DENISE: No I'm fine, sweetheart. So what happened then?

VALERIE: Larry fainted.

(Denise and Valerie burst out laughing. Denise gets up, out of breath.)

DENISE: *(to Valerie)* So great to meet you. So great. Can't believe I have to go back to the office. But you guys have to talk about me anyway.

VALERIE: Very considerate of you.

DENISE: You *(kisses Larry)* I'll see later. You *(kisses Valerie on both cheeks)* I'll see soon. Bye—

(Denise exits.)

LARRY: She'll see you "soon"? What did she mean by that?

VALERIE: I don't know. I'll see her soon.

LARRY: So.

VALERIE: So.

LARRY: So?

VALERIE: So.

LARRY: So what do you think?

VALERIE: What do I think.

LARRY: Do you approve?

(A beat.)

VALERIE: I really like her.

LARRY: *(relieved)* I knew you guys would get along.

VALERIE: She's amazing. She's a great person. And smart. And funny. Good funny.

LARRY: Yeah. I can't believe I was so worried. I think that's why it took me so long to introduce you—besides the obvious—I think I was nervous you wouldn't like her.

VALERIE: I really like her. And she's so beautiful too. I mean you said she was attractive but you didn't convey her level of beauty.

LARRY: She has a level of beauty?

VALERIE: Like if she weren't short, she could totally be a model.

LARRY: You think so? Yeah. Or she could just be a short model.

VALERIE: Petite model.

LARRY: Whatever. I am just so . . . I can't believe I was so worried. I'm so glad you approve. I would hate to have a girlfriend and have my best friend not approve.

VALERIE: I didn't say I approved.

LARRY: What?

VALERIE: Actually. I kind of don't approve.

LARRY: But you said you liked her!

VALERIE: I do like her.

LARRY: But?

VALERIE: But that doesn't mean she's appropriate for you.

LARRY: She's . . . not appropriate for me?

VALERIE: I mean, you can like two people, and they can like each other, and they can still be . . . completely wrong for one another.

LARRY: We're—wrong? Completely?

VALERIE: Just a first impression, Larry. That's all. I just don't see it. But it's you who has to date her.

LARRY: Valerie. You're my oldest friend. My best friend. We've always been here for each other. Be straight with me. What's wrong with her? I thought you guys got along so well.

VALERIE: We did!

LARRY: So, why are we—so wrong?
      (Beat.)

VALERIE: She's too good for you.

LARRY: What?

VALERIE: You don't deserve her.

LARRY: In what way is she too good for me?

VALERIE: In three ways.

LARRY: Three?

VALERIE: Let's not go into it.

(A beat. She changes her mind and decides to go into it:)
Okay. One is education. Now normally a little education differ-
ential in a couple is good. Stimulating, even. But with you guys—
it's a serious gap. She is so much more educated than you are.

LARRY: She is?

VALERIE: You dropped out of college. She has a JD, an MBA, and a
masters in economics!

LARRY: She does?

VALERIE: You didn't know?

LARRY: She has three graduate degrees?

VALERIE: Weird she didn't tell you, right? I guess she's learned not to
mention all her degrees to the college dropouts she dates. But
how long have you been going out?

LARRY: Five months.

VALERIE: Mmm. It should've maybe come up by now. You sure it's
been that long?

LARRY: Yeah five months. When did she tell you about her higher education?

VALERIE: In the ladies room. You always wonder what girls talk about
in the ladies room? Higher education. And fidelity. Which brings
me to problem number two.

LARRY: Which is what?

VALERIE: I observed you holding hands. She touched your hand . . .
extremely simply. Without guilt. So my intuition told me—she's
faithful to you.

LARRY: So?

VALERIE: So number two is I felt she was faithful to you. And number
three, really a subset of number two, is that I know she is faithful
to you.

LARRY: How?

VALERIE: I asked her in the ladies room.

LARRY: You did not!

VALERIE: Did.

LARRY: What if you did. She's not going to tell you if she cheated on
me. She knows your loyalty is to me, your best friend.

VALERIE: Doesn't matter. She could still tell me. It's the Code of Women. Code of Women trumps male-female friendship.

LARRY: Ah—ah—ah—the Code of Women who've met forty-five minutes earlier does not trump a male-female friendship spanning two decades.

VALERIE: You would think. But you have to remember we were in the Ladies Room, with its marble walls and revelations. There, the Code of Women is celebrated like nowhere else. Extenuating circumstances can be quickly forgotten, and female bonding heightened, in the glow of that recessed track lighting.

LARRY: Damn. I did always wonder about that.

VALERIE: And tonight there were marble walls. There was a wide, shared mirror, and there was a moment at which she would have told me, a complete stranger, very personal things. And in that moment, she said she was faithful to you in that same simple way she touched your hand, and I knew she was telling the truth.

LARRY: I would give *anything* to go to a ladies room.

VALERIE: So that's why.

LARRY: I don't understand any of your points, Val. You say she's got three more degrees than I do—

VALERIE: Four.

LARRY: Okay, four. But we're both smart. We both have good jobs. What does it matter how many times we went to school?

VALERIE: It doesn't now, but it could cause problems later. You'll start to resent her when she gets promotions and jobs you can't because she has those degrees . . . she'll start to resent you when it turns out your earning power is just as high despite her degrees, because you're a guy.

LARRY: Okay. Maybe you're onto something with point one. But your other points? Are that she's faithful. And you sense her loyalty. What's wrong with that?

VALERIE: Just that you don't deserve her. She's completely faithful. And you're not.

LARRY: What?

VALERIE: Larry. What's so difficult to understand. You've been a jerk. I think you've been a jerk. The girl is completely devoted to you, and you've cheated on her.

LARRY: But . . .

VALERIE: But?

(A beat. They both know what he's planning to say:)

LARRY: But I've cheated on her with *you!*

VALERIE: I still think it was jerky. She's so wonderful. And you're so . . . two-timing.

LARRY: With *you!* You can't disapprove of my cheating with you. Other than that, I've been totally faithful.

VALERIE: I can disapprove even more. Because I know the extent of it. Because I was there.

LARRY: Yeah. You were there. Because it was *you.*

VALERIE: Just because it's me doesn't make it any better.

LARRY: Of course it does. It's not like I went out and met a new person. You were already there. You and I had . . . unresolved issues before I ever met Denise. We discussed it. We discussed how we'd known each other forever, and always been curious, and it would just be a side thing. *(upset, almost teary)* I thought we had . . . a highly considered, intelligently planned out, extremely well-executed side thing.

VALERIE: Oh I thought we did too! But now that I see how utterly wonderful she is . . . I think it was wrong. I'm almost tempted to tell her—

LARRY: Valerie. Don't.

VALERIE: I probably shouldn't.

LARRY: Yeah and you probably shouldn't go to the Ladies Room with her ever again.
(softening:)
Valerie, honey.
(he touches her hair.)
Please.
(Valerie removes Larry's hand from her hair.)

VALERIE: Okay, Larry. I won't mention the past to her. That is your problem if you want to. But if you ever come on to me again, I will tell her right away.

LARRY: Oh, what, you'll call her? Her number's unlisted. And I've learned my lesson. I am not introducing you two anymore.

VALERIE: We exchanged business cards in the ladies room.

LARRY: You were only in there for three minutes!

VALERIE: We were efficient.

LARRY: You're beautiful when you're efficient.

(Larry puts his hand back in her hair)

VALERIE: We're having lunch Tuesday.

LARRY: What?

(He moves his hand away.)

VALERIE: When she said, see you soon? That's what that referred to.

LARRY: So you both arranged lunch without telling me?

VALERIE: Code of women.

LARRY: My stomach hurts.

(Instinctively, he leans toward her and holds her knee.)

VALERIE: Take your hand off my knee.

LARRY: Sorry.

VALERIE: I really liked her.

LARRY: I know.

(Lights down.)

Curtain

Café Grotesquerie

Andrew Biss

First produced by EndTimes Productions, Part of "Vignettes for the Apocalypse," their 4th Annual one-act festival dealing with dystopian, futuristic, and apocalyptic themes, Spring 2010. Cast—Dan Stern, Victoria Clare, Kevin Paul Smith. Directed by Leah Dashe.

CHARACTERS

Aubrey: . . . . Irascible, rather fusty, with a straightforward, no-nonsense sensibility. 30s–60s.

Audrey: . . . . Aubrey's wife. Supercilious, demanding, frustrated social climber. 30s–60s.

Sommelier: . Polished and professional, slyly sophisticated, with an insidiously patronizing manner. 20s–40s.

SETTING

The Café Grotesquerie

TIME

The present.

At rise: A small table in a dark, recessed nook inside the Café Grotesquerie. At the table are seated Aubrey and Audrey. Audrey is examining a menu. After a few moments, she swiftly throws it down onto the table and emits a heavy sigh of discontent.

AUBREY: For goodness sake, Audrey, do try to buck up a bit. You're beginning to put a real damper on things.

AUDREY: Well, why shouldn't I?

AUBREY: But I thought you liked this place.

AUDREY: I do like this place. I wouldn't be seen dead anywhere else.

AUBREY: Then why all the sighs and the long face?

AUDREY: Well, honestly, it's the same scenario all over again, isn't it? I mean, here we are once more, in one of the most exclusive restaurants there is, one that even the best people have to fight tooth and nail to get into, and yet again we're stuck way in the back at this poky little table instead of our rightful place at the big table.

AUBREY: But I told you when I made the reservation that they'd informed me the big table was already reserved for the—

AUDREY: Yes, yes, I know, I know—the Chinese Ambassador. And the last time it was the American Foreign Secretary, and before that... oh, who would even remember him now? Some little upstart with a lot of leverage. The point is we should be at the big table and we're not.

AUBREY: I rather like it back here. It's cozy, more intimate.

AUDREY: I don't want intimate, I want to intimidate. I want to radiate and dominate. Fat chance of doing that in this dingy little alcove.

AUBREY: Well, things are what they are, so I say let's just be grateful that we're here at all. You know, there's a great many people out there who will never have the opportunity to enter these doors—ever.

AUDREY: *(irritably)* Do you think I don't know that? And believe me, my heart goes out to each and every one of them. But I also think it's fair to remember that of all the hardships a person may be forced to endure, feeling less important than someone else has to be among the cruelest.

Audrey takes a sip from her glass, then pulls a look of disgust.

AUDREY: And to top it all, this blood is most definitely off.

AUBREY: Off?

AUDREY: Yes, off.

AUBREY: *(taking a sip from his glass)* Are you sure?

AUDREY: Of course I am. I'm surprised you didn't notice. Heaven knows you were gurgling and swilling it around in your mouth long enough in front of the sommelier.

AUBREY: Perhaps it is a little. When he comes by I'll have a word.

AUDREY: Ah! There he is.

(calling out)

You! Sommelier!

The Sommelier appears from stage R.

SOMMELIER: Yes, Madame?

AUDREY: This blood is off.

SOMMELIER: Off?

AUDREY: Yes, off.

SOMMELIER: How so?

AUDREY: I don't know how so. Perhaps it's corked?

SOMMELIER: Impossible, Madame. I opened it this evening in front of your very eyes. You both inspected the cork—it was flawless.

AUDREY: Look, I may not be a seasoned connoisseur of all the various blood groups in the world, but I do know when one is off, and this one is most decidedly off.

SOMMELIER: *(picking up the bottle and examining it)* Let me see, Sir ordered the . . . ah, that would explain it.

AUBREY: What would?

SOMMELIER: The Uzbekistan 2004. I'm surprised it's still on the list. It's our dirty little secret.

AUBREY: Was it a bad year?

SOMMELIER: It's never a good year in Uzbekistan, Sir. And of course, this is a varietal in name only. The blood is in fact a blend that is extracted—or rendered, if you will—from detainees hailing from any number of unspecified regions of the world, all with poor dietary habits. Combine this with the extremely unhygienic conditions under which the extraction takes place and what you are left with is not a varietal at all, but an extraordinary and barely palatable rendition.

AUDREY: Yuck!

SOMMELIER: Naturally, the quality and country of origin are reflected in the price, which is what makes this particular blood so appealing to the . . . how shall we put it . . . fiscally vigilant.

Audrey shoots an incriminating look at Aubrey.

AUDREY: I see.

SOMMELIER: Perhaps Sir would like to see the blood list again?

AUBREY: Yes, I think that–

AUDREY: No, he wouldn't. I think, under the circumstances, it might be wisest if you recommended something.

AUBREY: Steady on, Audrey.

AUDREY: Look, Aubrey, if I'm going to be stuck back here all night like some sort of social cast-off, then I'm damned well going to enjoy myself, and what's more, I'm going to do it at someone else's expense—i.e. yours.

(to the Sommelier)

Please continue.

SOMMELIER: Well, without knowing your dinner selections for this evening it's a little difficult to say, but to my mind a 1995 Srebrenica tends to compliment just about most things.

AUDREY: A Srebrenica? Mmm, that sounds yummy.

SOMMELIER: It's a full-bodied Bosniak, aged in oak casks in the picturesque mountains of the Republika Srpska. From there it is exported to Holland where, in a sleepy Dutch village where life just seems to happen without anyone noticing it, it is bottled with a mixture of willful abandon and callous indifference.

AUDREY: It sounds heavenly.

AUBREY: And, uh . . . what, um . . . what does that run at, then?

SOMMELIER: The price? *Very* high.

The Sommelier exits stage R.

AUDREY: *(excitedly)* Oh, look!

AUBREY: What?

AUDREY: The Chinese Ambassador's wife—she's heading to the ladies room. I'd better follow.

AUBREY: Whatever for?

AUDREY: To chitchat, of course.

AUBREY: What if she doesn't speak English? What if she comes back at you in Mandarin or some such nonsense? What'll you do then?

AUDREY: *(rising from the table)* Of course she'll speak English—they're all doing it now, all desperately trying to be more like us, bless them. Anyway, it doesn't matter whether we understand each other, silly. What's important is that we're seen talking.

(crossing stage L.)

Shan't be a tick.

Audrey exits stage L. Aubrey picks up a menu from the table and begins reading through it.

AUBREY: Dear, dear, dear. Why can't they keep things simple? There seems to be more and more on here every time we come. Look at this—it's just too much, it really is. A fellow shouldn't have to . . . look at all that . . . all there in black and white. Very troubling. Very troubling indeed. Best not to look, I say.

Aubrey snaps the menu shut and throws it back down on the table. Audrey suddenly rushes back in and returns to her seat, looking fraught with embarrassment.

AUDREY: Snubbed me! *Completely* snubbed me!

AUBREY: Dear, dear, dear.

AUDREY: Didn't you notice?

AUBREY: Wasn't looking.

AUDREY: Let's hope no one else was. Pinch-faced bitch.

AUBREY: What are you ordering?

AUDREY: Nothing Asian, that's for certain.

AUBREY: Fair enough. Are we going to have something to nibble on first?

AUDREY: I don't see why not. Any thoughts?

AUBREY: What about those little skewered things?

AUDREY: Skewered things?

AUBREY: Yes, you know . . . Mediterranean, I think.

AUDREY: Oh, Palestinians.

AUBREY: That's the ones—spicy little things.

AUDREY: Well, I know you're fond of them, but frankly I find them a little hard to digest.

AUBREY: That's because you don't chew them enough.

AUDREY: It doesn't matter how much I grind away at them, they still don't sit well with me.

AUBREY: Funny, it's never seemed to stop you before. I've seen you scarf them back like there was no tomorrow.

AUDREY: I most certainly have not!

AUBREY: Yes you have. You're like an animal with those things sometimes.

AUDREY: How *dare* you! How dare you compare me to an animal!

AUBREY: All right, all right, no need to overreact.

AUDREY: I don't know what's gotten into you this evening.

AUBREY: Forget I said it.

AUDREY: I'll never forget.

AUBREY: Well then, forgive and forget—minus the forgetting.

AUDREY: Forgiving does not come naturally to me, Aubrey, as you well know—not after what I've been through.

AUBREY: Oh, you're not going to drag that up again are you? Why can't you just let the past be and move on with your life, instead of continually stewing in it and lashing out at those around you whenever the mood strikes?

AUDREY: I have nothing further to say.

AUBREY: Nothing?

Audrey resolutely turns her head to one side and says nothing.
Pause.

AUBREY: Oh, I see—it's the wall of silence now, is it?

Pause.

AUBREY: All right, well, you just have a good old sulk behind it and let me know when you're done. I shall still be here.

Pause.

AUDREY: *(grudgingly) Not* that I have to defend myself to you or anyone else, but all I was attempting to say is that whilst you may be partial to Palestinians, I'm afraid I just can't stomach them, and no amount of teeth gnashing is ever going to resolve that.

AUBREY: Look, let's just forget about the Palestinians, shall we?

AUDREY: Yes, I think that's the wisest course of action, since this argument seems to be going absolutely nowhere. In fact, let's just forget about appetizers altogether. What are you having for an entrée?

AUBREY: Oh, I can't decide. There's too much on here.

(pointing to the menu)

I mean, look at it—who wants to wade through all that?

AUDREY: Oh, do stop complaining.

AUBREY: I would if there was nothing to complain about.

AUDREY: *(becoming exasperated)* Well then—just order from the specials when the waiter arrives.

AUBREY: Ah, good idea. That'll simplify things. Where is the waiter, anyway?

(scanning the room)

Waiter! Waiter!

The Sommelier reappears, holding a new bottle of blood and two new glasses.

SOMMELIER: Good evening, Sir, Madame.

AUBREY: What's happened to the waiter?

SOMMELIER: I am the waiter, Sir.

AUBREY: But you're the sommelier.

SOMMELIER: I am the sommelier and I am also the waiter. I do hope Sir doesn't find this arrangement too complicated.

AUBREY: But what happened to, uh . . . uh . . . oh, what was his name? Been here a while, I think. You remember, Audrey.

AUDREY: Abu? Bibu, was it?

AUBREY: No, no, no. Little Congolese boy, I think. You remember—one arm, big scar across his face.

SOMMELIER: Famelo?

AUBREY: Yes, that's it! Famelo.

SOMMELIER: Famelo is no longer with us, Sir. Unfortunately a number of the guests found his physical disfigurements unconducive to their fine dining experience.

AUBREY: Oh dear. Poor lad.

SOMMELIER: The scar on his cheek had become infected and maggot-ridden, as you may have noticed, so it seemed to be in the best interests of all concerned if we simply . . . how shall I put it . . . terminated him.

AUBREY: As quick as that?

SOMMELIER: Rest assured he's in a better place now.

AUDREY: How dreadful. Though in fairness, he never kept his fingernails short enough for my liking.

AUBREY: He only had one hand—probably took a bit of effort.

AUDREY: How much effort could it take? He only had five of them to trim.

The Sommelier holds the new bottle before them.

SOMMELIER: The 95 Srebrenica. Full-bodied, hard-hearted, and outrageously delicious. Though, of course, I myself remain impartial.

AUDREY: Yummy!

SOMMELIER: Now, perhaps Madame is ready to order?

AUDREY: Yes, my usual, please.

SOMMELIER: Which is what?

AUDREY: What I always have.

SOMMELIER: I have no idea what that is.

AUDREY: But I've been ordering the same thing for years.

SOMMELIER: Madame, I am not Famelo. I am your sommelier and I am also your waiter who is not named Famelo. I apologize for any confusion this is causing you.

AUBREY: For heaven's sake, Audrey, just tell the man what you want.

AUDREY: *(after an irritated sigh)* Somali orphan's head in a béarnaise sauce with potatoes insouciance.

SOMMELIER: Excellent. And how would you like that prepared?

AUDREY: Rare. And do remember to remove the eyes. I don't enjoy being stared at the entire time I'm eating.

SOMMELIER: Of course, Madame. And for you, Sir?

AUBREY: What are your specials?

SOMMELIER: Specials?

AUBREY: Yes, specials.

SOMMELIER: I'm sure Sir doesn't need reminding that everything we put our name to on our menu is, as Sir puts it, "special." We scour the four corners of the earth in search of the very finest ingredients to satisfy the rarified palates of our discerning clientele. There is no depth of human misery we won't stoop to in order to ensure our guests are catered to in a manner to which their bloated bank accounts and moral bankruptcy entitles them.

AUBREY: Yes, yes, yes, but what are you saying? Are you telling me that's it? That there are no additions to the menu?

AUDREY: Oh, do stop quibbling, Aubrey, I'm hungry. Just have the same as me.

SOMMELIER: Wait . . . wait just one moment, please . . .
(pondering)
Yes. Yes, we do have one addition to tonight's menu, now that I think of it.

AUBREY: Ahh!

SOMMELIER: And it is, as Sir might say, very special.

AUBREY: Mmm.

SOMMELIER: Utterly delectable.

AUBREY: Oooh.

SOMMELIER: And sinfully delicious.

AUBREY: I can feel my saliva glands excreting as we speak. Do go on.

AUDREY: Only make it quick.

SOMMELIER: I assure you, Madame, it will be both quick and painless.

AUDREY: Good, because I'm half-starved.

AUBREY: Well, come on, man, what is it?

SOMMELIER: We like to call it, quite simply . . . Self-Sacrifice.

AUBREY: *(ruminating)* Self-Sacrifice.

(beat)
That's a new one on me. Audrey, have you ever tried it?

AUDREY: Doesn't sound familiar.

SOMMELIER: It's a little creation our new chef, Radovan, dreamt up last week, inspired by the great Mother Teresa herself. In short, it's a tender mélange of nuns, missionaries, charity workers and Médecins Sans Frontières—or Doctors Without Borders, if Sir would prefer—slow-cooked for many hours until the very essence of human goodness has been reduced to a small, artistic arrangement on a plate for the consumption of those who can barely stand to look at their own reflection in the mirror.

AUBREY: Good God, that sounds divine!

AUDREY: *(impetuously)* I've changed my mind! I'll have that, too. You make it sound irresistible.

SOMMELIER: I should mention that we do not cull the saints among us ourselves. We use only the previously perished good Samaritans in our dish—the gunned down, ambushed, ransomed and pointlessly executed. You see, to us, 'Beauty Without Cruelty' isn't just a slogan, it's a cooking technique.

AUDREY: It's not how they died, it's how they taste that's important. Now do hurry up—we're famished!

SOMMELIER: Of course, Madame.
    The Sommelier makes to leave, then stops and turns back to address the table.

SOMMELIER: One last thing I should mention. If, during my absence, you should happen to cast an eye over the dessert list, kindly note that the Baked Antarctic Ice Shelf is now off the menu.

AUDREY: *(crestfallen)* Off the menu? But it's one of my very favorites. Surely you can rustle up a little piece just for me?

SOMMELIER: I'm sorry, Madame—it's all gone.
    The Sommelier exits.

AUDREY: Unbelievable!

AUBREY: Probably down to that Chinese mob.

AUDREY: More than likely. Look at them—acting as if they owned the world.

AUBREY: Still, you can't have everything.

AUDREY: What an absurd thing to say. One should have every right to anything at any given time.

AUBREY: Be that as it may, you heard the man—it's all gone, so you'll just have to have something else. What about the Petit Darfur?

AUDREY: *(scoffing)* Oh honestly, Petit Darfur—can't they move on? I mean, who eats that any more? Who cares? Talk about yesterday's news.

AUBREY: Well, perhaps there's something else on the menu you might enjoy.

AUDREY: Oh, I suppose so.
(listlessly picking up the menu)
Let's see...
(beat)
Oh... well, here's one I haven't seen before.

AUBREY: What's that?

AUDREY: It's just called 'Just Dessert.'

AUBREY: Just that?

AUDREY: Yes, 'Just Dessert.'

AUBREY: Sounds intriguing—let's go with that.

AUDREY: May as well, I suppose.
After several more moments of examining the menu, Audrey swiftly throws it down onto the table and emits a heavy sigh of discontent.

AUBREY: For goodness sake, Audrey, do try to buck up a bit. You're beginning to put a real damper on things.

AUDREY: Well, why shouldn't I?

AUBREY: But I thought you liked this place.

AUDREY: I do like this place. I wouldn't be seen dead anywhere else.

AUBREY: Then why all the sighs and the long face?

AUDREY: Well, honestly, it's the same scenario all over again, isn't it? I mean, here we are once more, in one of the most exclusive restaurants there is, one that even the best people have to fight tooth and nail to get into, and yet again we're stuck way in the back at this poky little table instead of our rightful place at the big table.

AUBREY: But I told you when I made the reservation that they'd informed me the big table was already reserved for the—

AUDREY: Yes, yes, I know, I know—the Chinese Ambassador. And the last time it was the American Foreign Secretary, and before that... oh, who would even remember him now? Some little upstart with a lot of leverage. The point is...

During their final exchanges, both lights and voice fade down until the stage is silent and BLACK.

END OF PLAY

Closing Time

Vasanti Saxena

Originally produced at Company of Angels Theatre, Los Angeles, April 2–25, 2010, as part of the L.A. Views: Hunger and The City short play festival. Directed by Lui Sanchez. Cast: Fred—Timothy Casto; Monica—Joyce F. Liu; Cass—Leilani M. Smith. The lead producer was Henry Ong (Literary Manager at Company of Angels):

CHARACTERS

Monica: Restaurant owner, 30s. Totally in control . . . of her professional life.

Fred: . . . Waiter, 40s. A hard worker, a gentle soul. Secretly in
love with Monica.

Cass: . . . Monica's ex-lover, late 20s–30s. She's a tenacious
dreamer whose bubble has burst.

SETTING

A small restaurant on the Westside of Los Angeles. Ten tables at
the most. 10:50pm. Tonight.

---

*(Lights up on Monica, cashing out the register. She counts money
while Fred puts chairs up on the tables. It's been a long, busy night.)*

FRED: How'd we do tonight?

MONICA: Not bad. Considering.

FRED: The economy?

MONICA: We did ok.

FRED: Considering?

MONICA: The economy.

FRED: It was pretty busy, huh?

MONICA: Damned right it was!
          (They laugh.)

FRED: Small plates were a great idea.

MONICA: Good for the indecisive people in this town.

FRED: And the ones who want to have it all.

MONICA: But in small portions. Like Table 4. What was the deal with
them?

FRED: Table 4?

MONICA: *(To jog FRED's memory)* Sesame crusted chicken wings. Sir-
loin sliders. Baked macaroni, four cheeses. Comfort food.

FRED: The couple?

MONICA: The couple. They didn't talk to each other all night.

FRED: They never do.

MONICA: Never?

FRED: They're married.

MONICA: Ah.

FRED: The only time they speak is to give me their order. And to ask for water.

MONICA: And more wine.

FRED: Always more wine with them.

MONICA: With those types.

FRED: That kind.

MONICA: Did you see when she was . . .
  (She gestures wildly like she's waving a knife.)

FRED: With her steak knife? I saw that.

MONICA: I thought she was going to kill him.

FRED: She does that a lot. When she's trying to think of something to say.

MONICA: It's that difficult?

FRED: They must've been married a long time.

MONICA: She could have put her knife down.

FRED: Maybe it was the only thing keeping her bound to the moment.

MONICA: You think?

FRED: The only thing keeping her . . . you know . . .

MONICA: What?

FRED: Sane.
  (They stare at Table 4. Monica shakes off her thoughts.)

MONICA: I got this, Freddy. I can lock up. You have a long drive.

FRED: 405 is clear this time of night.

MONICA: But you probably want to get home.

FRED: Not really.

MONICA: Why not?

FRED: No one will be awake.
  (Lights shift. Heightened reality. Monica freezes while Fred speaks the following.)
  I'll walk in the front door and my wife, my children. They'll be asleep. I'll walk to the room I share with my wife and turn on

the light. Just so I can see my way to the bed. And she'll cry out, so I'll shut the light off quickly and stub my toe on the corner of the bed frame. And not cry out because to do so would disturb her sleep. And her sleep is very important to the happiness of our household. I'll lay my tips on the nightstand so she has a bit of spending money for tomorrow. And I'll very, very carefully ease my body into my side of the bed and hope that the motion doesn't disturb her sleep because to do so would be to interfere with the happiness of our household. And she'll shift and murmur a bit. And I'll hold my breath until she settles. And I'll lie awake . . . thinking of you.

> *(Lights shift back to normal.)*

MONICA: You never know.

FRED: *(Hopeful)* What?

MONICA: She might have stayed up. Waiting. You wouldn't want her to worry.

FRED: No . . .

MONICA: See you tomorrow then.

FRED: Same time, same place.

> *(He goes to the door. Cass rushes in—beautiful, bedraggled, and a bit wild. She carries a huge purse, big enough to be an overnight bag.)*

FRED: Sorry, ma'am. Ma'am! We're closed.

CASS: Did you see that? Did you see that bus that just went by?

MONICA: Cassie?

CASS: Did you see it?

FRED: What?

CASS: The bus. The bus that just went by!

FRED: Heard it, I guess. Wasn't looking out the window though.

CASS: Well if you had, you would've seen her.

FRED: Who?

> *(Monica shakes her head "no" at Fred.)*

CASS: Her.

FRED: I'm sorry. I don't . . .

CASS: *(To Monica)* Did you see it?

MONICA: The bus your ex was in?

CASS: Not in. On. "New series premiering this Fall." On the fucking side of the bus. Her face bigger than . . . than my whole body!

MONICA: That's big.

CASS: Her face was plastered all over it.

FRED: Whose face?

MONICA: Her ex's.

CASS: The bitch. If you knew what I did for her. Then what she did to me . . . !

FRED: She's famous?

(Monica shakes her head emphatically.)

What's her name?

(Cass lets out an ear-splitting wail.)

Wow. Sorry.

CASS: I just want to get the image of her out of my head. But short of gouging out my eyes, there's no way.

MONICA: Sure there is.

CASS: No. Really. There isn't. No way in this town. Fucking buses. Benches. Billboards. Bullshit! And I was so close. So close to forgetting. But now with this . . . this "New series premiering this Fall" . . . Forget it! I'll never burn the image of her out of my brain. Wish I could. Could shove a fucking stake through my eyeball. Give myself a lobotomy. Still probably see her in my dreams. And that poster! Head cocked. Eyebrow raised all clever and so, so sexy. But I taught her that trick. Me! Hours in front of the mirror and I came up with that. To give her a bit a mystery. Camouflage the general . . . blankness.

MONICA: She won't last.

CASS: You think?

MONICA: Was she really that . . . blank?

(Cass nods.)

FRED: But she's sexy?

(Cass nods.)

Well . . . She might.

(Cass wails again. Throws down her purse and crumples into a chair. Bereft.)

Geeze. Sorry. I'm sorry. OK?

MONICA: Cass. Cassie. Honey. Why don't you come in tomorrow? A little earlier. We can talk then.

CASS: What are you talking about?

(Monica points to the clock.)

MONICA: We're closed.

CASS: I have ten minutes.

MONICA: We're closed.

CASS: Monica . . . Honey . . . Everyone knows that clock is ten minutes fast. I know your tricks. Everyone knows your tricks.

MONICA: You see any customers? No. You don't. There aren't any to see. You know why? Because it's late. The clock says it's eleven and there aren't any customers. So we're closed.

CASS: Don't I count? I could be a customer. I'm a person, right? *(To Fred)* Aren't I a person?

FRED: Of course you're a person.

MONICA: Don't encourage her.

CASS: Encourage me? I used to work here. I used to be your best waitress. You owe me.

MONICA: I thought we'd settled that debt.

CASS: I'm a person and I count. I'll even order something. You want me to order something?

MONICA: Kitchen's closed.

FRED: I could make you a sandwich.

CASS: Would you?

MONICA: You don't have to.

FRED: You girls sit and talk.

CASS: What a sweetie! Turkey on whole grain. Please.

FRED: Cheese?

CASS: Havarti.

MONICA: *Dill* Havarti.

> *(Cass is surprised that Monica remembers. Monica notices Cass's surprise. Meaningful.)*

And arugula.

> *(Lights shift. Heightened reality. Monica and Fred freeze as Cass speaks the following.)*

CASS: I can't believe you remember. I thought I wouldn't like it. That afternoon I first came in. My first week in LA and oh I wanted to try new things, but I wouldn't try arugula. I was a lettuce girl. Iceberg. Not even romaine. But you were making magic in that kitchen and I wanted to be a part of it. American cheese became havarti. Tomatoes became roasted red peppers. Mayonnaise became aioli. And I became yours. And even after. When I was lying in her bed. My stomach grumbling from being on whatever new diet she insisted on. I could taste your latest creation on my tongue. And couldn't help but lie awake . . . and think of you.

(Lights shift back to normal.)

MONICA: Roasted red peppers. And aioli. Light.

(Monica and Cass stare at each other.)

FRED: You got it.

(He exits.)

CASS: I heard about the remodel. Thought I'd check it out. Looks good. Kind of . . . sterile. But good. I've been hearing all kinds of good things. You know. About how you're doing. And, well, the economy isn't so great. It was tough making the rent with just me and . . .

MONICA: *(On guard)* You need help with your rent?

CASS: A couple of months ago, I did.

MONICA: And now?

CASS: I kinda need a place to stay.

MONICA: Where are you staying now?

CASS: Here and there.

MONICA: With friends?

CASS: They were all her friends. *(beat)* Or yours.

MONICA: So you've been staying . . . ?

CASS: Here and there. It's been a little colder.

MONICA: Colder.

CASS: And it's supposed to rain tonight. That's what they're saying. And. You know. I can deal with a lot. But I just don't know if I can deal with the rain.

MONICA: *(Realization dawning)* You want to stay with me.

CASS: Just for one night?

MONICA: You want to sleep in my bed?

CASS: For one night?

MONICA: Not ok.

CASS: Really?

MONICA: Not anymore.

CASS: You have a couch?

MONICA: I have cash. Get you a place for the night.

CASS: I'm not taking your money.

MONICA: You sure?

CASS: Come on, Monica. Would one night be so bad?

MONICA: I'm sorry.

CASS: *(False bright)* No worries. I'll just go to plan B. Always good to have a plan B, right?

MONICA: Sure.

CASS: That's what you always used to tell me. Remember?

MONICA: I know all about Plan B.

CASS: Plan A is better.

MONICA: Is it?

CASS: I think so.

MONICA: It's a good idea to stick around long enough to find out.

CASS: I didn't know the place was going to take off like this.

MONICA: Is that what it was about? This place? Funny. I thought it was about me.

CASS: It was. About you. Us. We didn't get to be Us because of this place.

MONICA: We were both here.

CASS: Working.

MONICA: That's what you have to do sometimes. Work.

CASS: I can do that.

> *(Fred enters with Cass's sandwich. He keeps his distance, listening.)*

CASS: I could waitress for you again. Maybe work off some of that debt?

MONICA: I can't hire anyone else on right now.

CASS: Why not? This place is really popular. People love small plates.

MONICA: It's been a little rough. Considering.

CASS: Considering what?

FRED: *(Bringing Cass the sandwich)* The economy.

MONICA: Right.

> *(Fred puts the sandwich down in front of Cass.)*

CASS: Pretty.

FRED: Thanks.

MONICA: You've always liked good presentation.

CASS: I'm more a fan of substance now.

MONICA: Are you?

CASS: You'd be surprised.

MONICA: It's a little...

CASS: Yes?

MONICA: Late.

CASS: Oh. OK. *(beat)* You know. Maybe I'll take this to go. *(She starts wrapping the sandwich up in a napkin.)* You're good people, Monica. And. Sometimes. You know. Sometimes it's really hard to find good people.

MONICA: Hey Freddy?

FRED: Yeah?

MONICA: You sure you're not in a hurry to get home?

FRED: Yeah.

MONICA: You think you could give her a ride to my place?

FRED: You sure?

(Monica takes a key off her key ring and gives it to Cass.)

MONICA: Yeah.

CASS: *(To Fred)* You don't have to.

FRED: Not a problem.

CASS: But...

FRED: It's on my way.

CASS: *(To Monica)* I can wait for you to close up.

MONICA: I still have some work to do.

CASS: I thought you were...

FRED: She has paperwork. Bills and...

MONICA: ...paperwork. *(beat)* You remember the trick with the lock? *(Cass nods.)* Ok then.

> *(Fred holds the door open for Cass. They exit. Monica looks after them, then locks the door to the restaurant, takes a few chairs off the tables, lines them up to make a makeshift bed, and lies down... eyes open, looking out at the audience. Lights fade.)*

END OF PLAY

Dante's Inferno: The Motion Picture

Philip J Kaplan

Production History: July 2010 Manhattan Theatre Source, NYC. Directed by Michael Boardwell. Cast: Tony—Ken Coughlin; Bridget—Kathryn Stevens; Sam—Ben Guralnik. October 2010, The Visceral Company, West Hollywood, CA. Directed by Dan Spurgeon. Assistant director Rochelle Perry. Cast: Tony—David O'Kelley; Bridget—Nicole Fabbri; Sam—Josh Fanaroff.

CHARACTERS

Tony: . . An ordinary guy, naïve and out of place. 30+

Bridget:. In control and professional. Mid twenties to mid thirties.

Sam: . . . A fast talking salesman type. 30+

SETTING

A non-descript office which is somehow a little off.

TIME

Now.

AUTHORS NOTE

Several Hollywood celebrities are mentioned in the play. They can be changed to make the script more current.

Set: An office.
(Tony is being escorted into an office by Bridget a polished professional woman. Tony is out of his element.)

TONY: Sit here?

BRIDGET: Yes. It's all yours.

TONY: I still can't believe it.

BRIDGET: That's the magic.

TONY: It's like a dream. Yesterday, a Bank Manager, today head of a motion picture studio.

BRIDGET: And time to get to work.

TONY: When I saw the listing on Craig's list, I thought it was a joke. Motion picture studio head needed, immediately.

BRIDGET: And here you are, ready for your first meeting.

TONY: Is that how they usually hire studio presidents?

BRIDGET: Absolutely, nothing suspicious about it. Oh, and your first appointment is here. In fact your only appointment.

TONY: Who is it?

(Sam, a fast talking salesman, enters carrying an easel with a chart. He puts the easel down, flips open the chart which says "INTRODUCTION")

SAM: I don't know what they've been telling you, but this movie is a blockbuster. This is TITANIC crashing into STAR WARS and being nailed by THE PASSION OF THE CHRIST till it bleeds and screams!

TONY: Good. I love blockbusters.

SAM: Then you're gonna love this! Do you like Romantic Comedies?

TONY: I prefer action movies.

SAM: Exactly, everybody loves Romantic Comedies. And when you hear "Dante's Inferno", what do you think?

TONY: People suffering the eternal damnation of hell?

SAM: Right! You think of Dante's eternal love for Beatrice. And that's why this Romantic Comedy is called DANTE'S INFERNO!

(Sam flips over a page on his chart, with the words DANTE'S INFERNO in big, red, cheesy letters.)

TONY: Are you the director?

SAM: No. No way. He never came back from Malaysia. The studio wouldn't pay for his ransom. You're the studio now, so you're retroactively responsible.

TONY: I'm sorry to hear that.

SAM: Don't be. He was a terrible human being. I'm glad he's gone.

BRIDGET: We all are.

TONY: So what's this movie about?

SAM: Cameron Diaz—

TONY: Oh, I like her—

SAM: —plays an expert on Quantum Mechanics but doesn't know anything about love. Ashton Kutcher plays the reincarnation of her lover and get this—he's her unborn embryo!

(Sam flips over the chart and it says "Romantic Complication")

TONY: I don't understand.

SAM: An embryo who can't commit! See the possibilities? Plus, Ashton Kutcher is your blockbuster insurance.

BRIDGET: It's true. Our research shows that people will see anything that Ashton Kutcher is in.

TONY: If he's an embryo how is he in the movie?

SAM: He shows up on the ultrasound. I mean who doesn't love kids or the unborn! This is the Romantic Comedy to end Romantic Comedies. And this is your film, Tony! This is how you'll be remembered.

TONY: So what do you want me to do?

BRIDGET: We had a sneak preview yesterday and we want you to review the audience comments.

(Bridget hands Tony a card. She will continue handing him cards which start out normal then get stranger and stranger, some dripping, some are objects, like knives, or watches.)

TONY: *(reading the cards)* "I will never go into a movie theatre again." "If I find the man who runs the studio who made this film, I will torture then kill him."

SAM: Not typical.

TONY: "I declare a Jihad against Tony." How did he know my name?

BRIDGET: We wanted you to get full credit.

TONY: "Tony will be in a lot of trouble if this movie doesn't make its money back."

BRIDGET: Nothing to worry about. Your name was signed to a few things.

TONY: How much did the movie cost?

SAM: Nothing. Loose change. Fifty.

TONY: Fifty? Fifty what?

SAM: Sixty million.

TONY: I don't have sixty million dollars!

SAM: In the first hour, DANTE'S INFERNO will make back its eighty million dollars or my name isn't Plartha Hrunga-Hrunga. Trust me. Take the lecture scene.

TONY: *(reads another card)* "Why was Cameron Diaz wearing a bikini when she was giving a lecture on the Dirac wave equation?"

SAM: I tried, I really did, but she won't do topless, it's in her contract.

TONY: How much did this cost?

SAM: A hundred million dollars, give or take.

TONY: Give or take!

SAM: Give or take another fifty million.

TONY: One hundred and fifty million?

BRIDGET: And every bit of it is coming out of your pocket.

(Sam flips over the chart to reveal a picture of a dollar bill with wings on it)

SAM: OK, we went a little over budget. But we had to shut down the Large Hadron Collider for an entire week—and pay for damages after. By the way, don't go to Switzerland, they're very angry at you. And definitely don't go to Vatican City, we destroyed some sacred relics there.

TONY: One hundred and fifty million?

SAM: The digital Humphrey Bogart was enormously expensive. We had to take out a mortgage on your house, and your parent's house, plus dip into your retirement to pay for it.

(Bridget hands Tony another card)

TONY: *(reads)* "I was terrified by Bette Davis. Each time she said, 'Pardon me, I have hepatitis,' I had an epileptic seizure."

SAM: Yeah, yeah, that's not the first time I've heard that. Pretty much everyone who saw the digital Bette Davis experienced an epileptic incident. But in my defense, to raise Bette Davis from the dead would not have worked. You can't light the undead for shit. So we went digital.

TONY: If the movie causes epilepsy won't people sue?

SAM: Ah, this country is lawyer crazy. You may get a few lawsuits directed against you.

(Bridget hands Tony a stack of papers.)

BRIDGET: Lawsuits. Nothing to worry about.

SAM: I take responsibility for getting his catch phrase wrong. I could have sworn it was "Pardon me, I have hepatitis." But no.

BRIDGET: We can save the movie! You should have seen the first version of ROLLER BOOGIE! We're all counting on you, Tony! What should we do?

SAM: Excuse me, I have ideas. As I mentioned, Romantic Comedy. That's the push.

TONY: I don't get it.

BRIDGET: No one actually laughed during the screening.

SAM: So we'll go with comedy as in the Shakespearean sense, where no one dies.

(Sam flips the chart. There is a picture of a tombstone with a not symbol drawn over it)

BRIDGET: And this is the problem we want you to fix. Many, many people die in this movie.

(Sam flips the chart which has a long list of names.)

TONY: That's strange. The third one on the list has the same name as my Grandma Netta.

BRIDGET: It is your grandmother. I'm sorry for your loss.

TONY: What? She actually died?

SAM: So did Timmy Christmas, the lovable scamp. Now that kid had potential. I say, "had."

BRIDGET: Timmy Christmas dies halfway through the film. It causes a slight plot hole.

SAM: But the good news is, we got it all on film!

BRIDGET: It's gruesome. Painful to watch.

SAM: But compelling. You just keep saying, "Why?"

TONY: Someone actually really dies in the middle of a romantic comedy?

SAM: It's gonna help box office. Look what Heath Ledger did for Batman. Look what Elvis Presley did for Graceland.

BRIDGET: Timmy's last words were, "I blame Tony for my death."

(Bridget cries.)

SAM: Don't feel guilty, Tony. Only 7 people died making this movie. Compare that to Hiroshima, and it's not so bad.

TONY: You left his death in the movie? Doesn't that make it a snuff film? Isn't that illegal?

SAM: Not in Palu, North Korea or the Island of Dreams.

BRIDGET: Of course in North Korea they only pay us in the blood of lambs.

TONY: I've got a hundred and fifty million dollar snuff film on my hands!

SAM: Two hundred million, plus your car.

TONY: Is there anything else that can go wrong?

SAM: Nah. That's pretty much it. Except the co-star was arrested last night for drunken driving, and he was caught on film slandering Jews, Muslims, and Christians.

BRIDGET: And Animal rights activists, Scientology and bikers.

SAM: Tony, you should choose your friends more carefully.

TONY: He's not my friend!

BRIDGET: Are you calling Mel a liar? I'd be careful, he's strong and crazy.

SAM: So since you're his friend, we added a scene to the movie.

BRIDGET: Ten minutes of you going to the bathroom.

SAM: Next time, remember to close the door.

(Bridget flips the chart revealing a drawing of a door.)

TONY: Why are you doing this to me?

(Bridget flips the chart. It shows a drawing of a kidney. Sam stares at it perplexed.)

SAM: I don't even know what that's for. Do you know? Oh, I remember! We had to take one of your kidneys.

TONY: What?

SAM: Actually three of your kidneys. Maybe we got the liver too.

BRIDGET: Normal people don't have three kidneys.

SAM: The liver then.

(Tony pulls open his shirt to discover a scar.)

BRIDGET: Think of it as your contribution. When you're dead, DANTE'S INFERNO will be the only thing you're remembered for.

TONY: I resign! I don't want to be studio head anymore!

BRIDGET: It's a little late for that.

SAM: Yeah. Look on the bright side. You still have your spleen.

TONY: This can't be happening! Wait! Wait! Am I in hell? Is this my punishment?

SAM: Yeah, that must be it.

TONY: But why me? What did I do?

SAM: You sold your soul. We have a contract. Signed in blood.

BRIDGET: Actually, he didn't.

(Bridget looks at a piece of paper.)

This is a little hard to read. He was either involved in the Rwandan genocide. Or he wasn't involved in the Rwandan genocide. Anyway, it doesn't really matter. You're here now. Hope you enjoy your stay.

SAM: So scoot, off you go to damnation.

TONY: My punishment is to hear bad news about a movie for all eternity?

SAM: No! That's stupid. What do you take us for? You have to stay here until the movie turns a profit. That's all.

BRIDGET: What should we do? We'll consider anything. Anything.

TONY: Oh. Well, what about a viral campaign? It's so bad it's good.

SAM: We can do viruses.

BRIDGET: Keep going. We've got all the time in the world.

(blackout)

Hole

Stephen Bittrich

Hole was first produced as a workshop production by The Drilling Company, Hamilton Clancy, Artistic Director, along with 8 other one-acts all on the theme of Faith in May of 2010 at The Drilling Company Theatre, New York City. It was directed by David Marantz; Set Design by Rebecca Lord; Light Design by Miriam Crowe; Sound Design by Chris Rummel. The production featured the following cast: *Brody—Dan Teachout; *Murphy—Billie Davis; **Millsap—Darren Lipari.

---

* The character names of Brody and Murphy have been traded in this updated publication version of this play as the female character gained a first name, and the author determine Ima Jean Brody was more musical than Ima Jean Murphy.

**Understudy Steve Sherman played Millsap for one performance during the run.

For Heather

CHARACTERS

Murphy.. mid-50s, male, a grizzled miner always with a story to
tell. Has lost his faith in mankind.

Brody . . . mid-30s, female, a compact and tough miner with
faith in herself.

Millsap . . mid-20s, male, a wide-eyed and green young miner
with faith in Jesus.

SETTING:

Summer, 1982. McDowell County, West Virginia, the southern-
most county in the state The dark. The hole. 700 feet deep inside
blessed terra firma. The light becomes another character in this
piece. It is recommended that as much as possible lighting instruments discovered on stage by the characters illuminate the scene—
matches, a lantern, a cap light.

---

*At rise: We hear a man playing a little harmonica intro and then
singing in the dark. This is Murphy. He sings the first two verses of
"Gold for Fools," an Appalachian-style Love Ballad. (Music and
lyrics by Stephen Bittrich available separately at: http://stephenbit-
trich.com/Gold_for_Fools.mp3)*

MURPHY: *(singing)*

Oh, Sally, Sweet Sally loved a young miner boy
When he took her a-courtin' she acted quite coy.

He said, "Sally, Sweet Sally, please give me a kiss.
I'm going down in the hole, down to the abyss.

She said, "When ya come home, I'll save ya a peck.
Just bring me some gold ta put 'round ma neck.

So down the deep shaft when the young miner boy
Ta seek him some gold for his love and joy.

But the hole it caved in, and the boy ne'er came home.
And Sally Sweet Sally heard the news at the gloam.

Yer young boy is dead now, his body's been found.
He's been bloodied and battered, his flesh took a pound.

So we cleaned him up nice and gave him fresh duds
Cleaned up his face, hands and his feet from the blood.

His fist was clasped tight with the strong grip of death.
And inside a gold nugget held 'til his last breath.

(A match lights.)

MURPHY: (CONT'D) Hey! Brody. Air's good. I checked the meter. You find some tobacco, girl? That why you feedin' that fire some of our blessed air?

(Brody, a compact and tough female miner answers, match to her face)

BRODY: I think I just unearthed the supply kit with the extra lantern.

(Millsap, a young wide-eyed miner in his chimes in)

MILLSAP: Good girl! Oh my dear Lord! And food and water too?

(She opens the supply case in the dark and turns on the lantern. Light flashes up on her face and then she takes it downstage and shines it on the other two. Murphy is center)

And the Lord said, let there be light.

(She finds food in the case)

BRODY: What do you want for supper, Millsap?

MILLSAP: Lord be praised. How's about some fried chicken and potato salad?

BRODY: Yeah, that'd be nice. How's about some peanuts and some water?

MILLSAP: That'll do.

MURPHY: Nice girlie. Every condemned man should be afforded a last meal.

BRODY: Stop yer bitchin', Murphy. That leg ain't so bad.

MILLSAP: Yeah, Murphy. Yer more of a woman than Brody is!

(Silence. The two of them stare Millsap down for very different reasons, then . . .)

I didn't mean that, Brody.

(They all voraciously devour the newly found treasure of food and drink)

MILLSAP (CONT'D): We should conserve the battery and only use it certain times.

MURPHY: Won't make no difference. Leave it on. Them new batt'ries will last for a fortnight. We'll be dead in 3 days.

BRODY: I don't accept that. Now that we have light, I'm gonna find a way out. You can believe that.

MURPHY: Well, you should make peace with yer maker nonetheless.

(Silence)

MILLSAP: Play another one, Murphy.

(Murphy plays about 6 bars of a little ditty, then launches into one of his familiar stories...)

MURPHY: Ya know if it t'weren't for John Red Deer, a barrel-chested, full-blooded Comanche Indian and my partner working a hoist while we was dragline mining up at e Creek in '78, I mayn't be able to grace you with the dulcet tones of this here fine instrument. No, sir.

(He moves his fingers in the light)

Where you see 10 fine digits ... I mighta gone down ta seven that day.

(beat)

Don't take two men ta run a hoist, but I was a dandy, as green as a new blade of grass, my first day on a mining job of any kind. Why I was greener than Miss Ima Jean here.

(Brody rolls her eyes at him)

And John Red Deer drew short straw and got ta be my wet nurse while I learnt the trade. They used to raz the dandies something awful back in them days, so when the hoist came asunder, split in two, I first figured mebbe I was the butt of some bad joke. But two men were riding the bucket down the seven hundred foot shaft, and it tweren't no joke. I yanked on the emergency brake, all for nought, cuz that burst apart too. As the drum unfurled like a giant leviathan on the end of a harpoon line, those two men in the bucket were surely off to meet their maker. Without a thought, John Red Deer pushed me outta the way like so much laundry, grabbed up some nearby guide timber, and levered it in between the frame and the drum, ripping off three-a his fingers in the process. But devil be damned he still pulled that makeshift lever down with the might of a man possessed and halted the drum. The men down the shaft were saved. The men down in the hole were save from a run away bucket. And because John Red Deer had pushed me outta the way, I didn't get any of my fingers tore off on my first day as a miner.

MILLSAP: Well, thank the Lord for John Red Deer.

MURPHY: *(to Millsap)* Back in them days, you'd never see a person of the female persuasion in the hole. Bad luck.

BRODY: Oh can it, Old Timer. We ain't on the high seas, and this ain't your ship, Captain Ahab. So don't give me that bad luck shit.

MILLSAP: Yeah, Murphy. Ease up.

MURPHY: Fer as I can see it, she don't need you ta answer fer her, boy. She's got a tongue sharp enough to cut diamonds.
(Beat)
Well . . . yer right Missy, it tweren't bad luck . . . just bad mining. Retreat mining is a fool's game, but the man above, and I don't mean Jesus, I mean, Luther Bilkis, our beloved CEO of Bilkis Bourbon Mines, has been a mining this way for decades.

MILLSAP: My Aunt Gemma says retreat mining is like living in house made out of pick up sticks and takin' another stick out every night before you lay down to sleep. 'Bout all I could do ta keep her from followin' me ta work every day ta give Luther Bilkis a piece-a her mind.

MURPHY: Yeah. That sounds like her.

MILLSAP: You know my aunt?

MURPHY: We used ta go . . . dancin'?

MILLSAP: What?? She never told me that!

MURPHY: Oh ho, you catch that, Girlie? He didn't like that—thinkin' about me and his Auntie! Don't worry, boy, a gentleman don't kiss and tell.

BRODY: I found a cap light.
(Brody turns on the other lamp, and it shines up in her face)

BRODY (CONT'D): It works!

MILLSAP: Lord be praised.

MURPHY: Tweren't the Lord. I put that lamp and grub in there. I check that kit every day.

(Brody fixes it on the hard hat and fixes the hat on her head, shining the light toward the men)

BRODY: I'm gonna go survey the cave-in a-fresh now that we got light again.

(Millsap rises to get the other lantern to go with her)

MURPHY: Don't let Millsap touch the lantern!

MILLSAP: That was an accident! I said I was sorry!

(Millsap and Brody are face-to-face center stage. The light from her cap light shines in his face and reflects back onto her face)

BRODY: Don't worry about it, Millsap. I'll be right back. Stay with Murphy.

MILLSAP: Be careful.

BRODY: I'm just gonna look. Piece of cake.

(She exits toward the cave-in. Millsap looks after her)

MURPHY: *(after a moment)* Yeah, she likes ya.

MILLSAP: Ya think?

(Murphy grins from ear to ear)

MURPHY: Nope!

MILLSAP: Oh keep quiet!

(Murphy plays around on harmonica. They sit for a moment without speaking. Just music. Millsap folds his hands and starts to pray, rocking back and forth ever so slightly)

MURPHY: Ain't nobody comin'.

MILLSAP: No, they're coming, Murphy. I know they are. The Good Lord wouldn't let us die down here. I got things ta do.

MURPHY: Like lose yer cherry?

MILLSAP: No, I done checked that offa my list . . . smart ass.

MURPHY: Boy, just because Miss Brody talks ta me like that, don't think that you can. Watch yer mouth.

MILLSAP: Sorry. How's your leg?

(Murphy ignores the question)

MURPHY: As sure as you have faith in the good Lord and the good will of mankind, so I have faith in the devilish and wicked nature of a man. And Luther Bilkis surely has a place set at Satan's great table in hell when his time comes. You know as well as I this mine was cited with 467 safety violations last year, 156 of which was deemed ta be serious in nature. That ain't too much different than the year a'fore and the year a'fore that. What runs this mine and most every mine is greed, plain and simple. And if we get outta here, it won't be due to the good graces of Mr. Bilkis.

(beat)

They'll call off the search in 4 ta 5 days if they don't break through. Cuz they'll figure we run out of water, run out of oxygen, run outta life.

(Brody has returned for part of this)

BRODY: Well, it's a good thing I don't have ta believe in God nor the questionable nature of man. Just myself. I think I found a hole I can fit through.

MILLSAP: No! Really?

BRODY: You may be able ta "butter yer bread yet," Millsap.

MILLSAP: I told you I ain't no virgin—! Oh forget about it. Anyways, I should be the one ta go.

(Brody prepares to leave, clipping the light to a miner's hard hat, finding some rope)

BRODY: You can't fit.

MILLSAP: And you can?

BRODY: Yes.

MURPHY: The hole ain't stable. And it may come to point. Like venturin' into a funnel. If there was a hole straight through, they'da found it already.

BRODY: You got better options? Besides waitin'?

MURPHY: No ma'am, Miss Brody.

BRODY: Well, ain't that nice? Suddenly I'm not "girlie" or "missy." I'm Miss Brody.

MURPHY: You get through that hole, I'll call ya the Queen-a England.

MILLSAP: I don't want you to go.

BRODY: I'll be right back. I promise.

(They look into each other's eyes, her light shining on him)

BRODY (CONT'D): I'll bring fried chicken and potato salad.

MILLSAP: Crap, I meant to ask you out.

BRODY: *(She touches his cheek tenderly)* I wouldn't have gone out with ya. Stay with Murphy.

(She turns to go, pauses, turns back around and gives him a brief, tender kiss. She exits. Millsap is a little beside himself, paces a little trying to figure out what to do)

MURPHY: I ever tell you, boy, about the Mole Man of Miner's Delight, Wyoming?

MILLSAP: *(annoyed)* What?

MURPHY: He was a small beady-eyed Mescun man from Chihuahua Mexico . . . like the dog. And he was never in the sunlight without his sunglasses, cuz the light was too intense for him to just walk around, just regular like in the daytime. But down in the hole, the Mole Man was like a damn superhero. He didn't need no torch. He could make his way around in near pitch black with only them beady eyes ta guide him. Eventually, he didn't come up at all. He just lived down in the hole. Some say he dug his own tunnels through the mine, his own drifts. One time, there was a cave in, and all was thought to be lost. Except that the trapped men had Mole Man with 'em—who knew that mine like a man knows his own dick. And don't you know, Mole Man found a way through the cave and to the other side . . . got 'em all rescued. That's a true story.

> *(beat)*

Go give yer girl another kiss. I can wait in the dark. I got my own mole eyes.

> *(Millsap takes the lamp, shines it one last time on Murphy and goes after Brody. Murphy in the pitch dark sings the 3rd and last verse of "Gold for Fools")*

> *Sally, Sweet Sally took the news awful hard.*
> *Like her heart was a-punctured through and through with a shard.*

> *She bid her mother and father good night*
> *And went up to her bedroom, donned a dress that was white*

> *She knelt by her bed, and she sent up her prayer*
> *Then she braided a rope made from her flowing hair.*

> *Her mother dear mother found her dead that next morn.*
> *A noose round her neck and her head freshly shorn.*

> *(End of play)*

"Honest Abe" Mazulu

Stephen Cooper

The first production of *Honest Abe Mazulu* was by the Theatre Odyssey of Sarasota, Daniel Greene, Director. Cast: William Muzzillo—Poulenc; Martin Taylor—Abraham Mazulu; David Taylor—David. Produced at 2010 Theatre Odyssey 10-minute play festival, Sarasota Florida. *Honest Abe Mazulu* was also produced at the American Globe Theatre, NYC. Katherin Carter, Director. Basil Rodericks—Abraham Mazulu; Robert Armstrong—Poulenc; Simon Siegel—David. Produced at the American Globe Theatre Short Play Festival, 2010. *Honest Abe Mazulu* was also produced at the Shepparton Theatre Arts Group, Shepparton, Australia, 2010.

CHARACTERS

Abe . . . . . (30–40 years), visiting from Gabongo. Abe's full name
is Abraham Mazulu. Abe is black. He is the well-
known fighter of corruption in his country, and is the
Minister of Corruption Control in Gabongo.

Poulenc . . (50–60 years), Director of Suisse Banc de Geneve,
Zurich, et Bern. This bank caters to people who want
secret Swiss bank accounts.

David . . . (20–30 years), Secretary to Poulenc.

SET AND TIME

The time is the present. The action of the play is set in the office
of Poulenc, the Director of the Suisse Banc de Geneve, Zurich, et
Bern. The office contains one large desk, a chair for Poulenc, and another chair for a visitor. On the desk is an intercom through which
Poulenc can request materials from his secretary, David. Other items
on the desk (high class pen and pencil set, in/out box, etc.,) indicate
that this is an office. There is an entrance to the office through which
David and Abe will enter. Ideally a door within a door jamb would
be best, but an imagined door with entrances mimed would be satis-
factory.

The the "M" before names in the script is pronounced "Mon-
sieur"

---

*Opening: At lights up we see Poulenc, wearing a conservative business
suit, sitting at his desk. He is busy writing, or he could be working on
a laptop on his desk. After a moment, David appears at the door followed by Abe, who is also dressed either in a less impressive business
suit or a dashiki. Abe is carrying an attache case or briefcase.*

DAVID: M. Poulenc, M. Abraham Mazulu is here for your two-o'clock
appointment.

POULENC: [*Poulenc puts away his writing or hhis laptop, then rises, comes out from behind his desk, shakes hands with Abe, and ushers him to the visitor's chair.*] Yes, M. Mazulu, come in. Very nice to meet you. Welcome to Geneva. Please have a seat right here. That will be all, David.

> [*David leaves and discreetly closes the door behind him. Poulenc returns to his chair behind this desk.*]

So, M. Mazulu, when you called you said you only had time for a short visit. You were lucky that I had this time open. I am very glad you were able to stop in. What can I do for you?

ABE: I have a simple mission. I am the head of the Corruption Control Office of Gabongo. I need your help with a problem that faces our country. Here is a letter from the President certifying my office while in Geneva.

> [*Abe reaches into his jacket pocket and takes out an envelope that contains a single page letter, crisply folded. He hands it to Poulenc, who opens the unsealed envelope, takes out the letter, and glances at its contents. Then gives back the letter.*]

POULENC: Hmm. Very impressive. I am at your service. How can I help you?

ABE: This should not take long. I am in need of the names of Gabongonese [*prounouced Ga-bon'-go-nay-say*] who have participated in corruption and who have exported our currency illegally. We need the names of those who have accounts in your bank. With this information we can finish off the corruption problems that have plagued Gabongo for years.

POULENC: But, M. Mazulu, that is impossible.

ABE: What do you mean? It is definitely possible. All you have to do is look in your account system and give me the names. Why is this a problem?

POULENC: M. Mazulu, I did not mean that it was impossible for for me to find the names—it is impossible for me to give you the names. It is our policy.

ABE: What do you mean? Informers have told us that illicit money from Gabongo has been deposited in your bank. We do not know the actual names of these criminals.

POULENC: The only problem is that the information you request cannot be given out. The Swiss Bank of Geneva is a bank that prides itself on protecting the privacy of our clients. We never divulge this kind of information. I think that makes our position and policy very clear. I am afraid that I cannot give you the information you seek.

ABE: M. Poulenc, I represent the Government of Gabongo. Sending money out of Gabongo is a crime—a serious crime. I am not sure you truly understand. Do you know who I am?

POULENC: [*Poulenc picks up a thin manila folder on his desk, opens it and looks at the single page in the folder. He reads.*] Actually I do. When David made the appointment for me, I looked you up on the internet.

[*Poulenc picks up a thin manila folder on his desk, opens it and looks at the single page in the folder. He reads.*]

Poor country teacher, grew up until you were thirteen as a close friend of the newly elected President of Gabongo. You were chosen by this boyhood friend to be head of the Department of Corruption Control and you succeeded beyond anyone's wildest dreams. And because of your honesty—in the face of overwhelming corruption and dishonesty—a newspaper called you "Honest Abe" Mazulu.

ABE: [*Light laugh or chuckle.*] I find that "Honest Abe" name funny. A man has his first name Abraham and because he is honest he gets the name "Honest Abe"—and just because Lincoln was honest. I guess the freeing of the slaves helped, and once one paper said it, the others just joined in. It wasn't my idea.

POULENC: I think you should be pleased to be called "Honest Abe". That name sounds good to me.

ABE: I must admit it was not easy being honest when I was young. Even after I began work as a teacher, I was poor. I wanted things for my family, my wife and children. I was tempted many times, but in the end I felt better for not giving in.

POULENC: An admirable feeling. And I am sure that your fellow citizens are grateful for your work and efforts at cleaning up the corruption problem.

ABE: When I first became the Minister of Corruption Control, Gabongo was completely corrupt. Parents would bribe teachers. Robberies and murders were ignored with the right payoff. Building permits were sold openly. Even after one skyscraper collapsed, the corruption went on. If we do not get rid of this problem, we will not attract tourists and the entire economy will suffer.

POULENC: I remember reading about that building collapse. I can imagine that one collapsed building could certainly make people pause before visiting Gabongo.

ABE: You take a few of the worst and subject them to death. Not just death, but actually a very public death, with much media attention, and after a while people begin to say no to corruption.

POULENC: I guess that's one way to cure the problem.

ABE: I was given funds to build an entire office with computer experts and accountants who were able to trace the movement of money. We were soon able to expose the corruption. Before we began, corruption was eating the soul of our country. People had to be dishonest in order to survive. I think they forgot what it meant to be honest. It was a difficult time and I was sorely tempted—many times—but I remained honest.

POULENC: I remember reading about the "Honest Abe" name. Le Monde said that you were the most honest man in all of Africa. Quite a reputation.

ABE: Thank you, M. Poulenc. But Gabongo is not cured. It is difficult to conceal a paper trail for money moving *within* a country. That is how we uncovered much corruption. But this approach is possible only when the funds were transferred *within* Gabongo. The problem still exists when money leaves the country. That is why I am here. We are looking for money that has left Gabongo.

POULENC: You think that some Gabongonese [*prounouced Ga-bon'-go-nay-say*] have accounts here in our bank? Accounts opened with stolen or extorted money?

ABE: [*Strongly, perhaps hitting his fist on the desk.*] We don't think; we know!

POULENC: [*Strongly and firmly.*] I think our conversation is going nowhere, M. Mazulu. I cannot help you with your investigation. I am very sorry. I cannot say whether there are accounts from Gabongo citizens. I am unable to tell you anything. We do not give out such information.
        [*Emphatically.*]
    At all!

ABE: Is there anything I can say that will make you change your mind? I really must have that information. Our country is desperate. And I am desperate as well.

POULENC: I am sorry, but the bank information is private and will remain so. I think our conversation is over. Thank you for coming in. Any further discussion is futile.

ABE: Just a moment more, M. Poulenc.

[*Puts fingers together in a thoughtful manner, as he thinks about what to say. Then he speaks slowly and deliberately.*]

My friend, President Lugando sent me here to eliminate the transit of money out of the country. He gave me three choices.

[*Pause*]

First, I could succeed and get the names from you and the government would take care of the problem. The guilty would be subject to the most public of deaths.

POULENC: Well, that choice is not possible. As I have explained in detail. You cannot get information about accounts in this bank.

ABE: The second choice is to fail, and if I fail to get the names, I shall return to the country and I will be the victim of the very punishment that awaited the criminals. I do not want to die. But if I were not to return to my country and stayed in Switzerland, the President has assured me that my wife and my three children, and my mother, will all face death in the same manner. So now I must return and face my own death rather than have my family suffer.

POULENC: My God. What a horrible choice. What is the third option? Is that a solution?

ABE: [*Slowly*] The third way involves you.

[*Abe reaches into his jacket or briefcase and takes out an automatic handgun. He points it at Poulenc.*]

I could redeem myself with the President by killing you.

POULENC: [*Surprised and shocked.*] But why me? I can't give you any names.

ABE: President Lugando gave me this third choice to ensure that I would not be weak in my resolve and that I would do everything in my power—and I do mean everything in my power—to get these names. I must have those names, or I am afraid I will have to kill you.

[*Pause.*]

You see, it is not only my country that is in need of the names, but I am in need as well. As you can understand from the choices, I am truly desperate. Desperate men will do desperate things. And I am truly desperate.

POULENC: But M. Mazulu. I am not sure *you* understand. This bank was founded in 1612. In a few years we will be celebrating our 400th anniversary. In all that time we have never given out account information. Not even one name. I cannot do it.

ABE: Then I am afraid you will have to die.

POULENC: Your threats cannot change this policy. You will not succeed.

ABE: As I have explained, I have no choice. I must get those names or you will die.

POULENC: M. Mazulu. Let me explain some things. There is even more than the history of this bank. My grandfather and my father were directors as well. They never told anything to anyone. I cannot give any information to you. If I did, I would not only soil the reputation and history of the bank, but the reputation and history of my family as well. And that I will not do.

ABE: Then you must be prepared to die. I am sorry. Truly sorry.

POULENC: One minute. May I speak to David. Can I call him in?

ABE: Yes, but make sure he doesn't try to resist.

POULENC: [*Poulenc bends over the intercom and pushes a button and speaks to David.*] David, will you come in? And please do not be surprised by what you see. Just be calm.

[*After a moment, David enters, is surprised to see Abe with a gun pointed at Poulenc, and waits to hear from Poulenc.*]
As you can see I may not survive this day. Let me just say "thank you" David, for your loyal service to me and the bank.

DAVID: What are you talking about M. Poulenc?

POULENC: I am afraid M. Mazulu is going to kill me. It is too long a story to tell you everything. I just want you to give my family some of my final thoughts.

DAVID: [*Speaking to Abe.*] This is crazy, M. Mazulu. What is going on?

ABE: David, as M. Poulenc said, it's too much to explain to you now. I need some information about some account holders and M. Poulenc seems to think it is better for him to die than to give out bank information.

POULENC: David, you must understand. I must die to protect the reputation of my family and the bank.

ABE: David, tell him he should give out the information. Otherwise he will die. And I am afraid, now that you have seen what is about to happen, I will have to kill you, too.

DAVID: M. Poulenc. This is crazy. You should not die for a few names. Give him the names, please, or . . . .

POULENC: [*Poulenc raises his hand to stop David from talking.*] David, I am ready. I would have only, at most, a few years left to live. But a soiled reputation will go on for thousands of years. I cannot bear that. I was entrusted with the integrity of this bank and I cannot destroy that name. I am ready to die. And I am sorry that you will die too. I cannot betray my trust.

ABE: [*Abe stands up and pushes the gun into Poulenc's face. Poulanc bends backward away from the gun.. Abe now speaks strongly and with fervor.*] I will give you one more chance, M. Poulenc. I need those names. I am desperate. I will do what needs to be done. I am a man of my word. Give me the names and you and David will live. Withold them, and you and David will die.

POULENC: Then I must die. I am sorry for David, but I have no other choice.

ABE: [*With rising voice.*] Is that your final decision? You will never give out the names?

POULENC: [*Emphatically.*] Never!

ABE: [*Abe puts the gun on the desk. He picks up the attache case, and puts it on the desk. He opens to case to show Poulenc what is in the case. The audience does not see the contents and can only guess what is in the case.*] Then I'd like to open a new account and make a deposit.

    CURTAIN or BLACKOUT

I Thought I Liked Girls . . .

Nicole Pandolfo

Productions: October 2010: Play-Makers Spokane, Auntie's Bookstore, Spokane, WA. September 2010: Briefs, Theatre Out, Santa Ana, CA. June 2010: Girl Play 2nd Annual Lesbian Playreading Festival, Women's Theatre Project, Ft. Lauderdale, FL. August 2010: Long Beach Poppin' Play Festival 2010, Alive Theatre, Long Beach, CA.

CHARACTERS

Lucy
Her Mom
Her Dad

TIME

Present day.

PLACE

The kitchen.\

At Rise: Lucy and her parents, Mom and Dad, are seated across from each other at the kitchen table.

LUCY: There's no easy way to say this, so I'm just gonna say it.
   Pause
LUCY: I'm straight.
MOM: Excuse me?
LUCY: I'm straight.
DAD: I don't understand.
LUCY: I like men. One in particular.
MOM: Wait a minute. I thought . . .
LUCY: I know. I was wrong.
DAD: You mean to tell me you're not a—
LUCY: Right. I'm not a lesbian.
MOM: Wait, wait, wait, wait, wait—
   Just, poof, you're not a lesbian anymore?
LUCY: Well, not exactly like that.
MOM: Then like what?
LUCY: It took me some time to figure it out, but now that I have, everything makes sense to me again.

DAD: You mean you're completely heterosexual?

LUCY: Yes.

DAD: So, these past 10 years have been a lie?

LUCY: I wouldn't call them a lie.

MOM: Yes. A lie! You don't just wake up one day and like men. Usually you wake up one day and realize how much you fucking hate them.

LUCY: There's more . . . I'm engaged.

Lucy Extends Her Hand With The Engagement Ring,
Pause,

LUCY: Aren't you going to congratulate me?

DAD: Is this some kind of a joke?

LUCY: No.
I love him, and I want your blessing to marry him.

DAD: But you're gay!

LUCY: No. I'm not. Not anymore.

DAD: I just don't understand how this could have happened!

MOM: Was it something we did? Were we not supportive enough of you?

LUCY: It's nothing you did.

Pause,

LUCY: I know this must be confusing for you.

DAD: The last 10 years we've been walking around thinking you like girls.

LUCY: I thought I liked girls.

Pause,

LUCY: But I don't. I prefer men.

DAD: So maybe you're bi?

LUCY: I thought that might be it. That maybe I like both. But no, I'm just not into chicks anymore.

DAD: Wait just a second! You just waltz in here, tell us you're not a lesbian, and then tell us your engaged?

LUCY: Yes.

DAD: Who the hell is he?

LUCY: His name is Harold.

MOM: Harold?

LUCY: Yes.

MOM: And what happened to Cynthia?

LUCY: You know we broke up like 8 months ago.

DAD: But I thought you were working things out?

LUCY: Working things out? She moved across state.
Dad, she left me because I stopped wanting to have sex with her. And now I know why. Because I'm not a lesbian.

DAD: Lots of couples stop wanting to have sex with each other—it doesn't mean you change your sexual orientation.

MOM: Yea, you gotta spice it up.

DAD: Why do you think your mom and I go to those swingers parties? To keep it fresh.

LUCY: You guys are swingers?

DAD: The first Tuesday of every month. The group meets for dinner at Chilli's then we go to someone's house for the after party.

LUCY: Oh my God.

MOM: We really like it.

LUCY: Stop talking!

> *Lucy looks disgusted,*

DAD: Does this Harold do something for a living?

LUCY: He's a doctor.

MOM: What kind?

> *No response,*

MOM: What kind?

LUCY: A gynecologist.

DAD: What is that some sort of a joke?

LUCY: No.

MOM: Cynthia was a poet.

LUCY: Cynthia was always broke.

DAD: Are you sure you're not just confused? Maybe this Harold, he's a good friend, has a good job. Maybe you're just confused.

LUCY: I'm not.

MOM: How long have you even known this guy?

LUCY: Five months.

DAD: Five months! And you're engaged?

LUCY: You guys got engaged after two weeks of dating.

MOM: But I didn't think I was a lesbian for 10 years!

DAD: And why does this Harold all the sudden make you straight?

LUCY: He didn't make me straight. I thought for some time that I was different- and then when I met Harold I knew for sure. I'm in love with him

> *Pause,*

LUCY: But there's one thing—he doesn't know I was a lesbian. And I don't want him to know.

MOM: What?

LUCY: He's a born again Christian, and if he finds out I was gay he'll leave me.

DAD: Oh my God. A born again Christian! Are you insane?

LUCY: You both have to promise never to tell him.

MOM: You're going to lie about the last decade of your life?

LUCY: Well I plan to just not mention it.

DAD: That's absurd!

LUCY: Please.

DAD: Honestly Lucy, how do you expect us to react?

LUCY: I expect you to be happy for me.

DAD: We were happy for you. When you were a lesbian.

MOM: You mean, all those times I dressed up for the pride parade, that was all for nothing?
I marched around with nipple tassels on for Christ sake.

LUCY: I thought this would make you happy. Isn't this easier? Now I can get married, have kids naturally.

DAD: What's so wrong with civil unions and adopting?

LUCY: Nothing, if it's a choice instead of the only option.

MOM: I see your point, but isn't that kind of a silly reason to turn straight?

LUCY: It's not the reason I turned straight Mom.

DAD: Then what is?

LUCY: I told you, I realized that I've been straight from the day I was born.

MOM: No, you decided to be straight.

LUCY: It's not a choice. Trust me.
Finally, I realized what I've been missing my whole life.

MOM: A penis?

LUCY: Yes.

DAD: The partners at my law firm are going be so disappointed when you don't bring Cynthia to the company party this year.

LUCY: Why? What do they care?

DAD: It adds to the company image to show that we're anti-discriminatory. That we do non-traditional things.

LUCY: Dad, I'm not gonna be a lesbian so that you can feel hip.

MOM: And what about me? I wrote a book called, "So My Kid is Gay... Now What?" What the hell am I supposed to do now? Write a new one called, "Just Kidding?"

DAD: You remember how long it took everyone to come to terms with it when you were 15 and you told us you were a lesbian? Right? And in the end we accepted you, embraced you. Do you remember what I said when you told me?

> *No response,*

DAD: Do you?

LUCY: Yes. You said, you'll accept me no matter what as long as I never tell you I'm a Republican.

DAD: And I meant it.

LUCY: So accept me now.

MOM: But, I got to go on a book tour...

> *Pause,*

LUCY: Look, I love Harold and I'm going to marry him, with or without your blessing.

> *Pause,*

LUCY: Well?

DAD: What?

LUCY: Are you going to support me or are we gonna have to do this the hard way?

MOM: We haven't even met him yet.

LUCY: Do you actually want to meet him?

DAD: Do we have to?

LUCY: Yes!

DAD: Fine.

LUCY: He's a great guy. I think you're really going to like him.

MOM: I doubt it.

LUCY: Please be open-minded.

MOM: Is he good looking?

LUCY: Yes.

MOM: Is he nice?

LUCY: Yes.

MOM: Does he make a lot of money?

LUCY: He's a doctor... Yes.

Pause,

LUCY: Will you two try and welcome him into the family? Please.

MOM/DAD: Fine./ I guess.

LUCY: Thank you.

Mom starts crying,

MOM: It's just so disappointing.

DAD: How are we supposed to explain this to everyone? Your grandparents? The shock could put Nana in the grave.

LUCY: I know this is hard, and it means a lot to me to have your support.

MOM: Our whole lives are going to change.

LUCY: I know. But if we could make it through me being a lesbian, we can make it through me being straight.

Pause,

DAD: You know we love you no matter what.

LUCY: I know.

MOM: Just give us time to get used to the idea.

LUCY: No problem.

DAD: You can invite Harold over for Sunday dinner next week.

LUCY: Thank you! And remember, don't mention the whole lesbian for a decade thing.

Lusy hugs them,

LUCY: I gotta run. Harold got us tickets for the opera tonight.

Lucy is about to exit when,

DAD: Luc, can we still all go to the parade together in the summer, you know, like we used to.

LUCY: Sure Dad.

MOM: Can I still wear my tassels?

Lucy hangs her head and exits. Lights hard to black,

THE END.

Last-Minute Adjustments

Rich Orloff

Last-Minute Adjustments was produced at Taipei American School (Taipei, Taiwan) in May 2010, Saint Bede Academy (Peru, Illinois) in November 2010, and Richmond Hill High School (Richmond Hill, Ontario, Canada) in December 2010. The play is also part of the author's collections *Nothing Serious* and *Oy!*

CHARACTERS

The Protagonist
The Supervisor
Assistant A
Assistant B
Radio Technician

The age and gender of all these characters can vary.

SETTING

A warm, comfortable place

TIME

The present

---

*The Supervisor and his/her two Assistants are speedily but not franti-
cally doing a last-minute review before the Protagonist is about to go
on a big journey. The protagonist has a huge tube attached to his/her
navel. The Radio Technician sits at a table with a kind of shortwave
radio apparatus on it. He/she wears a headset.*

SUPERVISOR: Ears?

ASST. A: Check.

SUPERVISOR: Nose?

ASST. B: Check.

SUPERVISOR: Chin?

ASST. A: Check.

PROTAGONIST: Why can't I become an aardvark?

SUPERVISOR: I told you. It wasn't our decision. Dimples?

ASST. B: One, on the left.

PROTAGONIST: I think I could do aardvark really well.

SUPERVISOR: Maybe next time. Tongue?

ASST. A: Check.

PROTAGONIST: Can't I at least have some feathers? Feathers sound so cute.

ASST. B: You'll have enough to deal with without having to worry about molting.

RADIO TECHNICIAN: She's just entered the hospital.

PROTAGONIST: Okay, let me make sure I've got this: Breathing, left to right.

ASST. A: In and out.

PROTAGONIST: The mouth, food goes in or out?

ASST. B: *(pinching the protagonist's cheek:)* That depends on how fussy you'll be.

RADIO TECHNICIAN: Contractions are three minutes apart.

SUPERVISOR: Okay, let's finish this sucker. Eyebrows?

ASST. A: Check.

SUPERVISOR: Eyelashes?

ASST. B: Check.

SUPERVISOR: Brains?

ASST. A: *(looks in an ear:)* Check.

SUPERVISOR: Soul?

> Both assistants look in the ear, see nothing.

SUPERVISOR (CONT D): Soul?

> The assistants look all around for the soul.

SUPERVISOR (CONT D): All right. Who was supposed to put in the soul?

ASSTS. A AND B: *(simultaneously pointing at the other:)* He was!*

> (*Or "She was", as appropriate, in this and all references.)

ASST. A: I remember distinctly. I was in charge of appendix; you got soul.

ASST. B: No, I was in charge of appendix.

SUPERVISOR: Okay, how many appendices does our little friend have?

ASST. B: *(checks, then:)* Two.

SUPERVISOR: Well, that'll give medical science something to have fun with. Okay, let's give our pal a soul before it's too late.

> The assistants hook up the soul transferring machine to the protagonist.

PROTAGONIST: Why do I need a soul?

SUPERVISOR: You won't be complete without one.

PROTAGONIST: I feel complete as I am. Completely complete. Fully equipped to have a rich, full life.

SUPERVISOR: You need a soul.

PROTAGONIST: I'd prefer feathers.

ASST. A: You need a soul to cope with disappointment, rejection, humiliation, cruelty –

ASST. B: And all the other perks of a full life.

SUPERVISOR: Please, you'll spoil all the surprises.

ASST. A: The soul connects you to wisdom.

PROTAGONIST: What's wisdom?

ASST. B: That's the knowledge you'll have where you'll have no idea where it comes from.

ASST. A: Like the stuff we're telling you now.

PROTAGONIST: I won't remember this?

ASST. A: In the beginning, you'll remember what your mother smells like, and that's about it.

PROTAGONIST: My mother, will I like her?

SUPERVISOR: Oh, you'll come up with plenty of answers to that one.

ASST. A: Ready for soul transmission.

PROTAGONIST: This really feels unnecessary.

SUPERVISOR: Okay, now just relax.

PROTAGONIST: Getting a soul, will it hurt?

ASST. A: Just for an instant.

ASST. B: A lifetime at most.

RADIO TECHNICIAN: Contractions, two minutes apart.

SUPERVISOR: Let's do it . . . Five, four, three, two, one.

The soul is transmitted into the protagonist.

SUPERVISOR (CONT D): How do you feel?

PROTAGONIST: Vulnerable.

ASST. B: Soul successfully attached.

RADIO TECHNICIAN: Time to start preparing to leave the womb.

PROTAGONIST: No!!!!!!!!!!!!!!!!!!!!!!!!!!!!!!!!!!!!

SUPERVISOR: *(used to this:)* What's the matter?

PROTAGONIST: All those things—humiliation, disappointment, cruelty—my soul won't be able to take it.

ASST. A: Give it enough light every day; it'll be fine.

PROTAGONIST: I'm staying in here where it's safe.

RADIO TECHNICIAN: She just broke her water.

SUPERVISOR: *(to the protagonist:)* Guess again.

PROTAGONIST: Why did you have to give me a soul? I suddenly feel terrified of everything.

ASST. A: Checklist complete.

RADIO TECHNICIAN: Contractions building.

SUPERVISOR: Okay, time to move 'em out.

PROTAGONIST: I'm not going.

SUPERVISOR: If you resist, you'll only make it harder on yourself.

PROTAGONIST: I'm staying.

SUPERVISOR: You want them to use forceps?

PROTAGONIST: They can use a forklift; I'm not moving.

ASST. A: You can't stay. Your lease is up.

PROTAGONIST: But I know my way around here.

ASST. B: Enjoy that feeling. It's the last time you'll have it.

PROTAGONIST: Why can't I be an aardvark?

SUPERVISOR: We didn't design you; we're only following the blueprint.

PROTAGONIST: But being a human sounds so stressful and exhausting. It doesn't sound nearly as good as waking up, wanting some ants, finding some ants, and eating some ants.

RADIO TECHNICIAN: She's eight centimeters dilated.

SUPERVISOR: Okay, no more procrastination.

PROTAGONIST: But what if I get hurt?

SUPERVISOR: You will get hurt.

PROTAGONIST: What if I'm disappointed?

SUPERVISOR: You will be disappointed.

PROTAGONIST: What if I'm disillusioned?

SUPERVISOR: You will be disillusioned.

PROTAGONIST: What if I turn moody, irrational and hostile?

ASST. B: It's called adolescence.

PROTAGONIST: I want you to take my soul back.

SUPERVISOR: That can't be done.

PROTAGONIST: Then when I get out there, the first thing I'm doing is getting rid of it.

SUPERVISOR AND ASSTS. A AND B: *(simultaneously)* Don't!

PROTAGONIST: Why not?

ASST. A: Because then you won't know love. Life'll just be an endless series of desires and gratifications.

PROTAGONIST: That sounds nice.

ASST. A: Love's better.

PROTAGONIST: Something's better than gratification? I know I'm only prenatal, but that still sounds stupid.

ASST. A: Love's better.

ASST. B: Much better.

SUPERVISOR: It's the touching of two souls.

ASST. B: No soul, no love.

ASST. A: Not even much like.

PROTAGONIST: But if I have a soul, I'm going to feel so much pain.

SUPERVISOR: That's true.

PROTAGONIST: Is love worth it?

    Everyone else gets very busy.

PROTAGONIST (CONT D): Is love worth all the pain?

RADIO TECHNICIAN: She's almost fully dilated.

PROTAGONIST: I'm not going out there until I get an answer.

SUPERVISOR: Look, kid, the only way to get an answer is to go out there.

PROTAGONIST: I'm not going out into that, that—uncertainty.

ASST. B: Look on the bright side. You'll be dead before you know it.

PROTAGONIST: You mean I'm going to go through a lifetime of work and pain and struggle just to end up dead?

ASST. A: That's what's on the schedule.

PROTAGONIST: When am I going to die?

ASST. B: About ten minutes before you've sorted everything out.

PROTAGONIST: It seems like such a waste.

SUPERVISOR: There's actually very little waste. We recycle almost all of you.

PROTAGONIST: I don't have a prayer, do I?

SUPERVISOR: Yes, you do.

ASST. B: You always do.

ASST. A: Always.

RADIO TECHNICIAN: She's fully dilated.

PROTAGONIST: That's her tough luck.

RADIO TECHNICIAN: They're all yelling "Push!"

SUPERVISOR: Let's help.

The two assistants grab the protagonist's arms and get ready to swing him/her out into the world.

PROTAGONIST: No!

SUPERVISOR: And a one!

The swinging begins.

PROTAGONIST: No!

SUPERVISOR: And a two!

PROTAGONIST: No!

SUPERVISOR: And a—

PROTAGONIST: I'm staying here!

SUPERVISOR: You can't stay here!

PROTAGONIST: Why not?!

SUPERVISOR: Because we need time to fix this place up for your little sister.

PROTAGONIST: Shit.

SUPERVISOR: Okay. This time like we mean it. On the count of three.... And a one... And a two...

PROTAGONIST: *(terrified)* Say something encouraging!

SUPERVISOR: Have a nice life!

The assistants toss the protagonist forward into the world.

PROTAGONIST: *(a scream)* Ahhhhhhh!!!!!!

The protagonist is hurled into the void.

(Perhaps a moment later, we hear a baby crying.)

The lights fade.

End of play

Lot Lizards

Kathryn O'Sullivan

Production History: Produced by American Globe Theatre and Turnip Theatre Company, 16th Annual New York City 15-Minute Play Festival, April 23, 2010. Directed by Paul Awad. The cast was as follows: Goldie—Lydia Mong, Donelle—Taifa Harris, Elena—Rachel Hardin.

Originally produced by the Source Theatre Company, Washington, DC, 23rd Annual Washington Theatre Festival, 18th Annual Ten Minute Play Competition, August 9, 2003. Directed by Paul Awad. The cast was as follows: Goldie—Jean Miller, Donelle—Millie Langford, Elena—Jessica Drizd.

345

CHARACTERS

Goldie: . . Truck stop prostitute, Caucasian, 50-60.

Donelle: . Truck stop prostitute, African American, late 20's.

Elena: . . . Truck stop prostitute, Russian, early 20's.

PLACE

A truck stop somewhere off of Interstate 95.

TIME

The present.

SETTING

An Interstate 95 truck stop.

AT RISE: Goldie, a prostitute that has worked her way up and down the East Coast for thirty years, sits on a bench fanning herself with a magazine.

Donelle, black, tough, applies sunblock and glances at a newspaper.

GOLDIE: Woowee. It's hot today.

DONELLE: Almost too hot to fuck.

GOLDIE: Really, Donelle!

DONELLE: All I'm sayin' is it's tough sellin' pussy at a truck stop when it's ninety five degrees.

GOLDIE: Must you curse all the time? It's so . . . unladylike.

DONELLE: I ain't trying to be a lady.

GOLDIE: If you did you might get more business. In my day if a woman talked like that she'd get a reputation.

DONELLE: That's exactly what I'm goin' for. (pushes up breasts) A reputation.

[*Goldie looks down the highway.*]

GOLDIE: Joe's late. The long haul fellas usually get here by now.

DONELLE: Yeah. Well. Maybe he'll be in the next shift. Afterall, it is an ozone alert day.

GOLDIE: That never stopped business before. What happened to the good old days?

DONELLE: Don't you start about how business was booming till they put in that fuckin' overpass. Trucks lining up at the truck stop two at a time for a blowjob.

GOLDIE: Your communication skills are seriously lacking.

DONELLE: I talk just fine. Matter of fact, my speech professor at the community college—He's this real cute dude with a tight ass. I'd do him for free if he weren't queer.—He said that I really know how to grab people's attention when I speak. He said talking well is what's gonna get me ahead in my career.

GOLDIE: I don't think he had this career in mind.

DONELLE: Maybe not. But come next month I'm ditching this life. I've got me enough saved to go to school full-time. Gonna get me a cosmetology license. Hey, Goldie. Why don't you go, too?

GOLDIE: I couldn't leave the fellas.

DONELLE: Come on. Ain't thirty years enough?

GOLDIE: And who would work the lot?

DONELLE: Elena.

GOLDIE: Ha! Elena wouldn't last a week by herself. Just look at that character Ronny she's mixed up with.

DONELLE: You don't know the half of it.

GOLDIE: What's that supposed to mean?

DONELLE: Now don't go getting your panties in a twist.

GOLDIE: Did Elena tell you something about Ronny?

DONELLE: No.

GOLDIE: Come on. Out with it!

DONELLE: Jees, chill, would you? *(searching through newspaper)* I didn't wanna say nothing 'cause this is how you get... Here it is. Look. Seems Ronny done went and robbed a bank. Shot a man, too.

GOLDIE: Lemme see that.

[*Goldie takes out a pair of reading glasses and reads the paper.*]

DONELLE: I thought someday he'd get caught for whacking off at old ladies or doin' it with cows on the side of the interstate. Guess he was thinking outside the box.

GOLDIE: There's a warrant for his arrest.

ELENA: *(O.S.)* Goldie! Donelle!

GOLDIE: Don't say a word.

> [*Elena, another lot lizard, rushes in. Her clothing has a slightly foreign look, something not quite American.*]

GOLDIE (CONT D): Elena. You're early.

DONELLE: Girl, do we got something to tell you.

ELENA: Me first.

GOLDIE: Say, are those new Candies?

ELENA: Yes. But –

GOLDIE: How many times do I have to tell you not to buy those cheap shoes? *(extends a foot)* You should try Clarks. They may not be fancy but they're like slippers the first time you put 'em on. Keeps me from getting those ugly spider veins. *(pulls up her skirt to show off her legs)* This is why men leave home.

ELENA: I like Candies.

DONELLE: Forget the shoes. We got something to tell you.

ELENA: Me, too.

GOLDIE: Donelle, don't.

DONELLE AND ELENA: Ronny is wanted by the police!

DONELLE: Well, fuck me doggie style. The girl already knows.

ELENA: I was watching TV with that man, John Welch —

DONELLE: Walsh. John *Walsh.*

ELENA: *Walsh.* Yes. Sorry. Mr. Welch say America is, what was the word, oh yes, he say America is gunning for Ronny. They have his picture. They show his tattoos and everything. All those people see my name on his ass. Isn't that cool?

DONELLE: Once they're on *America's Most Wanted,* they're good as dead.

ELENA: They're going to kill him?

GOLDIE: Not unless he does something stupid like resist arrest.

DONELLE: Which is real possible knowing Ronny.

ELENA: But they can't. He is famous now.

DONELLE: Ah, don't worry. Maybe they'll get him when he's sleeping. Like they did those sniper guys.

ELENA: Not possible. Ronny is an impotent.

GOLDIE: You mean an insomniac?

ELENA: What is difference?

DONELLE: (gesturing with a finger) One stays up all night.

ELENA: .... Oh. Poor Ronny.

DONELLE: Why you feeling so bad for that slug? From where I been sitting, it's not like he treats you so good.

ELENA: He does so treat me good.

DONELLE: Like the time you came home from working the lot and caught him banging some chick?

ELENA: You don't know him like I do.

DONELLE: And I don't want to.

GOLDIE: Why don't you leave Elena alone?

DONELLE: Why're you tryin' to shut me up? Just the other day you were sayin' we needed to talk some sense into Elena 'bout Ronny. Here's your opportunity for intervention.

ELENA: Intervention? What does this mean?

GOLDIE: It don't mean nothing, sweetie.

DONELLE: If Goldie don't care enough to tell you the truth then Donelle here does. Elena, you need to dump his ass. As a matter of fact, I say you call the cops and tell them where he at. Get the reward. Get outta this hole.

GOLDIE: And where's she gonna go? What's she gonna do?

DONELLE: She's gonna correct a mistake. 'Cause Lord knows ending up here sucking dicks and diesel is one huge mistake.

ELENA: The only mistake I ever make is watching American television.

GOLDIE: You got that right. (directed at Donelle) Television does nothing to improve one's vocabulary.

DONELLE: Like I need another way to say (to a man in the audience) Hey, mister, want me to suck your cock?

ELENA: (to Donelle) Why you hate Ronny?

DONELLE: Trust me. If Mr. Walsh wants Ronny, then he ain't no good.

ELENA: But you don't —

DONELLE: —know him like you do. Tell me. Does this sound like a good man? (reading from the paper) "On Tuesday, July 25th at approximately 10:42 AM Ronald Aaron Round, III allegedly walked into the Bank of America armed with a 9mm handgun and demanded $25,000 from teller Theodore White. Witnesses say that after Mr. White complied, Mr. Round became angry, insisting that Mr. White had given him 'a dirty look.' According to another teller, Mr. Round shot Mr. White twice in the face and once in the abdomen before fleeing."

ELENA: He never is violent with me.

DONELLE: If it looks like a duck and walks like a duck, honey, it's a duck.

ELENA: Ronny is no duck.

GOLDIE: Nick Gianetti always treated me like a queen. Never even raised his voice.

DONELLE: That's the mob, Goldie. They're used to keeping business separate from the slap and tickle.

ELENA: When I come to this country I have big dreams of going to New York City to be an actress. Like you see on television. But who wants Russian girl with no money and no English? I end up on streets. I think I am failure. How can I go back to my country? My whole family save to send me here. So I sit on the curb next to diner one night and cry.

GOLDIE: I met Frank Sinatra in a diner. Such a gentleman.

ELENA: Ronny came. He sit down next to me. Ask me what is wrong. I tell him. He tell me fame not come easy in America. That I have to work hard. He say I make good money giving head.

GOLDIE: Let me guess. He volunteered to be first in line.

ELENA: Yes. And he bought me a Twinkie after.

GOLDIE: What a guy.

ELENA: Showing men a good time give me my freedom.

DONELLE: Wake up and smell the exhaust fumes. This ain't freedom. Freedom is calling the cops and tellin' them where Ronny is. Freedom is gettin' that reward so you can get yourself a real man and get outta this highway hellhole.

GOLDIE: You're just determined to put her back in the gutter with no-body to care for her.

DONELLE: You want her stroking gear sticks her whole life?

GOLDIE: Of course not.

DONELLE: Then tell her to call the cops and get that money. Use it to start a new life.

GOLDIE: Doing what? She doesn't have any other skills. And what's she gonna do when that money runs out?

ELENA: If I collect money, can I still see Ronny in jail?

GOLDIE: Listen to her. You think she's ready to strike out on her own?

ELENA: You think I am loser?

GOLDIE: No, sweetie, of course not. You just have a lot to learn.

ELENA: That's what I want. To learn. Like Donelle. She says I could be real good at polishing nails.

GOLDIE: *(to Donelle)* This is what you've been filling her head with when I'm not around?

DONELLE: What's wrong with an education?

GOLDIE: Nothing.

DONELLE: Then it's settled. Elena calls the cops, gets the money, and goes to school with me.

ELENA: Why doesn't Goldie come with us?

GOLDIE: I couldn't possibly leave the fellas.

DONELLE: What fellas? There hasn't been a man come lookin' for you in . . . forever.

GOLDIE: Men drive fifty miles off route just to see me.

DONELLE: What? Oh, now you're gonna tell me about Benny Robinson? Goldie, that was nine months back. And don't get started on Elvis. That man done died on the crapper years ago.

GOLDIE: Joe's due any minute now.

ELENA: Who is Joe?

DONELLE: That's what I'm talkin' about. Joe's so far back it's before Elena's time.

GOLDIE: Joe's always been loyal.

DONELLE: I'm not sayin' he ain't. But you ever think the reason you haven't seen him lately might be 'cause he retired?

GOLDIE: He would have told me . . . He would.

DONELLE: So that's it? You're just gonna sit on your ass waitin' while life passes you by?

[*Goldie looks away.*]

DONELLE (CONT D): Fine. Have it your way. But Elena and I are leavin'.

[*Donelle grabs Elena's arm.*]

DONELLE (CONT D): I mean it. We're outta this dump.

[*Donelle watches Goldie then nods to Elena. They walk away.*]

GOLDIE: I'm the invisible woman.

DONELLE: What?

GOLDIE: The fellas don't see me like they used to.

DONELLE: Maybe you oughta get outta the heat. It's gettin' to you.

GOLDIE: It's not the heat that's getting to me. It's . . . I'm not nineteen anymore.

ELENA: You are still young woman.

GOLDIE: You see, when you two are around, men notice me. Maybe not exactly like they used to, but at least I'm still on the radar. If you leave, what happens to Golden Oldie?

DONELLE: Shit. You just need a new haircut. Hey, I could do it if you want.

ELENA: Please, Goldie. I do not want to go if you do not.

[*Goldie smiles then turns away.*]

GOLDIE: Joe will be here soon.

[*Donelle stares at Goldie a long moment.*]

DONELLE: Okay, Goldie. I'll make you a deal. If Joe comes, we'll stay and you don't got to worry about being the invisible woman. But if he don't, you walk off this lot with us and don't look back.

GOLDIE: That's ridiculous. I'm not going to make a decision like that based on Joe coming.

DONELLE: *(to Elena)* Sounds like she don't think he's comin'.

GOLDIE: You'll really stay if he comes?

DONELLE: You got my word. But if he don't, you leave. Take it or leave it.

ELENA: Come on, Goldie. What have you to lose?

[*Goldie looks down the road then back at Donelle and Elena.*]

GOLDIE: Okay. It's a deal.

[*Goldie searches the horizon. Elena squeezes Donelle's hand. They wait.*]

THE END

Love and Light

Jerome Parisse

Production: Otterbein University, Columbus (Westerville), Ohio; 15 May 2010. Directed / produced by Bryn Sowash. Cast list: Psychic—Jessica Parker; Tania—Grace DerMott; Bruce—Pascal Domicone

CHARACTERS

The psychic: . Female; sixty-something; elegantly dressed; well
           educated and conservative

Tania: . . . . . . Thirty-something; plump; neatly, but cheaply,
           dressed

Bruce: . . . . . . Tania's husband; slightly older than her; a little
           rough; wears a leather belt around his neck

SETTING

A room: a table, two chairs

TIME

Today

---

*Lights come up. A simple room: a table with a candle, two chairs. The
psychic and Tania are sitting at the table.*

THE PSYCHIC: So . . . did you bring a photo with you?

TANIA: I didn't know I had to bring one!

THE PSYCHIC: Don't worry, dear, it's OK . . . Would you have an object
that belonged to him by any chance? A ring, a watch, a piece of
clothing . . . ?

TANIA: I may have something. *(Tania searches in her bag and pulls out a
checkbook, which she places on the table)* How about this?

THE PSYCHIC: A checkbook? Um . . . I suppose that could work . . . All
right, then . . . *(The psychic lights the candle)* As I raise myself up
to the spirit world of love and light, I ask that only the purest
may enter. *(Bruce enters and positions himself behind the psychic.)*
I ask for hearing, vision and feeling to help Tania. May healing
also flow where it is needed . . .

BRUCE: Hello!

THE PSYCHIC: Ahhhh!!!!!

TANIA: What is it?

> *Bruce moves to the side of the table.*

THE PSYCHIC: He's here . . . Naughty boy, he gave me such a fright!

TANIA: Where is he?

THE PSYCHIC: Just here, standing by the table.

TANIA: Are you sure it's him? Without the photo . . .

THE PSYCHIC: He's about 6 foot, short brown hair, blue eyes, square shoulders, smiling in a handsome sort of way . . .

TANIA: Smiling in a handsome sort of way? That can't be my husband, I'm sorry.

BRUCE: Tania, be nice!

THE PSYCHIC: She can't hear you. If you want to tell her something, you will say it to me, and I will relay the message to her. *(To Tania)* He is wearing khaki shorts, a bright blue tee-shirt, red socks and a pair of runners.

TANIA: That's him, then. He's never had much dress sense . . .

BRUCE: Tania!!!!!!

THE PSYCHIC: *(To Bruce)* Quiet, please. *(To Tania)* Now, Dear, what is it you wanted to ask him?

TANIA: Well, three years ago Bruce opened a savings account . . . It was to buy a new car but with him leaving us so early, that sort of threw the plan out the window. Last week I went to the bank to sort out the paperwork but they told me he closed the account last year . . . So . . . all I want to know is where he's put the money.

BRUCE: And there was me thinking she missed me!

THE PSYCHIC: Bruce, you heard your wife, could you please tell her where the money is?

BRUCE: What does she need it for?

THE PSYCHIC: He wishes to know what you intend to do with those funds.

TANIA: But . . . that's beside the point! I . . . I don't know . . . Renovate the house, buy a new car as planned . . .

THE PSYCHIC: Very well. Bruce?

BRUCE: What do I get in return for saying where the money is?

THE PSYCHIC: Sorry?

BRUCE: It's all very well for her to ask questions! But I've got some of my own. When do I get to ask them?

THE PSYCHIC: He says he's got questions too . . . This is a bit unusual for a spirit I have to say . . .

TANIA: I'm not surprised; he's always been a bit difficult.

BRUCE: A bit difficult? Watch out!

THE PSYCHIC: She can't hear you, remember.

BRUCE: Aren't you supposed to repeat what I say?

THE PSYCHIC: Only if you're being nice.

BRUCE: Tell her she's a murderer!

THE PSYCHIC: Now, this is not what I call being nice.

TANIA: What is he saying?

BRUCE: He . . . he is blaming you for his passing.

TANIA: Typical!

BRUCE: I want to know what she thinks she's doing, mucking around with this Steven guy!

THE PSYCHIC: He is mentioning a . . . a . . . a friend called Steven. He would like to know what role he is playing in your life.

TANIA: *(To where she thinks Bruce is standing)* It's none of your business, you ratbag!

BRUCE: None of my business? Tell her she can forget about the money!!

THE PSYCHIC: I'm afraid your husband is quite displeased with what you just said, Dear, and for that reason he doesn't want to tell you where the funds are.

TANIA: What? He's left me with a mortgage and no job and he's taken the money! Who should be angry here?

THE PSYCHIC: Love and light!

BRUCE: I died for Goodness' sake! Where do you think I am? In Tahiti? At a Christmas party? Go to hell!

THE PSYCHIC: Love and light!

TANIA: What is he saying?

THE PSYCHIC: That you should show more understanding . . . considering he is now in the world of spirits.

TANIA: What's new? He's always drunk like a fish!

BRUCE: Look who's talking!

THE PSYCHIC: I'm afraid this is not working. I'd better call this session off. (She gets up) Love and light!

TANIA: Where are you going?

BRUCE: *(Overlapping)* Where are you going?

THE PSYCHIC: I can't help you if you behave like two silly toddlers.

TANIA: I won't do it again.

BRUCE: Please, stay!

THE PSYCHIC: All right, but I'm warning you, I won't tolerate such childish behaviour anymore. *(She sits down)* Where were we?

TANIA: I was asking him about the money.

BRUCE: And I wanted to know what she's doing with this guy.

THE PSYCHIC: He's insisting about this gentleman called Steven. Who wants to answer first?

BRUCE: Her!

TANIA: Him!

THE PSYCHIC: *(To Tania)* He says you.

TANIA: Hold on! I'm the one who's paying! This is not costing him a cent, he should answer first!

BRUCE: Let's get this straight, shall we? She tells me what's going on with that guy, and I tell her what she wants to know.

THE PSYCHIC: He says he will tell you where the money is only after your answer his question.

TANIA: That's not fair!

THE PSYCHIC: Your husband's got a point, Dear... You summoned him; it is only natural he gets something in return. He is a free spirit now so he can do as he cares.

TANIA: Are you on his side or what?

THE PSYCHIC: I'm on nobody's side, I'm just trying to help and provide you with the information you're after.

TANIA: What if he leaves without telling me where the money is?

BRUCE: Talk about trust!

THE PSYCHIC: He will abide by his word, I can guarantee you... He is not an evil spirit. Now, if you are not comfortable with the truth—

TANIA: That's not what it's about!

BRUCE: I'm ready.

THE PSYCHIC: He's listening.

TANIA: Steve and I.... are getting married.

BRUCE: What the fuck?!?!

THE PSYCHIC: He is nonplussed, dear.

TANIA: I've made up my mind.

BRUCE: I've only been dead three months!!!!!!!!!!

THE PSYCHIC: He says it's rather quick.

TANIA: It just happened.

BRUCE: You bastard!

THE PSYCHIC: He is not happy.

TANIA: Too bad.

BRUCE: Too bad my foot!

THE PSYCHIC: He disagrees.

TANIA: I'm not asking for his agreement.

BRUCE: Stuff you!

THE PSYCHIC: He's not giving it to you.

TANIA: *(To Bruce)* Tell someone who cares!

BRUCE: What about the two of us?

THE PSYCHIC: He is asking if you still feel something for him.

TANIA: Where's the money?

BRUCE: I'm not telling her.

THE PSYCHIC: Bruce, you gave your word!

TANIA: What's happening now?

THE PSYCHIC: He's changed his mind.

TANIA: Listen, you! I gave you the info you wanted so you'd better spit it out!

THE PSYCHIC: Love and light!

BRUCE: OK! Serves you right. There is no more money.

THE PSYCHIC: There is no more money.

TANIA: What??!!

BRUCE: I spent it. On booze, whores and poker.

THE PSYCHIC: He spent it. On alcohol, lady friends and gambling.

TANIA: Son of a . . . !

THE PSYCHIC: Now, now, Dear—

TANIA: Five years! I spent five years of my life married to him for nothing!

BRUCE: For nothing!? What about all those hot nights? Our bondage parties? Our slave and master sessions? Didn't they mean anything to you?

THE PSYCHIC: Please!

TANIA: What is he saying?

THE PSYCHIC: I'm afraid I can't bring myself to repeat such dreadful things.

TANIA: But that's what I'm paying you for!

THE PSYCHIC: I've had enough!! You two can sort out your problems by yourselves. I'm out of here. *(The psychic leaves)*

TANIA: See what you've done, you idiot! *(Tania throws the cheque book in the empty space and starts crying)*
> *Long pause. Bruce watches Tania cry.*

BRUCE: Honey...

TANIA: I can't believe you spent all that money without even telling me. I thought we trusted each other...

BRUCE: You silly goose! I transferred the money to another bank! I only said I spent it because I was angry with you; I was jealous...

TANIA: I didn't want you to die! It was a stupid accident!

BRUCE: Don't you think I know that?

TANIA: Bruce, are you still here?

BRUCE: Yes! I'm here, baby.

TANIA: You should never have asked me to put that strap around your neck!

BRUCE: I never said it was your fault.

TANIA: Bruce? Can you hear me? Bruce?

BRUCE: I've never left you, sweetheart.

TANIA: Oh, I wish you were still here...

BRUCE: Can't you feel me?

TANIA: I miss you so much!

BRUCE: I miss you too, honey...

THE END

Lovesick

Christine Croyden

Production Information: Most recently produced by ACOPA (Australian Centre of Performing Arts) October 2010. Producer/Director Lindsay Saddington.

CHARACTERS

Man:. . . . late twenties
Julian: . . . late twenties
Eveline:. . Blond, attractive and around 25 (She is supposed to
           look like a young version of the French actress,
           Catherine Deneuve.)

SET

A split set, a room with a door and an open window. The action inside and outside the door can be seen by audience but not by the actors.

TIME

Present

SUGGESTED MUSIC

Leonard Cohen's 'Hey, that's no way to say Goodbye.'

Music plays while Eveline is putting on lipstick and looking in her bathroom mirror. There is a man in her bed.

MUSIC: *I loved you in the morning our kisses deep and warm*
         Your hair upon the pillow like a sleepy golden storm
         Many loved before us . . . Fade

EVELINE: Oh no, another spot, I must need salt.

MAN: You don't need salt you need more sex.

EVELINE: Can I have it with salt?

MAN: If you like.

EVELINE: No . . . joke, I can't . . . sorry. Today's a full day *(she picks up her jacket.)* Where do you live? I can drop you somewhere.

MAN: *(He gets up. He is surprised.)* No. It's all right. I... I can catch the tram.

EVELINE: Are you sure?

> *He begins to get dressed. She is gathering things together and putting them into her briefcase.*

I can easily give you a lift... if it's on my way.

MAN: Where's your office?

EVELINE: St Kilda Road

MAN: Take me to the junction?

EVELINE: Not a problem.

> *He goes up to her and takes her arm.*

MAN: Did I miss something?

Maybe I... I just imagined the nature of our contact.

EVELINE: Sorry? *(He lets go of her arm).* No, you didn't.

MAN: So... this is the usual for you.

EVELINE: No.... I... *(sighs)* Please don't get complicated. It's 8am and I have to get to work.

MAN: Right at this minute.

EVELINE: Yes. I have an early meeting.

MAN: Is it an important meeting?

EVELINE: Reasonably. Look, I'm sorry if I seem....

MAN: Insensitive...?

EVELINE: I don't mean to... 4

MAN: It's a bit weird. I mean most women...

EVELINE: I've had problems with someone recently and I think it's going to be a while...

> *(Beat)*

MAN: You don't have to explain.

EVELINE: I know.

> *He shrugs and begins to put on his socks and shoes.*

MAN: What sort of problems?

> *She looks uncomfortable and is reluctant to answer him.*

MAN: *(to himself)* I will catch the tram.

> *(Pause)*

EVELINE: It was fun.

MAN: Yeah, I thought so.

> *(Beat)*

EVELINE: Someone's stalking me.

MAN: Stalking you?

EVELINE: Yes.

MAN: Have you told the police?

EVELINE: Yes.

MAN: Do you know who it is?

EVELINE: Yes.

MAN: You should be more careful.

EVELINE: I am.

MAN: Well... you're not... sex with strangers is not 'careful.'

EVELINE: you seemed...

MAN: What?

EVELINE: Decent

MAN: Decent?

EVELINE: You know... nice.

MAN: Well I'm not.

EVELINE: No?

MAN: Far from it. *(He tries to pull her back onto the bed but she walks away from him.)*

EVELINE: No, you're right... it is risky but... I guess when someone you know... someone you've known for a very long time turns into a psychopath strangers seem like a safer option.

MAN: Is he an old boyfriend?

EVELINE: I think so

MAN: Then... why don't they charge him?

(Beat)

EVELINE: He was there last night.

MAN: Where?

EVELINE: When you came up to me at the Bar... with that stupid line about me being the second most beautiful woman you've ever seen... I saw him walk past the window.

MAN: That wasn't a line it's true, you are

EVELINE: Come on... it was to make me curious and ask who's the first, There's nothing new about appealing to a woman's vanity.

MAN: Not at all

EVELINE: Yeah

MAN: That wasn't a line it's true, you are

EVELINE: Okay. I know once you make up a silly lie like that you have to stick to it.

MAN: *(serious)* I don't make up silly lies. It's a compliment. You remind me of Catherine Deneuve.

EVELINE: Who?

MAN: A French actress. She was in a film . . . well, she's been in lots of films but the one I love most is called *Belle de Jour* about a bored housewife who works as a prostitute during the day while her husband's at work.

EVELINE: *(She zips up her briefcase then remembers she's forgotten something.)* Oh very original . . . and let me guess, one of her clients falls for her?

MAN: No, not really . . . it doesn't have a happy ending. In the film her name was Severine . . . rhymes with your name, Eveline

EVELINE: Well there you go.

MAN: You're more cynical than I thought you'd be.

EVELINE: Am I?

MAN: I mean . . . . you didn't strike me as the cynical type.

EVELINE: You don't know me.

He picks up a book from her bedside table.

MAN: If I were . . . one of the characters in this book, would I be one you liked or one you disliked?

EVELINE: You're not a character in that book.

MAN: If . . . I said if . . . perhaps I'd be one you didn't like at the start and by the end you'd realise you do . . . like me, that is? Or, you didn't ever like me but because of some twist the author puts in at the end things change.

(She is still looking for something for her brief case)

EVELINE: I don't know.

Three loud, pre recorded, reverberating knocks on the door. Julian appears on the other side of the door. Eveline puts down her case then sits back on the bed and signals for the man not to speak.

JULIAN: Evie, are you in there? *(She doesn't respond.)* It's important. I need to talk to you. *(To himself)* Shit!

He hesitates and makes a call on his cell phone.

'Hi, Linda, Is Evie in the office yet?... Yes, I know she doesn't want to talk to me... this is important. Can you tell her I called?.... Just tell her!'

Julian hangs up his phone and turns to walk away then reconsiders.

If you can hear me for chrissakes Answer!

EVELINE: *(She indicates for man to keep quiet again and says firmly.)* I can hear you all right and I want you to go NOW.

JULIAN: Why didn't you answer me in the first place? What is this? Have you gone crazy?

EVELINE: Go now or I'm calling emergency.

JULIAN: Listen to your self... completely paranoid. It's me, Julian, the guy you lived with for the last three years... the guy who took out your garbage every week and rubbed stinky cream into your feet to get rid of your tinea. The one and only boyfriend your mother's ever liked. Remember?

(Beat)

Let me in we need to talk

EVELINE: We have nothing to talk about.

JULIAN: I saw you last night... in the Rouge bar.

(She looks at the man to confirm what she's told him.)

That guy, who was chatting you up, he's the one.

EVELINE: Please go away. I need to leave for to work.

JULIAN: Well come out and I'll walk you to your car.

EVELINE: You have got to stop this. Don't you have any self-respect? It's over.

JULIAN: Yeah I got that... a while ago. BUT you need to know that it's not me.

Man is picking more of her things up from her bedside table and looking at them.

EVELINE: Okay. What guy? I talked to more than one person last night and, anyway, what makes you think it could be him?

JULIAN: Pretty damn popular these days aren't you

EVELINE: You're so bloody obvious this is not about me at all. It's about you! You and your big, fat insatiable ego.

JULIAN: You're wrong... just for a change. I saw him following you to work the other day.

EVELINE: Really, so . . . where, exactly, were you watching me from this time?

JULIAN: I was on the tram. He happens to be the same guy you were getting to know last night . . . had his hand up your dress when I walked past the window.

EVELINE: Sure! *(She turns to look at man and he nods his head and rolls his eyes.)*

JULIAN: And you reckon it's me who doesn't have self-respect!

EVELINE: Okay that's it! Leave . . . or I'm calling the police.

JULIAN: Who would ever have thought we'd come to this?

EVELINE: GO!

> *He walks off stage. She stays at the door listening for a moment as the audience sees the guy picks up his tie.*

EVELINE: *(To check that he has really gone)* Julian?

> *She turns to face the man. For a moment she looks scared and he looks scary. She does a double take at him then composes herself and remains calm and in control.*

EVELINE: Aren't you ready yet. What are you doing?

MAN: *(man begins to put on the tie)* He seems pretty desperate.

EVELINE: Yeah. Can we get going?

MAN: Sure. *(He stands up)* Sort of romantic don't you think?

EVELINE: What?

MAN: To have someone . . . I mean to make someone lovesick for you.

EVELINE: I don't see it like that.

MAN: Don't you?

EVELINE: No.

MAN: But isn't luurrv just about the desire to be loved?

EVELINE: No *(she sits on the bed and looks up at him bewildered.)*

MAN: Well what is it?

EVELINE: This is heavy for so early in the day

MAN: I'm just curious

EVELINE: Maybe that's what it is for some people

MAN: Well what is it for you? *(He sits beside her.)*

EVELINE: I suppose I think of it as caring for someone more than you do for yourself.

MAN: So, it's sort of masochistic . . . martyr-type thing then?

EVELINE: No.

MAN: All good, completely sex less ... lacking erotic fantasy or the desire to control the other person.... or vanquish them or eat them?

EVELINE: *(She laughs a little nervously)* Come on let's go. I can see where this is leading.

MAN: I don't think you can

She smiles at him picks up her brief case and goes to open the door. She points to his coat on the chair.

EVELINE: Is that your coat?

He quickly comes up behind her and places his tie tightly around her neck.

Blackout.

Music plays into the darkness

But lets not talk of love or chains
And things we can't untie
Your eyes are soft with sorrow
Hey, that's no way to say Goodbye.

The Mascots

Chris O'Connor

Originally performed at Mile Square Theatre's *8th Annual 7th Inning Stretch: 7 10-minute plays about baseball* on March 13, 2010 at The DeBaun Center for the Performing Arts, Hoboken, NJ. Produced by Mile Square Theatre, Hoboken, NJ, Chris O'Connor, Artistic Director. Directed by Raymond McAnally. Cast: Vivian—Lisa Marie Fabrega; Arthur Pendafleur—Stephen Ellis; Charles—John McAdams.

CHARACTERS

Arther: . . male, early 20s, eager
Charles: . male, late 30s to mid-40s, aloof
Vivian: . . female, mid-20s to mid-40s, all business

SETTING

A talent agent's waiting room, New York City, the present

At rise, two men are seated in a talent agent's waiting room. Arthur is in his early 20s. He is anxious and hopeful. Charles, late 30s to mid-40s, is aloof. Arthur wears a stadium mascot costume, holding the headpiece in his lap. Charles in street clothes. There's a row of chairs, a sign-in table, and a coffee station.
   Arthur steals glances at Charles, trying to assess what he's about. They bide their time, Arthur somewhat uncomfortably, Charles non-chalantly. Perhaps Charles pages through a magazine. The auditions are running late.
   Vivian, the casting assistant, emerges from the office. She is extremely business-like. She looks at a clipboard. Looks at the two men. Arthur perks up noticably. She returns to the office.
   The men wait.
   Vivian returns. Arthur perks up. She pours a cup of coffee.

VIVIAN: Mr. Simon just needs a few more minutes.
   (She looks at the clipboard.)
   Which one of you is Arthur Pindaflower?
ARTHUR: *(rising)* Uh . . . Hi. That's me. I'm Arthur. And it's Pinda -
fleur.
   (Note: Arthur pronounces the last syllable of his last name VERY French. The more syllables, the better)
   My appointment is at—
VIVIAN: *(to Charles)* Pindafloor?
ARTHUR: *(rising)* No, Pindafleur. It's French.
   (Cold stare from Vivian)

VIVIAN: *(to Charles, warmly)* Then you must be Charles. So very nice to meet you in person. You'll be next, sir.
(Vivian begins to leave.)
ARTHUR: Uh, excuse me . . . When I'm called, does Mr. Simon want to see me with my head on or off?
(Vivian stops and again gives Arthur a cold stare. She exits slamming the door behind her.)
ARTHUR: OK.
(Another moment of silence between the men.)
CHARLES: Wear the mask.
ARTHUR: Excuse me?
CHARLES: When you enter that office. Wear your headpiece. The first impression is what defines you. Do you want them to see Arthur Picklefield or do you want them to see just another San Diego chicken?
ARTHUR: It's Pindafleur. And I would never even attempt to be the Chicken. The Chicken! My god, he's an icon. He's untouchable.
CHARLES: The Chicken, an icon? Rubbish.
ARTHUR: Oh, come on. If it wasn't for Ted Giannoulas, we wouldn't even be here today. He was a pioneer. And he had all the skills you could possibly want. He was an amazing improviser, had the physicality of a Charlie Chaplin or a Harold Lloyd. And his tolerance for heat stress was unmatched. Without the Chicken, there wouldn't be a mascot industry, let alone a mascot community.
CHARLES: A mascot community?
ARTHUR: Well, yeah.
CHARLES: And what other mascots do you 'commune' with?
ARTHUR: Uh . . . well, none really.
CHARLES: Aside from this humiliating exercise, have you even seen more than one mascot gathered in a single place?
ARTHUR: Well, no, but I know there are a lot of us out there. And we share a lot of the same problems and needs and goals and if we could organize as a group, we could—
CHARLES: Mr. Pencilfeld . . .
ARTHUR: Pindafleur.
CHARLES: How long have you been in this business?
ARTHUR: Well, I'm just getting started.

CHARLES: Allow me to give you some friendly advice. Mascots are little more than funny, fuzzy, lovable costumes that are worn by jaded, mostly alcoholic men who for some inexplicable reason love to be the center of attention in a stadium of thousands of nameless spectators. They perform in complete anonymity, for a laughable sum and are somehow addicted to the idea that they will eventually achieve the status of someone like your beloved San Diego Chicken. Though they are surrounded by the spirit of competition in the arenas they inhabit, the only competition they experience themselves is between each other when they are seeking their next job in dreary offices like this one. There is no such thing as a mascot community. We're a bunch of cutthroats. We loathe each other, and if given the opportunity, would gouge each other's eyes out or fracture each other's knees.

(Arthur is speechless.)

There, I've saved you the pain of figuring this out yourself. Do not try to befriend a mascot. Ever. That's the nature of the business.

(A long pause while Arthur tries to recover from his balloon being burst.)

ARTHUR: What gives you the right?

CHARLES: Excuse me?

ARTHUR: What gives you the right to attack a profession that brings nothing but joy and goodwill to people?

CHARLES: Well, I—

ARTHUR: You sit there without a single good thing so say about the profession that I bet has fed your soul for many a year. How can you be so cynical? What, is this just sour grapes because you're in the autumn of your career? Are you so pissed off since you can't book a job, that you have to take it out on the next generation of mascots? A generation that truly cares about where we're taking the art form? Are you jealous of me because I'm looking ahead to a life of mascot fulfillment while you are looking back at a sad trail of memories and regrets? I bet you haven't really done anything. And where's your costume? Do you even have one? I bet you're just a wannabe. Yeah, that's where your resentment comes from, isn't it? Who are you anyway? What have you done, Mr. Anti-Mascot Community? Mr. Allow-me-to-give-you-some-friendly-advice? Who the hell are you?

CHARLES: I'm Charles Bacon.

ARTHUR: Excuse me?

CHARLES: You heard me. I'm Charles Bacon.

ARTHUR: Yeah, right.

CHARLES: Whatever.

(Another long pause.)

ARTHUR: Wait a minute. You're Charles Bacon.

CHARLES: I am, sir.

ARTHUR: You're the Charles Bacon?

CHARLES: Is there more than one?

ARTHUR: Oh, my god. You're Charles Bacon. You're Charles Bacon! I'm in a casting office alone with Charles Bacon!

CHARLES: Settle down, kid.

ARTHUR: You broke the Antic Barrier. Before you, mascots could only lead cheers. You put the comic routine into the form. You were the first to actually do a comic bit with an umpire. You invented the Dugout Strut! Even the Chicken pays tribute to you. I am so embarrassed, sir. Please forgive me! I was just so caught up in defending mascots that I didn't recognize you. Of course you're not wearing a costume. You don't need to. You just say who you are and people know. Oh, please forgive me, Mr. Bacon.

CHARLES: It's really OK, Mr. Pendaflex.

ARTHUR: It's Pindafleur, but you can call me anything. Jeez, what an idiot I am. Again, I am deeply sorry.

CHARLES: Forget it, kid.

(Another long pause.)

ARTHUR: *(getting up)* Well, I don't know what the hell I'm doing here. I don't stand a chance of being chosen over the great Charles Bacon. I'm not in even in the same league as you, sir.

CHARLES: Where you going?

ARTHUR: Home. I really don't belong here. I'd just be wasting my time and Mr. Simon's.

CHARLES: Now, wait a minute. You've at least got to go in there and show the man your stuff. Saul Simon is the number one Mascot Talent Agent in the Northeast. Even if you don't get this job, he'll remember you and call you in for the next.

ARTHUR: You think so?

CHARLES: I know so. How do you think I became Charles Bacon?

ARTHUR: Good point. Hey, maybe I can show you part of my routine!

CHARLES: Well, I—

ARTHUR: No, I'll just show give you a little taste. Maybe you can give me a pointer.

CHARLES: I'm not really in the habit of—

ARTHUR: Please, Mr. Bacon. Just take a quick look and I promise I'll never bother you again. I would be so honored to show you my work.

CHARLES: This is hardly the place—

ARTHUR: Please, sir. I know I don't stand a chance in there. Just sharing a little bit of my work with the great Charles Bacon would mean more to me than anything at this moment.

CHARLES: OK, OK, what do you have?

ARTHUR: OK. This is what I like to do between the 7th and 8th innings, you know, they've just done the Stretch a half inning before, sung *Take Me Out to the Ballgame*, and maybe they've done the 'find the baseball under the cap' game on the jumbotron, and so they need something just a little crazy. So I seek out the homeplate umpire and I do this . . .

(Arthur puts his mascot head on, does a few stretches and goes into a frantic routine, using Charles as his umpire. The routine is hilariously bad and productions of the play are encouraged to make this as ridiculous as possible. Arthur clearly has no sense of his lack of talent. Towards the end of it, Vivian enters.)

VIVIAN: *(unseen by Arthur)* Excuse me. Excuse me!

ARTHUR: Oh, sorry. I was just warming up.

VIVIAN: Mr. Bacon. I'm sorry, but Mr. Simon wanted me to tell you that we won't need to see you this afternoon.

CHARLES: What do you mean, won't need to see me?

VIVIAN: Just that, Mr. Bacon. He's decided the Springfield Dodgers will be going in another direction for their mascot, so you can go home now.

CHARLES: Another direction?

VIVIAN: They're exploring going with a younger mascot performer.

CHARLES: Wait a minute. I drove all the way down from upstate. Saul said this meeting was just a formality.

VIVIAN: Well, I'm sorry, sir. I guess he's changed his mind. I'm sure you understand that that's the nature of the business. Now, Mr. Pindafeld, are you ready for your appointment? Mr. Simon is ready to see you now.

(Charles is crestfallen and suddenly looks all his age and then some.)

VIVIAN: Mr. Pindafeld?

(Arthur looks with concern at Charles.)

Mr. Pindafeld.

ARTHUR: Uh . . . can you give me just a moment, ma'am?

VIVIAN: Mr. Pindafeld, we have a very busy schedule and Mr. Simon has a conference call in 5 minutes. You are our final candidate for the Springfield Dodger mascot and I'm afraid this is his only opportunity to see you.

ARTHUR: Uh . . . You know what, ma'am. I think you can tell Mr. Simon that if the Charles Bacon isn't good enough for the Springfield Dodgers then neither is Arthur Pindafleur. I'm going home, too.

VIVIAN: OK, if that's the way you feel. I must tell you, though, you may not see another opportunity like this for some time. I don't think I need to tell you that this is a very competitive field.

ARTHUR: I understand that, ma'am.

VIVIAN: I'm sorry to hear that, Mr. Pendagrast. I'll let Mr. Simon know.

(Vivian exits.)

CHARLES: *(calling after her)* It's Pindafleur, lady. And don't you forget that name! Pin-da-fleur!

(Charles looks at Arthur.)

Thanks, kid. You didn't have to do that.

ARTHUR: Yes, I did, sir. She shouldn't have treated you that way. *(pause)* Now what do I do?

CHARLES: For starters, you might want to change that name of yours.

ARTHUR: My name? What's wrong with Arthur Pendafleur? That's a name they'll never forget.

CHARLES: Well, problem is, it's a name they can't even remember.

ARTHUR: Right.

CHARLES: And that routine of yours . . .

ARTHUR: It's something else, huh?

CHARLES: *(putting on his coat)* It's definitely that. How about we go downstairs and I buy you a cup of coffee and give you a few pointers.

ARTHUR: *(a realization)* Oh. You mean . . . Are you saying you'll work with me?

CHARLES: No, I didn't say that.

ARTHUR: The sensei master and his grasshopper! Merlin and his apprentice!

CHARLES: Don't press your luck, kid.

ARTHUR: *(exiting)* This is what I'm talking about. The mascot community!

> *(Arthur runs out the door ahead of Charles. Charles shakes his head, a little regretful, and a little happy to have found a younger, albeit less-talented, version of his former self. As he exits, he notices Charles'S mascot head, which was left behind. He picks it up and leaves, laughing at the absurdity of the moment.)*

> *End of play*

My Dinner with Rocco

Bob Manus

Produced by the WorkShop Theater Company, June 2–12, 2010. Produced by Scott C. Sickles. Directed by Liz Forst. Cast (in order of appearance): Anthony— Richard Kent Green; Rocco—Bob Manus; Frankie Two Shoes—Fred Velde.

CHARACTERS

Anthony: . . . . mid-level capo, nervous about his future—
30s to 50s
Rocco: . . . . don of a crime organization—40s to 50s,
Frankie Two Shoes: . deceptively genial hit man, takes pride in
his work—50s to 60s

TIME

The Present

PLACE

Upscale Italian Restaurant

Lights up on an upscale restaurant. Two sharply dressed men are seated at table.

ANTHONY: You'll like this place, Rocco. Try the veal. It's the best in the city.

ROCCO: I hope the food is good, Anthony, because I have a feeling the conversation will be less than stimulating.

ANTHONY: Class, Rocco. You got nothing but class.

ROCCO: Stop with the admiration society and start talking.

ANTHONY: Relax, Rocco. Let's just enjoy the ambiance of this fine establishment. We'll eat, drink, then ease into a nice little talk That is, if we can get a waiter. The food's good but I never said anything about the service. *(Loudly)* WHO DOES A GUY HAVE TO SUCK TO GET A DRINK AROUND HERE?

ROCCO: What are you nuts? Control yourself! You're embarrassing me.

ANTHONY: Oh, I'm sorry, Rocco.

ROCCO: *(As he stuffs a huge piece of bread into his mouth.)* You got no manners. This is how you do it. (He snaps his fingers.) See how easy it is?

ANTHONY: No one's coming, Rocco.

ROCCO: *(Snaps his fingers again, then snaps again—louder.)* What kind of fucking place is this?

ANTHONY: Rocco, we gotta talk.

ROCCO: Well, since we're not gonna eat, we might as well talk. What's on your mind, kid?

ANTHONY: They're foreclosing on my house. I don't want to lose my house, Rocco. I got a wife and kids. It's a nice house. We've lived there for years. I don't want to have to move back to Red Hook.

ROCCO: You expanded beyond your means. I tried to warn you.

ANTHONY: No. no, Rocco. It's this economic crunch. It's affecting everybody—American citizens everywhere.

ROCCO: You've done time. You're no longer a citizen.

ANTHONY: That's not the point. Things are bad. They're even foreclosing on Gotti's family. It was in the papers.

ROCCO: Don't mention that scumbag's name again. They should do more than foreclose. They should kill his kids, his pets, his servants. Wipe them off the face of the earth.

ANTHONY: You're right, Rocco. When you're right, you're right. But what I'm trying to say is—

(Just then a slender, well dressed "Guido" type walks up the table.)

ANTHONY: Well, look who it is. Frankie Two Shoes himself.

FRANKIE: How goes it, gents?

ANTHONY: Frankie is with the West Coast mob, Rocco. You remember Frankie.

ROCCO: Your reputation precedes you.

FRANKIE: Well, I appreciate that, Mr. DeAngelo.

ANTHONY: Frankie is the most feared trigger man they got out there. He doesn't kill you. He executes you. Frankie's responsible for the Jimmy Hoffa hit.

ROCCO: I'm well aware of that.

ANTHONY: Everybody thinks Hoffa was buried under the 30 yard line of Giants' stadium. That's so untrue. Where did you bury him, Frankie?

FRANKIE: That's a secret.

ANTHONY: C'mon Frankie, you are among friends. Where is he buried?

FRANKIE: Behind Lincoln's left eye on Mount Rushmore.

ANTHONY: Mount Rushmore! That's class, huh! Nothing but class.

FRANKIE: I was thinking of writing a book about my exploits. A sort of memoir, you might say.

ANTHONY: Really? What will you call it.

FRANKIE: Hit Men Think of Suicide When the Rainbow is Enough.

ANTHONY: Oh yeah? I'll wait for the movie. So what brings you to New York, Frankie?

FRANKIE: I was about to tell you. The specials for tonight are shrimp scampi over wild rice Very nice. We also have linguini with red clam sauce—very fresh, and made more special with a touch of pesto. Or perhaps you'd enjoy our veal special? Medallions of veal, wrapped around marinated artichokes and mushrooms in a delectable white wine and butter sauce . . .

ANTHONY: Whoa. Whoa! Wait a minute. What the fuck is this? You're our waiter?

FRANKIE: That's right.

ANTHONY: How could this be?

FRANKIE: Cut backs. Hit men are expendable on the coast. Nobody gets whacked out there anymore, so you might say I was laid off. And I can't exactly collect unemployment.

ANTHONY: I never heard of such a thing. What a shame.

ROCCO: I'll have the veal, Frankie.

ANTHONY: Yeah. Me too. Give me the veal.

FRANKIE: That's a good choice. It's the best in the City. I'll be right back with your drinks. We're giving you a glass of wine on the house for being so patient.

ANTHONY: What a guy.

FRANKIE: Don't mention it. Would you prefer red or white?

ANTHONY: Red. What would you suggest?

FRANKIE: We have an excellent Montepulciano.

ANTHONY: Sounds good to me.

FRANKIE: *(to Rocco)* And you sir?

ROCCO: Diet coke.

(Frankie leaves)

ANTHONY: Can you believe that, Rocco? That's just what I'm talking about. The economy has got us all by the throat.

ROCCO: That's his problem. What's yours?

ANTHONY: Well you see how it is. Dolores doesn't want to move. She belongs to the country club. She plays golf there. Angela is dating a real nice kid, comes from a good family. What can I say to them?

ROCCO: What can you say? You say, "Tough shit. Pack your bags. We're leaving."

ANTHONY: Heart, Rocco. The world is crying for a little heart.

ROCCO: I had that cut out of me a long time ago. Don't throw that crap at me. A man who can't take care of his own family is not a man.

Frankie returns with the drinks.

FRANKIE: Here you are gentlemen. Enjoy your wine. Your meal will be out shortly. *(He spills a drop of wine on Anthony's hand as he exits.)*

ANTHONY: *(Wiping the wine off his hand.)* What a tragedy. He whacked people better than he waits on them. *(He takes a sip of his wine.)* You gotta help me, Rocco. Come on.

ROCCO: *(Pulling a wad of cash out of his jacket pocket.)* You need a few bucks. Okay here. If I thought you were going to put the bite on me I'd have stopped off at an ATM.

ANTHONY: What's this? A couple of thousand bucks? Rocco. They are foreclosing on my house.

ROCCO: So what do you want from me? You're in charge of the drugs and sleaze. What's the problem?

ANTHONY: First of all, the drug scene is down 30 percent. The first thing people do when they're in a crunch is get rid of the luxuries. Drugs are a luxury. Second. Nobody goes to peep shows anymore. They're antiquated.

ROCCO: Antiquated? What's with the 50 cent words?

ANTHONY: They're obsolete.... OLD. People download their porn on the internets these days. Give me another source of income. Please. You want me to work over somebody, I'll do it. You want me to chop someone's arms and legs off. I'll do it. Then I'll kill him for you, if you so desire. I'll kill my own parents. Whatever.

ROCCO: Hey don't you every talk disrespectfully a bout your mother and father. Ever. Do you hear me?

ANTHONY: I didn't mean it Rocco. I was just speaking emphatically. *(He has started to sweat now.)*

ROCCO: There you go with the big words again. Emphatically? What? Did you read a dictionary last night? You thought that would impress me? We gave you nothing but opportunities and you blew it. You don't know how to take. I want something, I take it. You want something, you take it. You see that fat rich bitch over there with the diamond earrings as big as her nostrils? She wants something, she takes. What do you got hands for?

ANTHONY: Come on, Rocco, we go way back. *(He yawns.)* You gave me my first contract, remember? It was that hit on Joey Bonfanto. I walked into McHale's bar and the fat pig is sitting there at the corner table. I pull out my rod and point it at his head. He stares at me and says, "Anthony, what are you doing?" I pull the trigger. Nothing happens. I forgot to load the gun. I immediately remember it's April first, so I yell, "April Fool's!" Joey starts to laugh. He sits me down and buys me a few drinks. We laugh and drink for about a half an hour and then I sneak into the men's room. *(Anthony yawns again.)* Boy I'm getting drowsy. Well, anyway, I load the gun with bullets and go back into the bar. I walk up to his table and point the gun at him again. He says, "What's this, more jokes?" I pull the trigger. Bang! You should have seen the look on his face.

ROCCO: That was a good hit. I was proud of you. But that was then. This is now.

ANTHONY: What are you gonna do? Lay me off?

ROCCO: No. No, Anthony, I would never do that.

ANTHONY: I got a pain in my gut. I gotta go to the restroom. *(He exits running.)*

Frankie comes over to the table.

ROCCO: Whatever you put in his drink really worked.

FRANKIE: He'll be sound asleep within an hour—and he won't be waking up.

ROCCO: Well, it had to be done. He was getting sloppy. He was beginning to embarrass the organization. *(Rocco stands up, leaving cash on the table.)* See to it that he gets home alright. I want him to die in his own bed. I owe him that much.

FRANKIE: You got it, Mr. DeAngelo.

ROCCO: Come see me in the morning. Ten sharp.

FRANKIE: Thanks for the opportunity Mr. DeAngelo

ROCCO: That's alright. *(He begins to leave.)* Oh, and one more thing. *(He hands Frankie some cash.)* Buy yourself a couple of nice suits. I like my boys to look sharp.

FRANKIE: I'll do that sir, and thank you.

Rocco exits.

Dean Martin's "Ain't That a Kick in the Head" begins to swell as Frankie yanks off his tie and flips it on the table. Slow black out.

Passed Hordes

Mark Harvey Levine

2010–2011 Production Information: "Passed Hordes," part of "Cabfare For The Common Man," September 30th–October 23rd, 2010, directed by Andy Batt, assisted by Sarah Brunet. Cast: Paul—Josh Kessler; Isabel—Tricia Jones; Waiter—Stephen Woosley; Waiter—Nikki Smith; Waiter—Chris Youngblood; Waiter—Vicki Andronis. Produced by Madlab Theatre, Andy Batt, Artistic Directory.

Original Production Information: "Passed Hordes" was first produced by Theatre Neo (Los Angeles, CA) in April 2002 as part of Neo A La Carte. It was directed by Wendy Worthington, with the following cast: Isabel—Brooke Baumer; Paul—Mark Harvey Levine; Waiter—David Cheaney; Waiter—Denise Devin; Waiter—Patrick Gorman; Waiter—Flannery Lunsford.

Passed Hordes had its first Equity production at The Phoenix Theatre (Indianapolis, IN) in May 2005 as part of *Cabfare For The Common Man, An Evening Of Plays By Mark Harvey Levine*. Bryan D. Fonseca, Artistic Director. It was directed by Bryan D. Fonseca, with the following cast: Isabel—Deborah Sargent; Paul—Bill Simmons; Waiter—Jon Lindley; Waiter—Megan McKinney; Waiter—Sara Riemen; Waiter—Michael Shelton.

CHARACTERS

Isabel: . . twenties to forties, dour, serious, cynical but with hidden fire

Paul: . . . . twenties to forties, nervous, introverted, also has hidden passion

Waiters:. . as few as two or as many as your stage can hold. Manic, comic, acrobatic and elegant

SETTING

A party. (Can be a completely bare stage.)

TIME

The present.

A party. Isabel, a dour looking woman stands alone, holding a stemmed glass in her hand, which she does not drink from. A waiter with a tray approaches her. All waiters in this play offer their hors d'oeuvres with manic zeal.

WAITER 1: Spanakopita?

ISABEL: No thank y—

WAITER 1: —Bifteki?

ISABEL: No, tha—

WAITER 1: —Dolmathes?

ISABEL: No.

> *Immediately from the opposite end of the stage, a nervous guy with a stemmed glass in his hand is chased by another waiter.*

WAITER 2: Satsivi?

PAUL: No, thanks.

WAITER 2: Siomga?

PAUL: That's okay.

WAITER 2: Zakuski?

PAUL: No thank you.

The waiter chases Paul until he's next to Isabel, then both waiters briskly leave. Paul and Isabel try desperately to look casual. Pause. They watch other partiers.

PAUL: Know anyone here?

ISABEL: No.

PAUL: Me either.

ISABEL: Oh.

PAUL: Well . . . I'm Paul.

ISABEL: Isabel. I know.

PAUL: What?

ISABEL: The name. "Isabel."

PAUL: It's nice.

ISABEL: No, actually, it isn't.

Beat.

PAUL: I hate these things.

ISABEL: Me too!

PAUL: I never know anyone.

ISABEL: I don't fit in.

PAUL: I stand out from the pack.

ISABEL: The cheese stands alone.

Beat as Isabel mentally kicks herself and Paul looks confused.

PAUL: I don't know why I go.

ISABEL: I'm going to stop going.

PAUL: I only came as a favor to Louise.

ISABEL: You know Louise?

PAUL: Not really.

A waiter glides in to Paul.

WAITER 3: Carpaccio?

PAUL: No, than—

WAITER 3: —Provatura?

PAUL: No,—

WAITER 3: —Melanzane?

PAUL: What?

WAITER 3: It's a delicious combination of—

PAUL: —No thank you.

The waiter scurries off. While Paul was distracted, the other waiters surrounded Isabel and fixed her up a little bit— change of accessory here, adjusted her hair there, added a little makeup.

Neither Paul or Isabel are aware that this has happened to her.

PAUL: *(re: the other partiers)* They seem like they're having fun.

ISABEL: If you call that fun.

PAUL: You don't?

ISABEL: I wouldn't.

PAUL: Still . . . they LOOK like they're having fun.

ISABEL: Do they?

PAUL: Don't they?

ISABEL: Look at them.

PAUL: I'm looking.

ISABEL: Really look at them.

PAUL: What do you mean?

ISABEL: See them for what they really are.

PAUL: False?

ISABEL: Empty.

PAUL: Really.

ISABEL: Shallow.

PAUL: Well . . .

ISABEL: Vacuous.

PAUL: Not like us.

ISABEL: *(bitter laugh)* No, we're real.

PAUL: To think, I thought—

ISABEL: It's their plastic smiles . . .

PAUL: I mean, it looked—

ISABEL: . . . Plastic lives . . .

PAUL: But now I see.

ISABEL: . . . Plastic surgery.

PAUL: It makes you think.

ISABEL: It gives you pause.

PAUL: It colors your perception.

ISABEL: Life is perception—

PAUL: It changes your perspective.

ISABEL: —Or hadn't you noticed?
> *A waiter swoops in on Isabel.*

WAITER 4: Sui Mei?

ISABEL: Um, no.

WAITER 4: Fun Gwau?

ISABEL: I shouldn't.

WAITER 4: Wu Gok?

ISABEL: I can't.

WAITER 4: Har Gao?

ISABEL: I'm sorry.

WAITER 4: Gow Gees?

ISABEL: No!
> *Again, during this the other waiters fix up Paul, changing his jacket, combing his hair, etc. Neither Paul or Isabel notice.*

PAUL: *(the other partiers)* Some of them must be happy.

ISABEL: Nobody's happy.

PAUL: Nobody?

ISABEL: Not really.

PAUL: Some of them—

ISABEL: Take that couple, there.

PAUL: *(Gestures one direction)* Red Sweater and Unfortunate Haircut?

ISABEL: *(Gestures another direction)* Yellow Jacket and Regrettable Shoes.

PAUL: Oh, THEM.

ISABEL: Think they're happy?

PAUL: They're dancing.

ISABEL: Think they love?

PAUL: They're laughing.

ISABEL: Watch how she watches.

PAUL: His every move.

ISABEL: Look how he looks.

PAUL: At everyone but her.

ISABEL: See?
> *Again, the waiters swoop in on Isabel and Paul. During the following the waiters fix them both up in a flurry of activity. Again, neither notice. Both their glasses get removed, Isabel's hair is let loose as the waiters dance madly around them.*

WAITER 1: Burekas? Fattoush?

ISABEL: What?

WAITER 2: Taboulleh? Kenafeh?

PAUL: I don't know.

ISABEL: Have you tried any?

PAUL: Not yet.

WAITER 3: Lehmah Baajiin?

ISABEL: I've never—

WAITER 4: Çerkes Tavuk? Açili Ezmesi? Patliçan Ve Biber Kizartmasi?

PAUL: Um...

ALL WAITERS: Try one!

They've finished adjusting Paul and Isabel, who look at each other.

ISABEL: Maybe we should.

PAUL: What's the worst that can happen?

ISABEL: How bad can it taste?

PAUL: What the heck.

ISABEL: Why not.

They each take an hors d'oeuvre and pop it in their mouth.

PAUL: Hmmm.

ISABEL: Mmmm.

PAUL: Sort of—

ISABEL: Chewy.

PAUL: Tangy.

ISABEL: Yummy.

PAUL: Luscious.

ISABEL: Oh my God.

They hungrily fill their plates.

ISABEL: I used to work in catering.

PAUL: Did you, now?

ISABEL: But I never touched the passed hordes.

PAUL: The what?

ISABEL: The passed hordes. Passed hors d'oeuvres. Y'know? *(mimes a waiter holding a tray)*

PAUL: Oh.

ISABEL: Never touched them.

PAUL: Why not?

ISABEL: I don't know.

PAUL: Weren't you allowed?

ISABEL: We were allowed.

PAUL: But?

ISABEL: They were for other people.

PAUL: Now here you are—

ISABEL: Here I am.

PAUL: You are other people.

ISABEL: With my skewed perspective?

PAUL: I like the way you look.

ISABEL: You like the way I SEE.

PAUL: And I like the way you look.

ISABEL: You need glasses.

PAUL: *(confused)* I used to.

ISABEL: So did I.

PAUL: You have nice eyes.

ISABEL: They're squinty.

PAUL: See them as I do.

ISABEL: They're puffy.

PAUL: Watch how I look...

ISABEL: ...at me.

PAUL: ...at you.

ISABEL: *(Suddenly)* So is everyone else.

PAUL: What?

ISABEL: They're staring at us.

PAUL: *(Still staring at her)* Who?

ISABEL: The other people.

PAUL: *(Still staring at her)* There are no other people.

> *The waiters quietly leave.*

LIGHTS FADE

The Right Number

Deborah Savadge

The Right Number was given its first production as part of the New Play Festival at the historic Cherry Lane Theatre, New York City, on November 9, 2009. It was directed by Melissa Maxwell and produced by Joan Firestone, Rachel Reiner and the League of Professional Theatre Women. Cast: Ken—Brian W. Seibert; Jennifer—Lyndsay Becker; Matt—Jed Peterson. Costumes: Sarah Gosnell. Lighting: Pamela Kupper. Set: Kina Park.

It was presented at the Fifteen Minute Play Festival at the American Globe Theatre, New York City, in April and May, 2010 with the same cast, director and costumer. The Turnip Theatre Company, the American Globe Theatre, Gloria Falzer and Liz Keefe, produced. Audrey Marshall stage managed.

CHARACTERS

Ken. 20s
Jennifer . . 20s, Ken's girlfriend
Matt . . . . 20s, Ken's roommate

NOTE TO THE ACTORS

Slash marks (/) indicate the moment at which the next speaker interrupts.

SETTING

The primary living space of a very modest New York apartment.

Lights suddenly bump up to full.

JENNIFER: *(The middle of an argument)* You just said it. You just said / that exact thing

KEN: I don't say that. I never / said that

JENNIFER: Okay, okay, you implied it. You very snidely implied / it

KEN: I didn't. I just asked you . . . What does "snidely implied" even mean?/ What does that mean?

JENNIFER: It means: you smugly and snidely insisted that I tell you the gory details and / then you

KEN: No details. No details. I just / asked you

JENNIFER: You practically begged me to / tell you

KEN: You told / me and I

JENNIFER: You wheedled it / out of me.

KEN: You complained about / me. So I asked you

JENNIFER: And then when I told you, you pounced.

KEN: I didn't. I just . . . I was surprised / that's all.

JENNIFER: What is this—the nineteen fifties? Are we living in the / nineteen fifties?

Sound of a key in the lock. Matt enters.

KEN: No, we're not living in the . . . Anyone would feel the same way if their / girlfriend—

JENNIFER: Anyone would feel the same? You're saying anyone would feel the same. Okay, let's ask Matt. / Let's ask

MATT: Ask me / what?

KEN: Okay.

MATT: Dude, you can hear you guys all / the way up from the

KEN: Okay, we'll ask Matt.

MATT: Ask me what?

KEN: Matt, Mattie, if / you were with a girlfriend

JENNIFER: Okay, Matt. If you had a girlfriend, would / you

MATT: Yeah. If I had a girlfriend. Thank you SO much for bringing up what a loser I am that I don't / actually have a girlfriend

JENNIFER: You're not a loser, Mattie. You're hardly / a loser

KEN: Dude. You're cool. *(Indicating himself)* Look what a cool roommate you have.

JENNIFER: *(To Ken)* This is about Matt . . .

Wait a minute! I don't think we can ask him this without . . . I mean, I'm not sure I'm comfortable with asking him / because

KEN: It's just theoretical. It's just . . . It's, "If he had a girlfriend, would he be upset if—"

JENNIFER: No, no, no! "If he had a girlfriend, would he ever ask her—

KEN: Well, of course, he would. He would ask / her

JENNIFER: Maybe he would and maybe he / wouldn't.

MATT: Ask her what?

KEN: Maybe he wouldn't insist that she tell / him

JENNIFER: Well, that's the whole thing, isn't it? Wait / a second.

MATT: Ask her what?

JENNIFER: Ask her . . . Wait. If I ask him . . . this is / kind of humiliating

KEN: Ask her: How many guys she'd slept with.

JENNIFER: Well, now you've blurted out / the whole

KEN: No, because I didn't tell him . . .

MATT: Um, would I ask her? I mean . . . when? Like . . . when?

KEN: Well, not on the first date / or anything

JENNIFER: No, not on the first date

MATT: It's just: Would you want to know how many guys, like, she'd
     been with?

JENNIFER: He might want to know without practically breaking / her

KEN: I didn't. There was no physical / violence

JENNIFER: Without breaking her down.

MATT: Why? Did he break you down?

JENNIFER: Yes, I mean, I didn't mind telling him because it wasn't a
     number that I was uncomfortable with . . . I mean, it wasn't a
     big number . . .
        They both look at her. A beat.

MATT: Okay. You want me to say whether or not —

JENNIFER: No. I mean . . . It's just: he's making me feel like some /
     kind of

KEN: You're the one who brought up a number

JENNIFER: When we first met, you didn't think I was a virgin, did you?

KEN: Well, no, / but

JENNIFER: Well, then

MATT: *(Gesturing toward the door)* Um, do you want me to . . . ?

JENNIFER: / No.

KEN: No.

JENNIFER: I mean you know the whole thing now, anyway.

KEN: One of us was going to out for pizza anyway.

JENNIFER: I'll / go.

MATT: I'll go.

KEN: No, that's okay. I'll go.

JENNIFER: Yeah, you better. 'Cause if I leave you here, you'll just tell
     anyway.

KEN: That is low, Jennifer. I'm not . . . I wouldn't . . .
        . . . You want sausages and extra cheese on your pizza?

JENNIFER: Anything but the little fish. *(She gives him ten dollars.)* And,
     um, will you bring me a diet coke?

MATT: You want some money, Man?

KEN: That's okay. We'll settle up when I come back.
        And he exits.

JENNIFER: I'm glad you came home when you did, Mattie. This had
     HUGE FIGHT written all over it.

MATT: I didn't really *(do anything)*

JENNIFER: Yeah, you did. You absolutely did. You, you, diffused it, or /
    something.

MATT: Just call me, "The Diffuser."

JENNIFER: Yeah, Okay, "Diffuser Man."

MATT: "Diffuser Dude." He de-fuses at a moments' notice *(Singing)*
    Dum da da dum dum. *(As if announcing)* "Call for Diffuser
    Dude." *(He makes a Buzzer noise)* "Bahn bah bah bah Bahhhh."
    (They laugh, very comfortable with each other.)

JENNIFER: No, but really, we're in Big Trouble here. I mean, he was
    pretty unreasonable.

MATT: About . . . the Number?

JENNIFER: I mean, he was all Shocked, or something, about it. He
    said, he knew about my first boyfriend, and about my most re-
    cent boyfriend, but he didn't know there were . . . It was like he
    never thought there were any guys in between those two, or
    something.

MATT: So what are you going to do?

JENNIFER: . . . Do?

MATT: I mean, I like Kenny. We've been friends since, like, high
    school, but I mean if he makes you feel . . .

JENNIFER: . . . Cheap. He makes me feel cheap, which I am absolutely
    Not.

MATT: No, no, of course not.

JENNIFER: I thought he was kidding . . . at first. . . . But he wasn't.

MATT: Sometimes it's hard to tell with Kenny Boy.

JENNIFER: Is he just a jerk?

MATT: . . . um, a jerk? . . . Um,

JENNIFER: You can say what you really think.

MATT: *(Trying to decide whether or not to put the moves on her)* What I
    really think?

JENNIFER: I mean, I know you guys are really old old friends.

MATT: What do you want me to say here?

JENNIFER: I mean, what kind of a stupid double standard is it if he
    can . . . because I know he's been with like forty or fifty women.

MATT: Well, maybe not forty or . . . Well, maybe not fifty.

JENNIFER: I don't know. He cut a pretty wide swath / through the

MATT: A wide swath?

JENNIFER: You know what I mean.

MATT: Let's just say, he's had more girlfriends than I have had . . . ties.

JENNIFER: . . . But you never really answered. I mean, do you ask your girlfriends to tell you / how many

MATT: No. No . . . I don't . . . I wouldn't . . . But I mean, you kind of get a sense, like if she's always saying something like: "This guy I was with when I was vacationing in Tampa," and you know she was only IN Tampa for about fifteen minutes . . . I mean, you kind of get a sense.

JENNIFER: But I mean, would that rule her out? I mean, would you break up with her because she had had too many boyfriends?

MATT: No, no . . . . I mean, no. I mean, I haven't ever done that—But then it's not like I've been with some girl who's been with, you know, dozens and dozens of guys.

JENNIFER: Well, is there some, you know Number, that you would consider, like, too many?

MATT: It's not like that.

JENNIFER: What is it like?

MATT: You get to know someone. You get to know, if they're the type to, like, sleep with someone on the first date or / something

JENNIFER: You would rule out someone who slept with you on the first date?

MATT: Well, not Rule Out, no. But I mean, I wouldn't, I don't think, marry them, either.

JENNIFER: You wouldn't . . . you wouldn't dream of marrying someone who just fell, like, head-over-heels in love with you on the first date and wanted to, you know, have you back to her place?

MATT: Well, I guess, I mean, if we came home from a bar together and, like, fell into bed and the next morning we could barely remember each other's names, then I wouldn't expect we'd end up in church.

JENNIFER: What, are you, Catholic?

MATT: Yeah . . . Um, well, I was, but that was a long time ago.

JENNIFER: I think I have to get out of here.

MATT: Wait, no. What did I say?

JENNIFER: *(Collecting her shoes and her purse)* It isn't you, Matt. It's . . . I mean, I don't want whole relationships to be about The Number. And I don't think I want to be judged by what I might . . .

or might Not have done coming home from a bar one night if I was really really attracted to a guy and everything, and I mean, why is it fair that I should be judged, when guys are not ever— nobody ever . . . I think I just have to get out of / here.

MATT: But wait. I mean, wait. We're having pizza . . . and / everything.

JENNIFER: I'm just going to get my shoes on and and . . . I mean, I didn't even tell him . . . I mean, I mean, he asked me and I didn't even tell him the Actual Number. I mean, is this fair? I actually lied, because I didn't want him to give me a hard time about the real . . . Why am I telling you this? Damn. *(She exits.)*

MATT: Wait, Jennifer! At least wait until Ken gets back so you can

(Door slam.)

Woh.

> *Sound: Key in lock. Ken enters carrying a boxed pizza and a can of diet coke.*

KEN: She pushed right past me. What's that about?

MATT: I'm sorry, Dude. I think I said the wrong / thing.

KEN: It's okay, Man. I don't think I can stick with her. I mean, do you know how many guys she's been with?

MATT: Um, no.

KEN: . . . Promise you won't tell her I told you?

MATT: Um, promise YOU won't tell her I told you what she told ME?

KEN: What'd she tell you?

MATT: . . . No, I just meant, um . . .

What kind of pizza did you get?

KEN: Pizza! Sausage. Extra cheese . . . Should we save some for her or

. . .

MATT: I don't think we need to.

KEN: Is the difference between a guy and his girlfriend that he would never leave until he'd eaten the pizza?

MATT: . . . I think you're onto something, Man.

> *Ken pops the flip top on the soda can. Matt helps himself to pizza. Music up (possibly, "Girls Just Want to Have Fun.")*
>
> *Blackout*
>
> *End of play*

"Something of a Music Aficionado"

Brian Dykstra

"Something of An Aficionado " was originally commissioned and produced by The Drilling Company Theatre, artistic director Hamilton Clancy, for FAITH. It opened on May 6 , 2010. It was directed by Sarah Biesinger and featured the following cast: Jordan Feltner—Dean Wilkes; Anwen Darcy—Andrea Cooper; McKey Carpenter—Jake Paque. Sets by Rebecca Lord, lights Miriam Crowe, sound Christopher Rummel and web design by Phillip DeVita and Stage Management by Billie Davis. Hamilton Clancy, Artistic Director. Produced by Hamilton Clancy and The Drilling Company Theatrical Productions.

CHARACTERS

Dean Wilkes. . . . a twenty-something who believes that pro-choice has gone too far.

Andrea Cooper . a twenty-something who loves music from the 80s.

Jake Paque. . . . . a twenty-something who reads the anarchist cookbook and knows how to (although he never has) build pipe bombs.

SETTING

Post teen-aged wasteland. You know, like, wherever.

Dean, Andrea & Jake in the middle of it.

DEAN: Faith

ANDREA: Faith?

DEAN: Yeah.

JAKE: Oh, boy.

ANDREA: Okay. Fine. Faith.

DEAN: Yeah.

ANDREA: So it's ...Faith.

DEAN: (That's what I—)

JAKE: Oh, I know you know this shit.

ANDREA: Right into my little trap.

JAKE: Totally.

DEAN: (Are you guys—?)

ANDREA: Right? Father Figure. I Want Your Sex.

JAKE: Oh, I totally want yours, too.

ANDREA: Cute.

DEAN: (You—?)

JAKE: Thanks.

DEAN: (Wait...what?)

JAKE: Parts I and II, right?

DEAN: (You want—?)

ANDREA: I was going to say that.

DEAN: (You want—?)

JAKE: Cool. Sorry. Cool. I know you were. Sorry.

ANDREA: One More Try.

DEAN: Wait.

JAKE: Just let her—

ANDREA: Wait.

JAKE: Totally waiting.

ANDREA: Hand to Mouth, no, wait.

JAKE: Totally waiting.

ANDREA: First Hard Day, then Hand to Mouth—

DEAN: (What are you—)

ANDREA: Wait.

JAKE: Totally waiting.

ANDREA: There's another "hand" song, Wash Your Hands? "Wash your hands," listen to me, that's just stupid, Look at Your Hands.

DEAN: Look at my—?

JAKE: That's just the next song.

DEAN: The next song?

JAKE: Catch up, dude.

ANDREA: Then the monkey song.

DEAN: (The Monkey—?)

ANDREA: Monkey. It's called Monkey. Um... Kissing a Fool.

JAKE: Like the movie, but...not.

ANDREA: Hang on.

JAKE: Sorry.

ANDREA: Jesus.

JAKE: Sorry.

ANDREA: I'm almost there. Then the remix, the remix of Hard Day, then I Want Your Sex again.

JAKE: Ditto.

DEAN: (I'm—)

ANDREA: Cute. Or the reprise, or, no, it's um...Part III, I Want Your Sex Part III, but it's called something, it has a name.

DEAN: It has a name?

JAKE: Oh, totally.

ANDREA: Like The Last Resort.

DEAN: (The Last—?)

ANDREA: But no, that's the last song on Hotel California, isn't it?

JAKE: Totally. "They called it paradise, I don't know why..."

ANDREA: Right.

JAKE: "Call someplace paradise...

ANDREA & JAKE: ... kiss it good-bye"

ANDREA: Right. So, not Faith. The Last something else. The Last Mohican? The Last Round-Up? The Last Alabaster Disaster?

DEAN: The... what?

ANDREA: Totally kidding.

JAKE: Psyche.

ANDREA: But, what do I mean? Oh! Not The... A, it's an A!

JAKE: Totally.

ANDREA: Don't tell me.

JAKE: No worries.

ANDREA: ... A...A...A Last Request! Right?

JAKE: Totally.

ANDREA: A Last Request (I Want Your Sex Part III). Whew.

DEAN: Are you finished?

JAKE: She is.

ANDREA: Eleven songs. Faith. George Michael. Boom Chick-a Boom. Got 'em all.

DEAN: Are you the most biggest George Michael nerd of all time?

JAKE: Uh, top 100 albums of the eighties?

ANDREA: 85 weeks on Billboard 200?

JAKE: Top 500 all time according to Rolling Stone? You don't have to be a George Michael groupie to have a deep understanding of Faith.

ANDREA: You just have to be something of a music aficionado.

DEAN: I wasn't talking about Faith.

ANDREA: I fear you were.

JAKE: We both do. Fear that.

DEAN: No, I was asking about Faith. Real faith. Like faith, you know IN something, or FOR something, or, no, I guess IN something, or even THAT something. You know, Faith.

JAKE: You mean the thing George Michael is referring to when he named his album Faith?

ANDREA: Or when he called the first song Faith on the album he called Faith?

JAKE: Or, really, both.

ANDREA: Right.

DEAN: Or, okay, something like that.

ANDREA: Why didn't you say that?

DEAN: I thought I did.

ANDREA: Okay. I hear you.

DEAN: . . . So?

ANDREA: Okay, so, "Faith?"

DEAN: Yep.

ANDREA: I have faith that human beings will inexorably march to their own destruction by fucking things up from now until it's too late to save ourselves.

DEAN: You do?

JAKE: I do too.

DEAN: You do?

JAKE: Totally.

DEAN: Why?

ANDREA: Look at shit. There's nothing left to do. Not for us. This last spoiled brat generation or three who never had to sacrifice for anything and who could have done something if they weren't so effing selfish, has left us a toxic-shit septic planet (here comes another oil spill) to clean up, but have given us jobs in retail along with crushing debt. And with that we're supposed to take on corporate entities gilded with the armor of profits-over-sanity, and lobbyists buying present day considerations at the expense of survival. Faith? Please.

DEAN: You don't have faith in God?

ANDREA: So totally immaterial.

DEAN: Faith?

ANDREA: No, God.

DEAN: God is immaterial?

ANDREA: God's not going to fix this shit.

DEAN: God's not?

ANDREA: No. If I have faith in anything, I have faith in science.

JAKE: I knew I was here for a reason.

DEAN: Here on earth?

JAKE: No. Here. In this conversation.

DEAN: Why?

JAKE: She's totally right.

ANDREA: Thank you.

JAKE: And at the same time: Totally wrong.

ANDREA: I am?

JAKE: Totally. Just the fact you have to say that. Just the fact that the phrase "faith in science" is acceptable, means we have gone so far off the rails there is no hope.

ANDREA: That's what I said.

JAKE: And, that's the part you're right about, the no-hope part. Science isn't something we have "Faith" in. Science is Science. Suspectable (or should be suspectable) only to the scientific method. The fact that some of us place our "faith" in science or (inexplicably) choose to not place our "faith" in science is a catastrophic failure of human kind.

DEAN: It is?

JAKE: It can't be a question of faith.

ANDREA: I agree.

JAKE: But it is!

ANDREA: I agree.

DEAN: You do?

ANDREA: I do.

JAKE: Huge steps backwards. Huge.

ANDREA: I agree.

DEAN: You do?

JAKE: The Age of Enlightenment was called "The Age of Enlightenment" because it was a time when we began to grasp the fact that there was such a thing as science and the scientific method. The dark ages were called "the dark ages" for the simple reason that there was too much God.

ANDREA: Or too much faith.

JAKE: Right. Faith. God is immaterial.

ANDREA: Right.

DEAN: God is not immaterial.

ANDREA: It is for this discussion.

DEAN: It?

ANDREA: He, she, it, whatever.

JAKE: The problem we got now, is too many motherfuckers are desperate to deny what is provable and move backwards into some
place where they want to embrace voodoo or magical thinking
at the expense of science. And we can't afford to do that, because
there are way too many other fundamentalists (barely one generation off the camel, by the way) who only embrace faith and
ignore everything else. So women are to blame for their own
rape, in spite of the burka. Which wouldn't be so much a global
problem, but these faith-addicted fundamentalists have become
the world-wide nouveau riche and spend it like they don't give a
shit, cuz they all know they're getting rewarded with 70 virgins
in heaven if they can only get their hands on a nuclear weapon
to make a mushroom cloud over New York City, or wherever the
"cultural elite" are hanging out so we get stuck with more jack-
asses from Alaska, or fat white dudes from Nebraska leading us
closer to the cliff of even more "Faith" to nudge us over the edge,
where we can all (ahhhhhhhh!!!) fall to our death, which they
don't give a shit about because they have faith they're getting
their own reward (albeit not 70 dark-haired virgins) in their
equally messed up version of heaven. Great. Right?

DEAN: So, "faith" is the enemy?

JAKE: No question. Oh, no question. Not even a question.

ANDREA: I agree.

DEAN: But miracles happen every day.

ANDREA & JAKE: No they don't.

DEAN: They don't?

ANDREA: Or, if they do, they get counter-balanced by all the human
nature that's going on to counter-balance anything you might
call a miracle.

DEAN: Babies get born every day.

JAKE: That's biology, dude. Like amoebas splitting.

DEAN: Another miracle.

ANDREA: If you say so.

DEAN: What do you call it?

ANDREA: What did you call it?

JAKE: Biology.

ANDREA: Biology.

DEAN: Which is kind of a miracle.

ANDREA: If you say so.

DEAN: That's what I thought. You don't have faith in anything.

ANDREA: I told you, I have faith that we're going to fuck this shit up.

JAKE: Don't know if that's really faith.

ANDREA: No?

JAKE: More like following empirical evidence.

ANDREA: Okay.

DEAN: What empirical evidence?

JAKE: You got one?

ANDREA: Well . . . Oh, well, like what he said, like Saudi Arabia.

DEAN: Saudi Arabia?

JAKE: Good one.

DEAN: What about Saudi Arabia?

ANDREA: The Saudis are sitting on the largest fresh water aquifer in the world. It's huge. Larger than any oil deposit anywhere.

DEAN: So?

ANDREA: And, among other things, they use it to water golf courses & run huge water parks.

DEAN: So?

ANDREA: They use it 20,000 times faster than it can replenish itself.

DEAN: So?

ANDREA: So, they're going to run out. And pretty soon. And when they run out, they're going to be Saudi fucking Arabia with no water. And all the desalination plants in the world can't keep up with the kind of demand they're going to have when they run that aquifer dry.

DEAN: So?

JAKE: Seriously, dude?

DEAN: What's your point?

ANDREA: Seriously, dude?

DEAN: What?

ANDREA: If human beings can't be bothered to give a shit about running out of water because they want pristine fairways in the middle of the fucking desert, how are they ever going to give a shit about an overheating planet if they want the engines of commerce well-oiled and spitting out profit.

DEAN: Something always happens.

JAKE: What do you mean?

DEAN: Something always comes along and fixes shit.

ANDREA: Like what?

DEAN: I don't know.

JAKE: There were four ice ages that we know about. They fixed shit.

DEAN: No, I—

JAKE: And that asteroid fixed shit for the dinosaurs.

ANDREA: Well, that's true.

JAKE: The black plague came along and—

DEAN: No, that's not what I'm saying. I'm saying something always happens. Something always comes along to make sure human beings gain the upper hand. We're going to invent something, or there's going to be a natural occurrence where all that carbon isn't such a big a deal. Human activity isn't really going to effect the weather. Not really. Not badly. Or, if so, something's going to come along and fix it.

ANDREA: Something like what?

DEAN: I don't know, Noah built a boat.

JAKE: Noah built a—

ANDREA: "Elephants and kanga-roosies roosies—

JAKE & ANDREA: "Children of the Lord."

DEAN: Yeah. Some guy with a good idea. Or, maybe, in Saudi Arabia, they're going to make way better desalination plants and who needs your giant aquifer? And if there's some kind of harmful by-product from that, someone else will come along and make something to deal with that. Because God (who is not immaterial) isn't going to let us just die off.

JAKE: Why not?

DEAN: We're his creation. He's not just going to give up. Not on us.

ANDREA: Seriously, dude?

DEAN: Of course.

JAKE: No, seriously?

DEAN: Of course!

ANDREA: And you know this, how?

DEAN: . . . Faith.

ANDREA: I was afraid you were going to say that.

DEAN: And your lack it, of faith, is cynical and curmudgeonly.

ANDREA: Curmudgeonly?

DEAN: It's a word.

ANDREA: Jake?

JAKE: Yeah?

ANDREA: We can't be friends with Dean any more.

DEAN: What?

JAKE: I know.

DEAN: What?

ANDREA: He's standing in the way. You're standing in the way.

DEAN: Of what?

ANDREA: You're the problem. People like you. People with faith in "Poof," . . . when there is no "Poof." We have to actually do things. And praying is not doing.

DEAN: It certainly is!

ANDREA: Jake?

JAKE: Yeah.

ANDREA: You want to go listen to George Michael?

JAKE: I want your sex?

ANDREA: Yeah.

JAKE: . . . Parts one, two, and three?

ANDREA: Oh, yeah.

DEAN: Wait.

ANDREA: What?

DEAN: After all that, after telling me I have to do something, you're just going to crawl off and listen to George Michael? That's what you're doing?

ANDREA: Yeah. But not with you. You're the enemy.

DEAN: So, what are you doing?

ANDREA: Us?

DEAN: Yeah.

JAKE: We're giving up.

DEAN: And what's that doing?

JAKE: It's giving up. Fuck survival, let's dance. Let's trash the hotel so when we check out, the party's already over.

DEAN: There's no checking out. Things are going to be fine.

ANDREA: Great. You have your faith, we have ours.

JAKE: And never the twain shall meet.

DEAN: God in not immaterial!

ANDREA: Neither is George Michael.

JAKE: Dude, dude, dude, can I borrow a condom?

DEAN: What?

JAKE: Totally kidding, dude. I'm covered.

ANDREA: Cute.

DEAN: How do you think you know any of this?

JAKE: Seriously?

DEAN: Of course.

JAKE: . . . I am so fighting the impulse to say something.

DEAN: Like what?

ANDREA: Wait. You really don't know what he's fighting the impulse to say?

DEAN: No.

ANDREA: Don't say it.

JAKE: Okay.

DEAN: You know what it is?

ANDREA: Of course.

DEAN: What?

ANDREA: I'm not saying.

DEAN: Why not?

ANDREA: It's too obvious.

DEAN: You don't know. You don't know what he wants to say.

ANDREA: Oh, yes I do.

DEAN: You're bluffing.

ANDREA: If you say so.

DEAN: How do I know you're not just bluffing? How would anyone?

ANDREA: You want to take this, or should I?

JAKE: Let's go together.

ANDREA: Oh, okay. Ask that again.

DEAN: Ask what?

ANDREA: What you just asked. How do you know I'm not bluffing?

DEAN: Okay. How do I know you're not just bluffing?

JAKE: One, two, three . . .

ANDREA & JAKE: Have faith.

As Andrea & Jake leave:

DEAN: That's not what you were going to say.

Andrea turns back.

ANDREA: Okay.

And they leave together. A pause.

DEAN: Fuckin' heathens.

End of Play.

The Story of Little Sanchez and How We Lost Our Mother

Daniel Talbott

The Story of Little Sanchez and How We Lost Our Mother was first produced by Red Elevator Productions at HERE Arts Center as part of Too Little Too Late, February 3–14, 2010. It was directed by Portia Krieger and featured Craig Jorczak, Jacob Murphy, Anna O'Donaghue, Laura Ramadei and Claire Siebers. It was remounted by Krieger as part of The Meet at CenterStage, August 18–20, 2010 and featured Daniel Abeles, Craig Jorczak, Anna O'Donaghue, Laura Ramadei and Claire Siebers.

CHARACTERS:

D . . female, mid-twenties, a teacher, sister to J, B and T

J . . . male, mid-twenties, married to C, brother to D, B and T

C . . female, a physical therapist, mid-twenties, married to J

B . . female, mid-twenties, mother to Jalen and Briarlyn, sister
    to T, D and J

T . . male, early thirties, brother to D, J and B

SOME NOTES ON THE TEXT AND FORMATTING:

Some of the dialogue should overlap like a real conversation, some
of it may be whispered, they may only partially be listening at times.
They've known each other a long time, they're family.

A slash (/) can be the start of a new line, an overlap of two voices,
people coming in on top of each other, finishing each other's
thoughts.

Some conversations are set off to the side—the same thought
being worked through at the same time, or a new/parallel thought,
everyone is listening, sometimes partially, to everyone, the overlapping comes easily and naturally.

All of this constitutes an idea—the play should happen as much
as possible like an actual conversation and the rhythm of it should be
discovered by each individual cast, and the slashes and parallel text
are just an approximation of hopefully a helpful idea of how to begin
to approach it.

Note about the use of " . . . "—this constitutes a beat, a breath, a
change in thought, a shift, maybe a thought within a thought.

Lights up mid-conversation.

A cabin at the top of a mountain surrounded by snow in California.
A fire.

You can hear a TV in the background playing 'The Lord of the
Rings'.

It's pitch black outside, frozen, cold and late.

*Five young adults—three girls, two guys—sit around on sofas, the
floor, a rug, chairs, whatever, lounging, sore, exhausted from a long
day of skiing.*
   *There's a pizza box, a bowl of chips and some guac and salsa,
maybe some french onion dip, beers and leftover bags of fast food, some
large cokes from Jack in the Box, etc.*
   *Two of the girls (D and C) sit side by side, texting, curled up on a
couch. They are still part of the conversation while they text.*
   They are all related by blood or marriage and are waiting.

D: *(texting)* No his name was little Sanchez.
J: Little / Sanchez?
B: That was not his / name!
D: *(texting)* It was!
T: And he was a sex offender?
C: Yup.
   A registered one.
         C reading a text response to D from her iPhone.
   "Fail.
   Fail.
   Fail.
   Fail.
   Fail."
   He just keeps writing 'fail' over and over again like a psycho.
D: His name was little Sanchez.
   Art Sanchez. /
   Little little Sanchez.
C: Lucky Sanchez.   J: *(laughing)* Little   D: Yes!
                        Sanchez.   Art Sanchez.
                                                 But we called him Art. /
                                                 Little Arty Sanchez.
                                                 I swear.
C: *(reading new texts as they come in)* He's fucking crazy.
   This is crazy.
   "Fail.
   Fail.
   Fail.
   Fail."
D: *(texting as she talks)* He's just lonely.

c: That's / not lonely.

b: *(about the texting)* That's scary.
    It's scary. /
    It's really scary.
    It creeps me out.

c: *(reading more posts)* He's not lonely. He's pathetic.

c: *(cont'd. reading.)* He's a fucking loser.

t: Can I text him?

d: No.

t: I'll fucking text.   b: Just stay out of it.
    I'd love to text him.

d: No!

t: How bout call him?   c: You should totally let him call
                             him.
                         d: No.
                         So little Sanchez!

j: Little Sanchez.   d: Little Sanchez.   t: Little Sanchez the
                                             child molester?

d: He wasn't a child molester.

c: Yes he was.
    He was totally / a child molester.

t: Leave it to my sister.

d: He baked bread.
    He was like a little middle-aged man.
    Like an Ewok.

t: *(laughing)* An Ewok!?

d: Yes a little / Ewok.

t: Out of like / fifty guys.

d: He was / like five four.

t: Like fifty / guys D.

d: He / had no hair.

t: Fifty / fucking guys.

d: He was nice.

t: It's a really nice house. /
    Anybody would live there.

j: It's a steal.

c: Jeff didn't like them.

He didn't like them. /
He didn't like any of the young ones.

J: But he liked Sanchez.

C: Yup.

T: The / registered sex offender.

C: He loved Sanchez.
Cause he knew Dayna wouldn't / want to fuck him.

D: He was nice.
He was like a neat freak and would stay home all day and cook things. /
He was really cool and kept the house really clean.

C: He'd watch porn.

T: What?

C: Tons of porn.
All day while D was at school teaching third graders.

J: Irony.

C: When your mom kicked him out. She got a cable bill for like four hundred dollars for On Demand / porn.

T: Dayna that's insane! /
That's crazy!

C: He'd sit home all day and jerk off / on her couch.

B: That's disgusting.   D: You don't know that.

C: He didn't have a	D: I didn't know when	T: You're fucking
TV.	I rented to him!	crazy.

J: How did you find out?

C: Jeff. /
(reading more posts)
"Fail.
Fail."

D: Jeff's paranoid.

C: He's paranoid about child molesters.
(from the texts)
"I'm crying you suck
You fail.
You bitch. You bitch..
You fuckin two face whore bitch.
Bitch.

...."
(of Jeff)
Cause of his kids.

T: I can't believe you're dating a guy with three kids Day.

B: By two mothers.

C: Two different / mothers.

B: Who sells pot that his parents grow for a living.

C: Jeff goes on the site every week to check things out and I'm not
    shitting you.
    On the front page.
    A big ole picture. /
    Of Art.

J: *(laughing)* Of little / Sanchez?

D: Of little Sanchez. /
    Little lucky Sanchez.

C: Smiling.

D: He's smiling. /
    Like it's picture day at school.

J: You need to get a Japanese kid.
    Like one that doesn't speak English.

T: Did you see fucking *Audition?*
    The movie *The Audition?*

D: No.

T: With the throw up and the bag? / And the acupuncture needles?

B: There's something / so wrong with you.

T: You don't need anyone Japanese.

D: Mom didn't believe him.

C: Your mom's at the office.
    Dayna calls and tells her.

D: She's like no way.

C: They pull it up. /
    Her secretary pulls it up.

D: There's / Art.

C: There's little Sanchez. /
    She literally screamed.

D: *(laughing)* He was really cool   C: *(reading more posts)*
    though and he kept the house   "You're a whore.
    really clean.   You're a whore."

D: *(texting)* He did steal shoes though.

T: What?!

D: He'd steal like one shoe and....

D (CONT'D): He was doing dirty things with those shoes.

D: And cameras too every time we'd have a party some girl's camera would get stolen.

T: It's fucking crazy.

C: *(reading)* "You're a cum siphon."

C: *(reading texts)*
"You siphon cum.
You siphon cum.
You siphon the world's cum for a living."

C: *(reading texts)* "Cum siphon. Cum siphon."

C: "Fail.
Fail.
Fail."

C: *(reading texts)* "You suck dick.
You suck dick.
You broke my hearf.
Black black black dick.
Black dick."
I can't do this any more.

B: It's crazy.   J: It's insane.

T: *(overlapping)*
You need to figure this out Day.
This is insane. /
This guy's insane.

C: I'm turning your phone off.

D: No!
No. No.
Let me say goodnight.
She takes her phone back and gives C her phone.
She starts to text.
C turns off her own phone.
The Lord of the Rings in the background.

J: When was she supposed to be here?

B: Like now.
Like an hour ago.
She said she'd call.

C: Was Dave with her?

B: I don't think so.

C: You should call her.

B: I did. /
    I tried.
    Like an hour ago.

J: Call Dave.

T: Why was she driving up here this late?

B: I don't know.

D: Cause she's tough. /
    She's mean.

J: Cause / she wants to see all of us.

T: Get off your fucking phone.

D: I am.
    Do you remember when she walked in on that party with me
    and Kayla and the bikinis in the hot tub?
    And threw everybody out?

C: Yes.

D: She beat me up.

T: Good.
                    She finishes.

D: *(to the phone)* There.
    Goodnight.
                    She turns it off.

T: Take it away from her.
            C takes the phone and throws it to J, who puts it in his pocket.

B: Jalen loves that story. He can tell you the whole thing word for
    word. /
    She went ballistic on them.

T: Wasn't Kayla really sweet / before you turned her into a—like a
    skank whore?

D: Kayla ran out the—snuck out the window in the bathroom and I
    tried / but she caught me.

C: Your mom / went crazy.

T: She said. She said. She lost it. After so many months of it. Of all
    the crap. She lost it.
        At like two o'clock in the morning and Mom's in her Lexus
    across the street watching the house for like an hour and every
    fuckin ghetto guy in Stockton is comin out of it.

B: Our family.
Like a miniseries.

J: Like a fuckin miniseries.

B: Seriously.
C: She's insane.

T: She goes in there. You and Kayla are in the hot tub and there's 30 Mexican guys in there and no other girls.

D: They weren't all Mexican.

J: *(to his sister D)*
You're crazy.

D: *(a joke)* Some of them were *bona fide* Latinos.

B: Dayna you need to get out of Stockton.

D: I teach there./
That's where I teach.

J: How are you a teacher?

B: Exactly.
How?
How?
It makes me paranoid.
I think every one of Jalen's teachers is like a hooker / or a titty dancer in disguise.

D: Fuck you.
I'm a good teacher. /
I don't drink on school days.

C: You guys are exhausting.

T: Tell me about / it.

J: Keeps us all on our toes.

D: I just need a normal guy who makes a lot of money but doesn't want to work very often.
And a big dick.

J: *(to D)* What?!

T: Dayna!

D: What?!

T: What is wrong with you?!

J: You need some / serious help.

T: You're fucking crazy.
Do you—

B: *(to C)* It's really late.
(pause)
It's weird.

C: *(to B)* What?

B: That she hasn't called.

C: Do you think maybe she lost cell reception?

B: Maybe.

C: Are you worried?

B: No.

Do you know what country we
live in?

D: Jeff meets that criteria.

T: Cause he's a fucking drug
dealer.

J: Cause he sells pot.

D: I know.
What's wrong with that?
It's medical.

T: You are so full of shit!

D: It's medical.
Its legal.
He has a prescription.
He makes a lot of money.
It's medicine.

B: Are any of you wigged out that Mom's like three hours late and
nobody's called us?!

T: No!

J: No.

T: No.
Why do you do that?

B: Do what?

T: Do that.
That thing.
Get all crazy and shit and spooky?
Like put bad fucking stuff in the air?
In the room.
Don't be paranoid.
You're always like that.

B: I am not.

T: I hate that.
I hate it.
It's disturbing.
. . .
It's dark.
It's snowing.
It takes fucking forever to drive up here.
Stop.

C: Do you want me to try her
again?

B shakes her head.

> *(to C)*
> Don't you have any males in your office?
> Someone to introduce her to?

c: Yeah there was one but he has a girlfriend.

t: Can't you break them up?

j: Please honey?

d: I just need someone that already has money. That has lots of money. / Like an inheritance.

t: *(sarcasm)* You're definitely / going to find that in Stockton.

c: And that isn't insane.

d: And that doesn't want to work. Or have to work. / Or doesn't work at all.

j: And doesn't post shit on your wall like you're a black black black sucking dick whore and you siphon cum for a living.

d: I just need to marry Caitlin.
> *(to C)*
> Hey Caitlin can you just strap it on?
> Will you marry me?

t: What?!

d: Just do it.
> Please.
> *They all laugh.*

d: Hope you don't mind Jeremy.

t: *(smiling)* Is that alright Jer?

j: *(laughing)* ... hey.

b: There is something / so deeply wrong with all you.

t: Two for one. /
> Two for the price of one.

d: Can threesomes get married?

b: Not to your brother and his fucking wife.

t: It's California.

b: Prop 8 fuckers! Prop 8!
> You're all disgusting.
> They won't even let gay people get married.
> They're certainly not going to be to keen on an incest trio.
> The Mormons people.
> The Mormons.

> *She gets up and goes over to her brother J and takes D's cell
> phone out of his pocket as they all continue to laugh, the way
> you can only laugh at stupid shit when you're really really
> tired and a little worn out and buzzed.*
> *She dials.*

D: We could film it. /

Make money that way.

T: Little Sanchez could be the director. / Do the art direction.

J: Little Sanchez!

D: He's the producer!

He's the producer!

Oh my god.

He's our producer!

I think I found my hobby.

J: Your life calling.

D: I could be little Sanchez's Queen roller. /

His chief bitch.

T: His cum siphon.

D: Make tons of money. /

Tons.

J: Get me a website. / I won't ever have to work again.

D: We could film at the school.

Use it as a set.

At night.

> *J and T and D are all laughing.*
> *T starts singing Journey's 'Don't stop Believing'. J joins in.*
> *They both forget the lyrics and begin laughing.*
> *T takes a swig off of one of the cokes.*
> *Lord of the Rings in the background.*
> *B hangs up the phone. Stands.*
> *She rubs her eyes.*

C: I'm tired.

B: Me too.

Does anybody want anything?

T: *(still laughing)* No thanks.

B: *(to C and D)* You want some tea?

D: *(dramatically)* Not me.

J: She better fucking get here soon or I'm going to pass out.

C shakes her head.

B: *(to J)* You good?

J: Yup.

(Yawns.)

Yup.

I'm good.

I'm good.

Just tired.

She stays standing.

Hesitates and then goes and sits back down.

They stereo suddenly turns on, blaring Rihanna's 'Hard'.

It's extremely loud and scares the shit out of everybody.

B goes over quickly and tries to turn it off. She hits it, searching and finally figures it out and succeeds.

Silence.

The Lord of the Rings in the background.

B: Fuck.	D: Oh my god.	C: That scared the shit
Fuck.	Oh my god.	out of me.
	Oh my god.	

B: That scared the shit out of me. /

Fuck.

Fuck me.

D: Me too. /

Oh my god.

C: I love that song.

D: Me too. /

Oh my god.

B: Oh.

Oh god.

Oh my god.

I hate this house.

I hate it.

I just hate it.

. . . .

David wanted to buy it and he never even comes up here.

It's like the fucking 'Shining' or some shit.

I hate it.

It fucking terrifies me.

B (CONT'D): The minute we drove up that hill, that drive way and I saw it I was like we shouldn't even be here.

. . .

We had this toy we had bought for Jalen so it was older but we saved it for Briarlyn and it was in our room and it has this little like globe thing with animals that you have to spin and it goes doo-doop, doo-doop, doo-doop. But you have to actually spin it and every like quarter of a turn that's when it would make a noise so it would go (motioning) doo-doop, doo-doop, doo-doop you know like all the way around. And you know at like three o'clock in the morning we're totally asleep and /

D: It went all the way around?

B: Oh my god I'm getting goose bumps. This is like freaking me out. But it was all . . . . It woke me up. It was all doo-doop . . . doo-doop. Doo-doop. Doo-doop. And it kept going and going— (looking at goose bumps) oh my god I'm freaking out it's totally freakin me out. I started to cry. It like totally freaked me out. / And it's not easy to move. So it can't be like the wind or something.

C: Of course —

B: And I tried not to move like oh my god—and my friend Sarah says that the activity that happens you, you know like spirits and blah blah blah blah it happens around three o'clock and um . . . I think I grabbed David and am like did you hear that and I just didn't really get up and like I was asleep and then. We have tons of alarms in our house and stuff and I swear. Every single alarm in the house went off. Like all the sudden all our alarms, like all the sudden in the whole house—like the smoke alarms, the car alarms, the house alarm, pool alarm, like upstairs and downstairs, started going off.
Screaming.

C: I hear something—

T: Somebody's / crying—

C: Somebody's screaming / and crying—

J: *(calmly)* It's the baby.
It's the baby.

B: *(joking)* Is it three o'clock?

B gets up and goes to check on the sleeping kids.

Turns lights on as she goes.
Silence.
Lord of the Rings.

T: Mom was really sensitive to that stuff.
She said she had lots of problems with it as a kid.
She'd see stuff.

  ...

She used to hate our house.
She wouldn't even go down to the bottom level. Downstairs.
She used to yell down for us from above.
That's why they installed that intercom thing.

D: Totally.

J: It was great. You knew you were totally safe down there.
Friends used to pay me money in high school to use the guest room.

C: Like a fucking bordello.

J: Yeah. It was genius.
We made so much money.
   B comes back.

T: Was she crying or was she just talking?

B: Crying.

C: Is she okay?

B: Yeah.
She went back down.

T: We were talking about the old house.

B: Mom was scared to death of that place.

C: Jalen hated it too.
He would never go down there.

B: *(to C)* I know.
Mom was always like go play.
Go play in the toy room and he'd just sit there.

T: Oh god the toy room.
I swear.
It totally freaked me out playing in that room. I was down there with Bailey one night and I literally felt like I was being watched by like thirty people or something. And I'm not kidding you like I literally was in that room and I even think I said something to you about it I said there's something down there, like...

I seriously like /
There was something.

B: Kids are / sensitive that way

T: There was definitely / something down there.

B: It was like all the sudden too. Like I was fine with the place and then all of the sudden like one day I would go downstairs and I'd like try to go into my room and like the feeling from—I'm freakin out—the pressure from both sides of like that little hallway.

T: Yeah—

B: Would like take me in and I would like pretty much run. Run upstairs. /
Like a little kid.

> *D begins to cry, silently. Not forcing it. Not knowing why or it being demonstrative in any way. But tears are silently, quietly streaming down her face, almost like blood out of a cut. She's stunned by it.*
> *No one notices at first.*

T: Yeah.

B: Seriously.

T: Seriously / I'm telling you . . .

J: You guys are fucking crazy.

> *C notices. She takes D's hand.*

T: Seriously, there was something. / There was something downstairs there.	C: What? What? Dayna what?
J: You're / crazy.	*D is shaking her head overcome and almost laughing at herself, confused. She can't stop crying.*
B: I was terrified of that place.	
	D: I don't know. *(laughing)* I don't know.

> *B, J and T all notice. D's laughing at herself, pushing the tears away. She can't stop. It's like she's bleeding from the eyes.*

B: Dayna. / Dayna.

T: Are you okay?

D: Yeah.

T: Are you sure?

D: Yeah. Yeah.

> I don't know what's . . . .
> I don't know what it is . . .
> I don't know . . .
>> *D's iPhone rings. They all look at it. It's a ring tone like Ke$ha's 'Tik Tok'.*
>> *B answers it quickly.*

B: Hello.

> Hello.
> Hello?!
> Hello.
>> *She pushes end call.*

T: Was it Mom?

B: Blocked caller.

D: At 2 in the morning?

> *A short silence.*
> *The Lord of the Rings.*
> *The phone rings again.*
> *B answers it.*

B: Hello.

> Hello.

D: Who is it?

> *A strange electronic ding is heard in the house.*

B: *(into phone)* Who is   D: *(about the ding)*
this?   What's that?

B: May I ask who's   C: What was that?
speaking?   D: That was weird.

B: Hello.

> *She pushes end again.*

B: The driveway.

> It was the driveway. /
> It lets us know someone's here.

C: It must be your mom.

J: It's totally got to be Mom.

> She drove five miles an hour or some shit all the way up here.

B: Yeah.

> Yeah.

They all wait and look out the window into the darkness.
The Lord of the Rings in the background.
The sound of fire, maybe wind.
They wait.
They begin to see something.
The phone rings again.
Lights in the darkness. The phone continues to ring.
Red and blue flashing lights from a state trooper's car.
The lights grow on their faces.
The phone rings.

Blackout.

End of play.

Ted's Head

Kathleen Warnock

Ted's Head was originally produced by Vanguard Repertory Theatre, at The NoHo Actors Studio, North Hollywood, CA, from Oct. 15–24, 2010. Director: Tony Christopher. Cast: Ted—Randy Marquis; Mreen—Susan Marlowe; Baz—Quentin Miles.

CHARACTERS

Baz . . . . scientist, late 20s/early 30s.
Mreen . . . . Baz's supervisor, 30s-40s.
        (Both parts can be played by either a man or a
        woman, and cast color-blind.)
Mr. Williams . . an old man, whose remains consist of a head in
        a jar.

TIME

350 or so years from now

PLACE

A recovery center

NOTE ON LANGUAGE

The scientists communicate in an English that has evolved in the several hundred years since our own time; it's a compressed language, with some words having different meanings from our time. It uses fewer articles and modifiers, and repetition to indicate superlatives (i.e., "smart smart" rather than "very smart") and sounds as different to us and ours would to an English-speaker of Shakespeare's time. Still, the audience should be able to pick up what's being said from action and contact. Here's a glossary of several terms used that might not be clear:

> Appos=apologies
> Bezble=baseball
> Dudle=stupid
> Jetplay=jet plane
> Yay yay=Yes

We hear the sounds before the lights come up: first the crack of a bat, the plop of a ball into a glove, crowds cheering, of machine guns, whining jet engines, the sound of the ocean lapping against a boat, the cast of a fishing rod, children's voices, unclear, giving way to adult voices of men and women. A heart monitor, the heartbeat fading. A long tone. The sound of an infant crying. The sounds overlap and fade in and out, first one getting louder, then the others. There's a crescendo of all the sounds coming together, then fading, leaving the crack of the bat. Then we hear a voice, at first indistinct, then becoming clearer. It is a man's voice, Ted's voice, and it seems to come from all around us.

TED: *(voiceover) (Grunts, breaths hard, then:)* I'm Teddy BALLGAME *(grunts, crack of bat).* Teddy Ballgame. *(grunts, crack of bat).* of the Major FUCKIN' League. *(Grunts, crack of bat).* Teddy BALLGAME. *(Grunts).* Major LEAGUE… *(continues, with slight variations, fading down to a mutter when other voices come in.)*

   The lights slowly rise on a table that holds a sort of clear globe, in which the head of a man can be seen, it's Ted. Ted's head is that of an old man, his face battered and swollen, his eyes closed. Electrodes are attached at various points around his head, which twitches as it is stimulated by some kind of current. Two figures stand by the table, touching instruments on it.

BAZ: Synaptic activity occurs.

MREEN: Affirm connection. "Ball Game?"

BAZ: Bezble.

MREEN: "Ball Game" old handle for Bezble? Yay yay.

BAZ: Teddy: head's old handle. Hey… head don't HAVE handle! *(He laughs. Mrene does not).*

MREEN: Stim cortextual affirm?

BAZ: Yay yay.

   Ted's eyes twitch, blink, at first slowly, then finally stay open. They work hard to focus. His lips move, but any words he forms or sounds he makes don't come from him, but rather from his projected voice, which continues to resonate from a speaker.

TED: Teddyteddyteddy… sonofabitch…. hurt… legs hurt… chest hurts… no one… John! John Henry! Son? I'll sign whatever you want. Yeah. Says here what? Cryo… what? It hurts, son. I'll sign whatever you want… we'll all be together. Yes.

BAZ: Ted.

MREEN: Ted.

TED: Can't SEE you! John? I'm cold. I'm FROZEN!

BAZ: Ahhh.... the docu here. Wait. Yes: *(obviously reading from something)*. "Come-well to the future, insert name. Check... scratch... Mizz Theodore "Ted" William plus one. No... scratch. Williamzzzz. Happy things! You are awoke from long, long sleep. Captain strides been making... *(what?)*

MREEN: No! MAJOR strides been making in sci, dudle. Not take langs at uni?

BAZ: Oldie langs? Not need... I THOUGHT!

MREEN: Need more than good sci cert for this gig, newbie. Appos, Ted, Appos! Baz begins. You his first frozen guy wakeup.

BAZ: I sci guy! Not lang guy!

MREEN: No excuse. He real person. Big big big man.

TED: If there was ever a man born to be a hitter it was me.

BAZ: OLD English... stupe. Why talk that?

MREEN: His lang. Respect, Baz. Learn not at uni?

BAZ: Best best best in class! Work hard hard hard. Smart me, stupe... him.

TED: Baseball gives every American boy a chance to excel, not just to be as good as someone else but to be better than someone else. This is the nature of man and the name of the game.

BAZ: Bezble? Who members? Stick and bell?

TED: There's only one way to become a hitter. Go up to the plate and get mad. Get mad at yourself and mad at the pitcher

MREEN: BALL! Ted hit ball best.

BAZ: Who cares? Not count now.

TED: I was a guy... who practiced until the blisters bled... and then practiced some more... Teddy Ballgame of the Major Fucking Leagues.

MREEN: Ted: I Mreen. I splain you. *(Pause; Mreen struggles with unfamiliar words and phrasing)* Ted! You choosen, many times ago, to cold your own self in way, way past. We make you wake. Things is cured! Put... energy in your head. Wake up Ted! Wake up! Now is future! Smart smart smart we!

TED: I always envied my brother Bobby... the father he had, a father who was close to him, telling him what to do, encouraging him... Son, John Henry?

BAZ: Son of you. He froze too ... but some frozens can't brungen back. Too dead.

TED: John Henry? Son? We'll all be together.

MREEN: Sometime, Ted. Head too dead.

TED: Too dead?

BAZ: YOU not too dead, Ted!

MREEN: Yay yay, Ted! Some frozen guys NOT come back. You do. Special you! Very miss old life? Wanting back, Ted?

TED: ... my son ... the tension, my father and mother never really together, my brother always in some kind of scrape. I tried to give my mother everything, but I could never give her all I really wanted to ... because she would have given it to my brother.

MREEN: Your scendants prob want see you.

TED: I'll sign whatever you want.

BAZ: You old old old unfrozen head guy. Frozen bodies come AFTER you head frozen.

TED: The Keys. They were supposed to scatter my ashes in the Keys. Florida! Florida!

BAZ: Ted, sad time frozen wake up. Join this world now.

TED: ... not all my difficulties were funny to me ... I didn't know how to handle them.

BAZ: No hands, Ted.

MREEN: Baz! Splain more, not haha with Ted.

TED: A man has to have goals—for a day, for a lifetime—and that was mine, to have people say, 'There goes Ted Williams, the greatest hitter who ever lived.

MREEN: Rights of you now have as alive. What unfrozen head want, can happen.

TED: By the time you know what to do, you're too old to do it.

BAZ: Mrene! Not time, head not ready. Later ...

MREEN: Body he misses. That one, body he USED.

TED: If there was ever a man born to be a hitter it was me.

BAZ: Bezble, yay yay. Captain player!

MREEN: MAJOR player. See pix him? Read bout him?

BAZ: ... no.

TED: I'm hit ... I'm hit ... My wing's on fire ...

MREEN: Ted great great great in bezble, Ted in jetplay, enemyshoot. Wah Wah Too. Krene Wah. Later, Ted fisherguy, great all.

BAZ: Body need for those.

TED: I've found that you don't need to wear a necktie if you can hit.

MREEN: Time diff now, ours from his.

BAZ: Prob mine? No! Waken up frozen head guys. Job mine, not thinken why? Good? Bad? Crazymake do THAT, Mrene!

TED: The water... the light on the water... Hall of Fame. Hall of Fame.

MREEN: TED! Wanting what?

TED: I hope somebody hits .400 soon. Then people can start pestering that guy with questions about the last guy to hit .400.

MREEN: Ted. You. Now future now. What?

TED: Baseball's future? Bigger and bigger, better and better! No question about it, it's the greatest game there is!

MREEN: No, Ted. YOU. I tell you, you tell me. Where? What? For you.

BAZ: M'reen, not! Not ready, Ted.

MREEN: Yay yay, Baz! Ted head make decide!

BAZ: Not making trub, going away. (He leaves).

TED: Splinter... Splendid... let him go.

MREEN: Plugpull, Ted?

TED: A kid copies what is good. I remember the first time I saw Lefty O'Doul, and he was as far away as those palms. And I saw the guy come to bat in batting practice. I was looking through a knothole, and I said, 'Geez, does that guy look good!' And it was Lefty O'Doul, one of the greatest hitters ever. The Kid... The Kid... Say goodbye, Kid.

MREEN: Bye bye, Ted? Sure? Not stay with us?

TED: Hitting is fifty percent above the shoulders.

MREEN: Also below. Body man. Fish, fly, hit. No body for everybody. Oh, Ted. So, so sorry. Really go?

TED: You have to hit the fastball to play in the big leagues.

> *Mreen waits a moment. Ted looks her in the eye. She makes a decision, and touches something at the base of the globe. A change in the light. Once again the sounds of Ted's life that accompanied his waking play; starting quite loudly, very fast, abruptly cutting off. Mrene watches as his eyes close for the last time. She puts a bag over the globe, removes it. Baz returns. Looks at her. Looks at the container she holds.*

MREEN: Ted's head.

BAZ: Ted sad sad sad. Why?

MREEN: We know sci. Know lang. Know good life now. But we un-smart bout heads. Old heads.

BAZ: Take Ted's head where?

MREEN: Fla . . . old handle Flo-ri-da.

BAZ: Flo-ri-da Doors?

MREEN: Keys. Flo-ri-da Keys.

BAZ: Come with?

MREEN: Not fraid of trub?

BAZ: YOU get trub. Me newbie. *(Pause)*. Right right right thing for unfrozen Ted. Sci not everything. Sometimes here *(he points to his own head)*. Sometimes here *(he points to his heart)*. Not fraid.

MREEN: Baz. Learning you. You come with. *(Pause)* Ted's head . . . wrong here. Nofault us.

BAZ: Mrene . . .

MREEN: Baz . . .

BAZ: If wego like headguys . . . sleep now, wake future . . . things all diff. Sad sad couldbe we?

MREEN: Herenow enough. When done, done.

BAZ: Also me. Like Ted.

MREEN: Like Ted.

BAZ: Bye, Ted! Cold no more.

MREEN: Bye, Ted.

> *They leave. As lights go down on empty table, we hear the crack of a bat, crowd noise fading, taken over by the sound of a heat beating slower and slower. Then a long uninterrupted beep.*
>
> *Silence.*
>
> CURTAIN

Rights & Permissions

(NOTE: to obtain a performance license for any play licensed by Smith and Kraus, go to www.smithandkraus.com. Click on "LICENSING," then click on "10-MINUTE PLAYS.")

AFTER © 2010 by Glenn Altermann. Reprinted by permission of the author. For performance rights, contact Smith & Kraus (www.smithandkraus.com).

AIRBORNE © 2010 by Laura Jacqmin. Reprinted by permission of Derek Zasky, William Morris Endeavor Entertainment. For performance rights, contact Derek Zasky (dsz@wmeentertainment.com)

AMENITIES © 2010 by Gregory Hischak. Reprinted by permission of the author. For performance rights, contact Smith & Kraus (www.smithandkraus.com).

THE BABY © 2009 by Ron Burch. Reprinted by permission of the author. For performance rights, contact Smith & Kraus (www.smith andkraus.com).

BEMUSED © 2009 by Mrinalini Kamath. Reprinted by permission of the author. For performance rights, contact Smith & Kraus (www.smithandkraus.com).

BEST FRIENDS © 2010 by Jenny Lyn Bader. Reprinted by permission of Jack Tantleff, Paradigm Agency.. For performance rights, contact Jack Tantleff (jtantleff@paradignagency.com).